Beyond Traditional Marketing

Innovations in Marketing Practice

Lead Author and Editor

Kamran Kashani

Contributors

Jacques Horovitz
Jean-Pierre Jeannet
Seán Meehan
Adrian B. Ryans
Dominique Turpin
John Walsh

John Wiley & Sons, Ltd

Other Wiley Editorial Offices

John Wiley & Sons Inc., 111 River Street, Hoboken, NJ 07030, USA

Jossey-Bass, 989 Market Street, San Francisco, CA 94103-1741, USA

Wiley-VCH Verlag GmbH, Boschstr. 12, D-69469 Weinheim, Germany

John Wiley & Sons Australia Ltd, 33 Park Road, Milton, Queensland 4064, Australia

John Wiley & Sons (Asia) Pte Ltd, 2 Clementi Loop #02-01, Jin Xing Distripark, Singapore 129809

John Wiley & Sons Canada Ltd, 22 Worcester Road, Etobicoke, Ontario, Canada M9W 1L1

Wiley also publishes its books in a variety of electronic formats. Some content that appears in print may not be available
in electronic books.

Library of Congress Cataloging in Publication Data

Kashani, Kamran.
  Beyond traditional marketing : innovations in marketing practice / lead author & editor,
  Kamran Kashani; co-authors Jean-Pierre Jeannet . . . [et al.].
    p. cm.
  Includes index.
  ISBN-13 978-0-470-01146-1
  ISBN-10 0-470-01146-7
  1. Marketing. I. Jeannet, Jean-Pierre. II. Title.
  HF5415.K2875 2005
  658.8—dc22

                                              2004029129

British Library Cataloguing in Publication Data

A catalogue record for this book is available from the British Library

ISBN-13 978-0-470-01146-1 (PB)
ISBN-10 0-470-01146-7 (PB)

Typeset in 10/16pt Kuenstler by Integra Software Services Pvt. Ltd, Pondicherry, India
Printed and bound in Great Britain by TJ International Ltd, Padstow, Cornwall, UK
This book is printed on acid-free paper responsibly manufactured from sustainable forestry in which at least two trees
are planted for each one used for paper production.

To our families

Contents

Contributors

This book is written by authors who are passionate about improving the practice of marketing. They all have received their advanced marketing education in great schools from around the world, but what binds them together is their common faculty experience of working with literally thousands of managers and senior executives who come to IMD for executive education. It is the authors' intimate knowledge of what these practitioners face in their industries and companies that has informed their research and writing. It is also this knowledge that has allowed them to identify and address gaps in traditional marketing thought, the focus of this book. Together, the authors have written 97 books and numerous articles published in reputable management journals. They are recognized among their peers and practitioners alike as international thought leaders in marketing.

Kamran Kashani – Lead Author and Editor

Kamran Kashani is Professor of Marketing and Global Strategy at IMD. He teaches topics in marketing, brand building, global strategy and international management. His special interests span across industrial, business-to-business, and consumer marketing.

Jean-Pierre Jeannet

Jean-Pierre Jeannet is Professor of Strategy and Marketing at IMD. His areas of special interest are global business and marketing strategies, and market orientation.

Jacques Horovitz

Jacques Horovitz is Professor of Service Strategy, Service Marketing and Service Management at IMD. He focuses on how to compete through service and improve customer satisfaction with heavy emphasis on service as a strategy for differentiation, on customer loyalty and on creating a service culture.

Seán Meehan

Seán Meehan is the Martin Hilti Professor of Marketing and Change Management at IMD, Lausanne, Switzerland. His teaching encompasses marketing and corporate strategy. He has designed and/or delivered management development programmes for companies such as PricewaterhouseCoopers Corporate Finance, COSA, Hilti A.G., Swiss Re and Toyota.

Adrian B. Ryans

Adrian Ryans is a Professor of Marketing at IMD. His areas of interest include marketing strategy and strategic market planning. He has particular expertise in business-to-business marketing and in strategic market planning for companies operating in fast-moving technology-intensive markets.

Dominique Turpin

Professor Turpin is the Dentsu Professor in Japanese Management at IMD, and specializes in marketing and strategy. He is co-director of the Programme for Executive Development (PED), a ten-week programme which brings together high potential upper- and mid-level managers from all over the world in an integrated learning experience to explore the latest management issues.

John Walsh

John W. Walsh is Professor of Marketing at IMD. His research interests include the application of economic and econometric models to marketing issues, managerial and consumer decision-making, and competitive marketing strategy.

IMD

IMD is one of the world's leading business schools. Located in Lausanne, Switzerland, IMD has been helping organizations improve their performance for over fifty years. Its high standards are recognized by hundreds of the best companies around the world.

IMD was founded by a group of leading corporations to address the real challenges that international business executives face and, in the final analysis, need to win. To this day, IMD remains focused on real-world management issues – developing leadership capabilities and offering state-of-the-art concepts and tools. While other business schools primarily teach full-time graduate university students, IMD keeps an unwavering focus on the learning needs of executives and their organizations.

Executive Development from IMD

The book series *Executive Development from IMD* provides cutting-edge thinking from the faculty of one of the world's leading business schools.

Each book presents concepts and insights for today's most important business and management challenges. The tone is straightforward. The message is practical. The ideas are tested and ready for managers to apply in their companies.

Each book follows a similar format: key-point summaries reinforce the message of each chapter and learning points translate concepts into action. Every chapter is illustrated with relevant international case studies that bring the discussions, analysis and recommendations to life.

Executives attend IMD programmes not only to learn but also to be inspired. The books in this series, like IMD programmes, provide executives with inspiration as well as with tools to improve themselves and make an immediate contribution to their companies. The focus is executive learning – engaging, energizing and impactful.

Preface

This book is written for the thoughtful executive who is looking for new ways of improving the marketing practice in his or her organization. Markets change constantly, but marketing as a discipline doesn't change with the same speed. Often, marketing practice leads and the discipline follows, and the gap between the two can take a long time to close. Our book, inspired by innovations in practice, is about addressing some of the more important gaps in the traditional marketing literature that represent the core ideas in the discipline. The gaps appear even in highly popular textbooks. These publications definitely have their place; they provide the needed foundation and structure for the discipline. But, as classics, the textbooks are not expected, or able, to address the emerging issues in marketing. By the time they do, those issues are no longer emergent or, alternatively, relevant. But the practitioners cannot afford to wait; they must devise their own ways and innovate their own solutions.

The idea for the book was born out of a brainstorming meeting among the authors, all members of the IMD marketing faculty, who were troubled by the fact that today's practitioners are ill-served by many of the existing books on marketing. Our conviction has come about from years of working with executives in leading international firms, many of them clients of IMD. We have seen how these managers have struggled with thorny marketing problems that have been ignored by well-known authors in the field. We have also marvelled at how some have managed to find innovative solutions to these problems – solutions that could well serve the interests of others facing similar issues. We decided to capture in this volume some of these innovations, such as value chain marketing, aligning with customers, 'passion branding' and discriminate pricing. We also wanted to put forward our own fresh ideas, inspired by innovative practices, on the marketing of services, a framework for marketing decision-making and the role of value creation in today's organizations striving for customer satisfaction and retention.

The book begins with an overview of the major developments that have transformed industries and provided the impetus for many of the changes in the field of marketing. Each of the chapters that follow focuses on one or more areas where new thinking in marketing has led to innovations in practice. The book is rich with examples of real-world companies who have dealt effectively with the emerging issues, and others who have not. To be useful for busy managers, each chapter ends with summaries and managerially oriented guidelines for action.

Kamran Kashani
Professor
IMD
Lausanne, Switzerland

Acknowledgements

This book would not have materialized if my six colleagues in marketing had not shown a collegial willingness to undertake this collective effort and if, in addition, they had not shown the required discipline to draft, write and complete their chapters in timely fashion. My sincere thanks, therefore, to Jean-Pierre Jeannet, Jacques Horovitz, Seán Meehan, Adrian Ryans, Dominique Turpin and John Walsh. You are great colleagues.

IMD's president, Peter Lorange, inspired this collection by encouraging the authors to work on a collaborative project and to 'make good even better'. On behalf of my co-authors I thank Peter for his encouragement and persistence. I also owe a word of thanks to Gordon Adler, IMD's director of communication and PR, for contributing substantively to the original concept of this book. His advice was critical at the early stages and over time; I am indebted to him. Others deserving special mention for their contribution are research associates Inna Francis, Rebecca Chung, Martha Lanning, Henri Bourgeois and Joseph Hartzell. They helped with our research and fact-finding. We should not forget the help all of us received from Michelle Perrinjaquet for her quality control at a crucial stage.

Finally, Caroline Taggart had a lot to do with assisting me and my colleagues to get the final drafts in a form that would fit into a single volume. Her helpful editorial suggestions created a coherent style and presentation throughout the book. Thank you, Caroline. You are wonderful to work with.

Kamran Kashani

1
Introduction

Professor Kamran Kashani

Marketing has traditionally prided itself on being the discipline in management that is most alert and responsive to the business environment and its changing demands. A review of marketing's early evolution gives ample justification for this pride. For example, marketing originally defined itself around the task of selling what the business produced, a focus that reflected the rapid industrialization, growth and prosperity of post-World War II economies. It was the right definition for its time. Later the focus on demand promotion changed to the 'marketing concept' to reflect the many changes that were taking place in the marketplace. Customers were becoming more sophisticated and demanding; competition, on the other hand, was getting more severe as growth in many markets slowed down and the fight for market share intensified. The marketing concept that promoted the idea of focusing the business organization towards identifying and satisfying customer needs was the discipline's response to the new business realities and a more exacting marketplace. And it was the right response for its time.

The adaptive early history of marketing notwithstanding, the truth is that the discipline's record of keeping up with more recent developments in the market environment has been disappointing. One could persuasively argue that the fast changes in the marketplace have outpaced marketing's ability to adapt and respond. Take the example of bundled services. For a growing number of sectors and companies, the distinction between products and services has disappeared. The customer-value proposition is an integrated offer of both tangible products and intangible services. Companies such as Otis or Schindler, for example, not only sell new elevators but also maintain, service and modernize the old ones in their installed base. Likewise, computer companies like IBM and HP sell hardware but also an increasing volume of bundled services, including business consulting. In both cases the customer offer is an integrated package in which the depth and breadth of the service component are increasingly the sources of differentiation and profitability.

Despite the emergence of add-on and integrated services, however, the traditional core ideas in marketing, including the ever-present marketing mix (Product, Price, Place and Promotion), continue to be tangible product-centred – a relic of a distant past. The discipline has had difficulty integrating the bundled product–service strategies into its core concepts. Consequently the marketing of services (as stand-alone 'products') has developed as a separate branch and a niche discipline for some academics and book publishers. But for a growing population of practitioners, the complexity of profitably marketing integrated products *and* services remains an issue for which the discipline does not offer much help.

To understand the shortfalls of traditional marketing in today's demanding markets, we must begin with a review of the changes that have fundamentally transformed the marketing environments for many firms – the changes have outpaced the discipline's historical ability to adapt. The present chapter highlights some of the more relevant and pervasive changes in the structure of markets and their behaviour. These changes have also inspired innovations that have bypassed the traditional boundaries of the discipline – innovations that are the subjects of future chapters. The list of highlighted changes is not meant to be exhaustive, but a useful backdrop for the rest of the book. This introduction also offers a quick overview of the next seven chapters, each devoted to an in-depth treatment of a topic and related innovative management practices. Given the diversity of topics and their coverage, the reader is advised to begin with the current overview before delving into the chapters.

Forces of change

Market change is a constant source of problems for some firms and opportunities for others. The particular changes that are highlighted in the following paragraphs have for the most part brought new managerial issues to the surface and, in doing so, have challenged our traditional ways of thinking about marketing. If marketing is to remain a central and relevant discipline in business, it must find ways of addressing these deep and intertwined shifts in the environment. Only then can it guide managers in their never-ending search for effective practices.

- **Commoditization** An unrelenting change in technology, in addition to well-informed customers and fast-moving competition, has made sure that many once unique products or services have rapidly lost their intrinsic differentiation value and become 'commoditized'. Take the example of PalmOne, the original makers of palm-sized personal digital assistants (PDAs). The company that spends close to 10% of its turnover on new product development, and enjoys one of the strongest brands in the business, still finds itself suffering from the effects of commoditization – i.e. declining customer franchise due to the emergence of rivals with similar or enhanced offerings, and the resulting pressure on prices and margins. Competition from Hamstring (later acquired by the company), HP, Dell, Toshiba, Sony and a number of others has had a devastating impact on the pioneer of PDAs. Since 2001, the company's turnover has declined by 45% (to $872 million in 2003) and its net income has sunk from a profit of $57.5 million in 2000 to a loss of $64 million in 2003, dragging share prices down from the split adjusted level of nearly $1600 in 2000 to around $22 in mid-2004.[1]

PalmOne is not alone in feeling the effects of commoditization. Managers in a growing numbers of industries as diverse as IT, pharmaceuticals, branded consumer products and banking services, just to name a few sectors, complain of the ever-shortened lifecycles of their product or service offerings and the resulting negative impact on profitability. How to pre-empt or slow down the commoditization process remains the single most crucial issue for many marketers. Marketing innovation (as opposed to product innovation) can form the centrepiece of such strategies, but it also remains an area to which traditional marketing has paid scant attention. Innovations in segmentation and target marketing, in pricing, distribution, communication and services are all areas where management practices have bypassed the discipline in countering commoditization.

- **Consolidation** A real force for change in many markets is the growing concentration of sales and profits among a handful of major customers. A good example is the global automobile manufacturing industry, in which suppliers find themselves relying on a shrinking number of OEM (original equipment manufacturer) customers, a process that is accelerated by mergers, acquisitions and alliances among previously independent automakers. Other sectors facing similar consolidation in their customer base include health care and pharmaceuticals, shipping and transportation, paper, fast-moving consumer goods (FMCGs) and retail distribution, to name a few.

The steady and highly visible process of consolidation in distribution has led to the emergence of powerful retail chains and buying groups (a collection of smaller chains and independents joining forces together). Sony, the global leader in consumer electronics, sells a growing share of its worldwide production through fewer and fewer mega retailers. As of a few years ago the company sold more than 40% of its volume in Europe through no more than ten retail chains and buying groups. That percentage has kept rising steadily, bringing increasing pressure on manufacturer prices and margins.

The central issue for marketers facing consolidation among their customers is to find ways of acquiring and retaining their ever-larger accounts, and of doing so profitably. The recent focus on key account processes and customer relationship management (CRM) systems is a reflection of changing times where gaining or losing a single customer could have a major impact on profitability. The focus also reflects a major shift in perspectives, from transactional mass marketing, the discipline's traditional preoccupation, to customer- and account-specific relationship marketing. The discipline's need for new models and tools for managing important and long-lasting customer relationships cannot be overstated.

• **Power shift** A direct consequence of the trend towards consolidation among customers is a general shift of bargaining power away from vendors to their buyers. Perhaps nowhere is this trend more in evidence than in retailing, where the ever-larger chains and buying groups have gained the upper hand *vis-à-vis* their suppliers, including producers of many branded products. Wal-Mart, the world's largest retailer with sales of nearly $260 billion, uses its enormous buying power to drive down prices paid to its suppliers and, in addition, to dictate its strict policies on quality, logistics and vendor services. That power has allowed the retailer to enter and prosper in product categories not normally associated with mass discounting. To illustrate, Wal-Mart became the largest seller of DVD players in the US market thanks to its aggressively low prices (with some models selling for as little as $39), made possible by its huge purchasing power. A latecomer to DVD retailing, Wal-Mart stole shares from specialist chains like Circuit City and Best Buy with prices they could not profitably match.

The growth of private labels has been a factor in boosting retailers' power *vis-à-vis* their branded-goods suppliers. In some markets the penetration of lower priced private labels in food and other grocery categories is as high as 40%, if not more. Another factor contributing to the shift in power is the retailers' increasing access to relevant and timely information on consumer shopping behaviour. The advent of bar codes and intelligent cash-register systems has allowed retailers to know a great deal about consumers, and they are using that knowledge to their advantage in dealing with their less-informed suppliers.

Outside consumer retailing, a shift in bargaining power downstream, to customers and, in turn, to their customers, has taken place across a wide spectrum of industries, including computer parts and electronics, auto parts and components, packaging material and systems, speciality chemicals and professional services, to name a few. The complex set of issues arising out of marketing to powerful customers has not been adequately dealt with in traditional marketing literature. Innovations like the 'Intel inside' brand campaign that bypass the immediate industrial customers to promote the company's ingredient products to final end users are examples of how companies might effectively use downstream marketing tactics to rebalance their bargaining power *vis-à-vis* their large and powerful buyers. Such innovative practices aside, the discipline is far from ready to tackle the compelling issues surrounding the power shift.

- **Margin erosion** The combined effects of commoditization, consolidation in customer base and shift in bargaining power have had a predictably negative impact on producer margins. Levi's, the iconic brand for jeans, is a recent victim of margin erosion. Faced with multitudes of rivals marketing low-priced denims, the company has launched a new line of discount jeans selling through mass distributors like Wal-Mart and Target. Called Levi Strauss Signature, the line sells at prices nearly 50% below those of the company's traditional jeans, and offers margins that are significantly below those of its core line. The entry into low-margin discount jeans was a strategy that the struggling Levi's had for a long time tried to avoid. But its hand was forced by the seemingly unstoppable loss of market share to its lower priced competitors, including private labels. And it remains far from clear if the low-priced line can catapult the company back to profitability.

Nokia is another example of a company that has seen its margins erode as it tries to combat the growing competition in its sector. The company's enviable global market share and operating margins in handsets have come under pressure thanks to the entry of new players like Samsung and LG Electronics on the one hand and the revival of old competitors like Motorola on the other. To regain losses in market share (down 10% from a high of 40%), the company has had to slash by more than 20% its average selling prices. The net effect on operating margins has been dramatic: a reduction from 23% return on sales just a few years ago, down to a projected 16%. The news of a shortfall in profitability has had a devastating effect on the company's market capitalization, with stock prices dropping by nearly 40% in the course of a few months.

The cases of Levi's and Nokia, two truly global brands, are by no means exceptional. An OECD survey of major international companies shows that the trend of margin erosion is a pervasive one. The survey illustrates a clear degradation of operating margins among the 147 Fortune Global 500 firms for which data was available. For the period under consideration, the survey shows, the average domestic operating margins for these firms declined from nearly 10% in 1990 to just about 7% in 2001. For non-domestic margins the decline was even larger, from 10% to close to 5% over the same period.[2]

The growing issue of margin erosion has coincided with the general pressure on management to increase profitability and shareholder value. Over the last decade managers have turned their focus towards cost cutting under different banners such as 're-engineering', 'streamlining the business', or 'reducing complexity'. Whatever the euphemism used, the reality is that today's marketers are under pressure to 'make the numbers', which often means cutting back on both short-term marketing expenses and long-term investments. For many top managers eager to deliver on tight financial targets, it is easier to cut back on advertising than on IT budgets, or to downsize and even eliminate the marketing department than to do the same with procurement and supply-chain planning. Business priorities are shifting and marketing has to learn to go about its mission in leaner times.

The inherent risk in margin erosion is that it can lead to a myopic view of marketing that would further accentuate the profitability problem. More specifically, many value-adding strategies meant to improve a producer's ability to charge higher prices and improve margins require investments that might be considered excessive or even dispensable under a cost-rationalization regime. Investments to improve customer-service capability, modernize the product portfolio, strengthen the brand or upgrade skills for key-account personnel all require commitment of financial resources that could only be justified over the longer run. In their absence, the firm falls victim to its own short-term priorities that could simply accelerate commoditization and put even greater pressure on margins and profits.

Traditional marketing practices offer little in the way of combating margin erosion or doing more with less. As top-of-mind issues for today's corporate managers, measuring and increasing the productivity of marketing expenditures are not adequately addressed by the discipline. The reputation of marketers as free spenders continues to be more than just a caricature. It rings true in many companies.

- **Value focus** The tough market changes highlighted above are compelling companies to re-examine their past strategies and embark on new directions that aim to offer customers novel and differentiated values – values that combat commoditization and the accompanying margin erosion. While the other forces are all external to the firm, the renewed focus on value creation is an internal push for change. Such efforts take place under different banners, but almost all incorporate at least two ingredients: a drive towards a customer-oriented organization; and a greater focus on value innovation. The first ingredient is centred on making the entire organization more knowledgeable about the customers it serves and enabling it to be more responsive to their unmet needs. The second is about finding innovative ways of fulfilling those needs profitably. Both ingredients are essential for a customer-focused strategic renewal.

For Nestlé, the world's largest food company, value focus has meant a renewed emphasis on innovation as a pillar of the company's growth strategy. The brand managers are being exhorted to seek consumer insights that lead to innovative products and marketing practices. In this light, the firm makes a distinction between 'renovation' and 'innovation', with the first aiming to keep pace with changing consumer expectations, and the second striving to leapfrog ahead of the consumer with novel product ideas. A new and improved formulation of Nescafé, the company's global brand of instant coffee, is an example of the former; the launch of Nespresso, a highly successful roast and ground coffee-making system incorporating hardware and services, is an example of the latter. The drive towards renovation and innovation is led from the CEO's office and is being felt all across the company's global organization.

The push towards new customer values can take the strategy beyond a company's core, and often commoditized, markets. The Swedish company SKF, the world's largest producer of ball bearings, has stretched beyond its core by turning its know-how in rotation technology into innovative products and services for its customers in the manufacturing sector. The services division presents plant managers with a pallet of modular packages including preventive maintenance, technical service, training and even management assistance, all aiming to enhance factory productivity. These value-added services, offered with performance guarantees, have made the division the most profitable in SKF, with returns several times above those of the core business of ball bearings.

Similarly, IBM's spectacular turnaround in the mid-1990s was built on a move towards new value-adding services that took the company beyond its core of mainframe computers. The old IBM-centred and hardware-focused philosophy had to be transformed through a customer-centred strategy that combined products, including those produced by competitors, with services into innovative solutions for business problems. Examples of IBM solutions range from helping retailers to increase revenues from each customer visit with smart shopping carts that help shoppers to navigate comfortably through crowded aisles, to running a global company's accounting and finance department, and business consulting services on e-commerce strategies. While hardware sales have declined, revenues from the highly profitable and fast-growing business services have risen to $43 billion.

Without a doubt, the changes implied by value focus are no less than a rediscovery of the spirit of the marketing concept, a working philosophy that was almost forgotten during the heyday of corporate re-engineering. But while customer-value creation is on the top management agenda, in most companies the marketing people are not driving it. Contributing to this fact is the misconception that marketing is all about short-term action, while value innovation is a strategic responsibility best assigned to new business development, strategic planners or even R&D. The result: business strategies that are elegant but fail to take into account customer needs, and new products and services that are innovative but lack consumer appeal. Side-lining marketing has not been in the best interests of business.

The marketing discipline has only itself to blame for the current state of affairs. The field has failed to rise above its traditional preoccupation with tactics; it has failed to address the big picture – the issues surrounding the business strategy, the organization and its culture, and the transformations required to link a company's priorities with those of its customers. The discipline that invented the all-important marketing concept is excluded from participating in its implementation.

Figure 1.1 depicts the five forces highlighted above and their interrelationship. The two forces of commoditization and consolidation are the primary drivers; they provide the engine behind power shift, margin erosion and the push for value focus.

As mentioned, the preceding list of market forces is not meant to be exhaustive of all changes that have challenged traditional marketing. Marketing's slowness to adapt can also be seen elsewhere. Where the traditional ideas in marketing have been of little use, the practice has bypassed

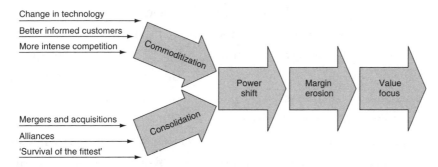

Figure 1.1   Forces of change in the marketing environment

the discipline. Through trial and error, innovative management action has filled the gap.

The book's coverage

This book is about fresh ideas that go beyond the traditional boundaries of marketing, ideas that are for the most part inspired by the recent innovations in practice. Our work does not claim to address all the gaps in the discipline, nor suggest a 'new and improved' marketing mix for the twenty-first century. Those noble and much-needed contributions are far beyond the scope of this book. Rather, the authors have selected a number of areas where modern marketers have devised innovative ways of addressing the emerging issues in their businesses and, in doing so, have contributed to the practice of marketing. The discipline can learn much from these practices.

What follows is an overview of each of the next seven chapters with a summary of the core ideas presented under each heading. Chapter 2 begins the sequence with value chain marketing, a topic that examines opportunities for marketing downstream to the customer's customer. The following three chapters view novel value creation and differentiation through aligning with major customers, the effective marketing of services and two-way (internal and external) branding. Chapter 6 offers a robust conceptual tool for analysing market opportunities and devising profitable marketing strategies. Profitability is also a concern of Chapter 7, which delves into the emerging practices of price discrimination – a by-product of the growth of database marketing. The last chapter addresses the issue of organizational structure and how it can help or hinder customer-value creation and responsiveness.

A short abstract of each chapter follows.

- **Chapter 2: Value Chain Marketing**

  Much of traditional marketing theory and practice is focused on a firm's immediate customers. Typically, they are defined as the 'next in line' institutions who are the direct users of a company's products or services. Many vendors have found that this narrow view, focusing on the nearest set of buyers, is insufficient for sustained competitive advantage. Instead, companies have learned to look down the entire value chain to understand the behaviour of the customer's customers, sometimes several steps beyond the immediate buyers. We have named this process of identifying, understanding and at times even influencing the downstream customers *value chain marketing*. Chapter 2 covers this concept and explains how it can best be employed to strengthen a firm's marketing operations.

- **Chapter 3: Countering Commoditization: Value-added Strategies and Aligning with Customers**
  Commoditization of products and services has forced many industrial vendors to look beyond their core businesses for growth and profitability. Attempts to overcome commoditization have led to novel value-added strategies that range from customization to system development and solutions innovation. In addition, a growing number of firms are engaging their major customers in what could best be described as 'collaborative marketing': attempting to align their own operations and/or strategies towards serving a small number of important customers in ways that traditional marketing never conceived of. Instead of arm-wrestling with their major accounts for value capture, these vendors collaborate with them to create a larger value pool on which both parties can draw. This chapter lays out the logic of such alignments and explores ways in which suppliers can collaborate for greater value creation and capture. The chapter also highlights the barriers and gateways to aligning with customers.

- **Chapter 4: The Marketing of Services: How is it Different?**
  In this chapter we will look at what is different about intangible services – as opposed to tangible products – and what it means for marketing, in particular what needs to be done differently to attract customers and to retain them. In this context the following issues will be addressed: making the intangible tangible, selling the service and the ability to serve, pricing for peaks and troughs, quality of delivery (doing it right the first time) and managing the customer mix and involvement. The chapter also includes a useful classification of service businesses and the different roles of 'soft factors' in their success. It ends with an examination of

the role of the marketing function in a service organization and the specific issues related to the internationalization of services.

- **Chapter 5: The Missing 'P' in the Marketing Mix: Putting Passion into Brands**

  Traditional marketing has recognized that strong brands are the rewards offered by the market for good management of those brands. Many businesses have focused on communicating the benefits of their brands externally; but few have gone the extra mile to create and manage the extra 'P' (for Passion) in their marketing mix: turning strong brands into 'passion brands'. Innovations in brand building show that managing passion brands is not only about external communications; it is also about communicating effectively internally and about making sure that employees become the best brand ambassadors by creating a strong emotional link between the company and the market. Only then can executives expect to dramatically differentiate their brands of products and services from their competitors'. Building on the experience of companies such as Starbucks, Nike and Ducati, the chapter will also suggest why internal branding is a worthwhile exercise; what an appropriate internal marketing strategy might be; and what tools are necessary to better engage employees for better results.

- **Chapter 6: Beyond Beating Competition: Shaping Markets for Profitable Growth**

  Many traditional marketers are too focused on winning and beating competitors, sometimes at almost any price. However, a few leading companies focus not only on winning, but also on ensuring that the market will generate attractive margins for them. This requires marketing executives to think beyond their customers and competitors, and focus attention on the other market forces that impact profitability. These include potential entrants, substitute products and services, complementary products and services, and suppliers. This chapter will explore some of the many strategies and tactics that companies can, and do, use to manage each of these market forces and thus increase the likelihood of achieving high profits in a market. Moves that on the surface make good sense can sometimes have serious, unanticipated, deleterious impacts on the long-term profitability of a market. The strategies and tactics will be illustrated with examples drawn from a variety of industries.

- **Chapter 7: New Frontiers in Pricing for Profit**
  Until recently, many marketing managers grappled with setting the one 'right' price – set too high or too low and profits suffered. Opportunities to price-discriminate were few and far between. Today the combination of databases and technology presents marketers with a multitude of ways in which to offer different prices to different customers. While the opportunity here is clear – charging more to those willing to pay more – the pricing decision has become much more complex. It has moved from setting just one number to setting many, and to determining a plethora of payment structures. This chapter will deal with the economic and psychological factors at play in this new world that permits almost infinite flexibility in pricing. What should managers consider in setting their price structures? And how should we handle customer perceptions of differential pricing? Issues covered include: the impact of technology and customer information on price setting; a survey of approaches to price discrimination; the psychology of pricing and its potential impact on consumer behaviour.

• **Chapter 8: Beyond the Matrix: An Organization-wide Solution for Creating and Sustaining Customer Value**

For decades companies have struggled with what exactly is the role of the marketing function and indeed what is its role, if any, in driving or realizing a customer-value orientation. The startling evidence from several studies is that the concept of focusing the entire firm on customer-value creation simply hasn't caught on in practice. At best customer satisfaction and retention rates are mediocre, companies struggle with implementing a customer-value orientation and CEOs often subjugate it to the interests of other stakeholders. This chapter will examine how organizational structure and company culture work hand in hand to focus the entire organization on customer-value creation. It will reveal how, counter to prevailing notions about empowerment and network organizations, customer-value orientation thrives in environments where clarity and simplicity are valued and hierarchy is appreciated. This organizational vision demands that we revisit traditional notions of structure. We recommend revisiting the traditional matrix organization and respecifying the role of marketing.

References

[1] Sony, facing declining margins, recently announced its withdrawal from the PDA markets in North America and Europe. Others are likely to follow.

[2] Ghemawat, Pankaj, 'The Forgotten Strategy', *Harvard Business Review*, November 2003, Vol. 81, Issue 11, p. 79.

2
Value Chain Marketing
Professor Jean-Pierre Jeannet

T he situations described below represent a new type of marketing challenge that may be found worldwide across many industries.

Exa, a small start-up firm pioneering a non-abrasive cleaner that generates no toxic waste, had difficulty marketing its process. The firm developed low pressure blasting tools for cleaning services and distributed them through the building trades. After a disappointing reception, it realized it needed to influence not only its direct customers but also members of the building services' value chain: building owners, building managers and other related service companies.

Bukser & Berging, a Norwegian tugboat operator, developed a new tugboat design to assist steering and harbour placement. Conceived for slow-moving ocean vessels operating in narrow harbours, fjords or channels, the design innovations placed the fin first and changed the hull from V-shaped to a shell. The new design cost more, and harbour operators as direct customers were slow to adopt it. The company found it necessary to work downstream with harbour customers such as oil or chemical companies.

A supplier of polyurethane materials developed a new system for use in car seats. The company could not convince car seat manufacturers, its direct customers, to switch to its more expensive product. It addressed automobile manufacturers, for whom saving a few centimetres in cushion height translated into gaining interior head room, a detail so important that the added cost was easily justified. The customer down the value chain most influenced the decision.

An agrochemical company developed new chemical treatments for a variety of crops. These treatments were customarily marketed and distributed to farmers through agricultural co-operatives and dealers. Downstream participants in the farm produce value chain required the company to change its marketing and pitch not only to farmers, who were yield-driven, but also to food processors and retailers concerned about chemical residue.

Blocked market access: a common theme

The stories above have a common thread: each company arrived at a point where traditional marketing approaches became ineffective. Established firms (the agrochemicals and polyurethane examples) found that downstream players affected marketing results. The start-up (cleaning agent) failed to penetrate established markets with new technology or to attract attention from distributors and customers. The firm with a design innovation (tugboat) was forced to work with downstream customers.

The phenomenon that we call blocked market access results from heightened competition and from the introduction of new technology. As companies innovate to escape the threat of commoditization (a subject we shall discuss in detail in the next chapter), having a breakthrough product does not guarantee success. Behaviour changes are required, both along the channel and by the customers. Market bottlenecks and limited market absorption are likely to become increasingly common across companies and industries.

Traditional marketing[1] has limits. The fact that companies need new approaches for different technologies has led to what we call 'value chain marketing'. 'Traditional marketing' refers to practices aimed at existing target customers, with existing sales or promotional practices, employing existing arguments and approaches. To break out of this behavioural stranglehold and differentiate from competitors, we offer the concept of value chain marketing with the view that, while not yet established, it will become imperative for firms that wish to succeed in the future.

The concept of value chain marketing

The marketing function has typically provided competitive analysis on products and services offered by other firms. Analysis has focused on offerings closely related in purpose and function. Any firm in the market could become the focus of analysis, comparing direct competitor products and companies in great detail. However, as companies apply standard marketing concepts, they are challenged to differentiate their products and services and to capture and retain advantage in crowded markets. To break through marketing clutter, companies need to understand customer processes and the processes of their customer's customer. In this chapter, we argue that companies need to search for new ways to render marketing operations more effective.

Over the past decade, competitive analysis practised by business analysts and company strategists has given way to the industry view, based on gaining insight from analysing an entire industry. The main proponent of industry-based competitive analysis is Michael Porter, who wrote two seminal books, *Competitive Strategy*[2] and *Competitive Advantage*.[3] According to Porter's thesis, the entire industry becomes the focus of analysis, including players both upstream and downstream from a given set of competitors. This calls for coverage of participants not usually included in traditional analysis.[4]

With this more coherent view, a rich set of insights can be gained on the dynamics of an entire industry, leading to an understanding of requirements for all competitors. We will revisit these requirements later as key success factors (KSFs), essential building blocks in the development of competitive strategy.

Analysis is usually left to corporate strategists and not picked up by marketing management. Underlying this chapter is the assumption that developing competitive marketing strategy requires a focus on the industry and its value chain. We use the term 'value chain marketing' to refer to the practice of influencing an entire industry value chain for the benefit of the marketing function.

The industry view of competitive struggle yields important insights on the role the marketing function can and should play in an integrated business strategy. It is essential that marketing managers learn to apply the industry view and incorporate its conclusions to build marketing strategy.

Value chain marketing requires marketers to develop an enhanced understanding of their industry, including activity at successive steps throughout the value chain, and to apply marketing tools to maximize effectiveness of the marketing programme up and down the value chain. New analytic tools to understand the industry must be deployed, and new tools to maximize marketing effectiveness must be developed. Value chain marketing challenges marketers to step into a broader framework where the dividing line between business strategy and market development is sometimes blurred.

Analysing the macro business system

The basic building block for understanding any industry is the macro business system. It includes all industry participants, connected in a successive chain of value added, from raw material production to OEM customers, wholesalers, retailers, retail customers and in some cases recycling. As in macroeconomics, where macro denotes the behaviour of the economy as a whole, the term 'macro business system' applies to an entire industry and all players upstream and downstream from a given competitor.

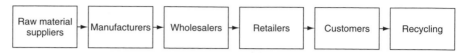

Figure 2.1   The macro industry business system

We define the macro business system as the industry value chain.[5] Later we will distinguish the macro from the micro business system, which we define as the value chain within a company, consisting of value-added steps and processes as they take place within a firm. This is consistent with Porter's definition of the firm value chain.[6] However, since analysis of the macro business system differs from analysis of the micro business system, we use both terms to describe the business system (see Figure 2.1).

Identifying participants in the macro business system

Macro business system firms participate in the flow of goods from raw materials to finished products to customers or consumers. The number of stages in a macro system depends on the industry structure and the extent to which free-standing activity exists among firms. For any step in a macro value chain represented by a significant number of entities, a separate participant category should be identified for analysis.

Although we can speak of a standard business system (see above), any experienced analyst knows that each industry may present a unique business system. Thus participant categories may differ among industries, as well as the types and numbers of participant groups. The methodology, however, is consistent and requires us to flow chart the value-added stream, identifying each step represented by any group of firms.

The starting point is to define the industry. This has preoccupied writers in the past. Traditional marketing theory has approached this question from a 'business definition' viewpoint.[7] However, the term 'business' has typically referred to the organizational unit.

Past and present writers have accepted that it is as much an art as a science to define an industry by drawing a line around its boundary. For the purposes of this book, we define an industry as a set of interrelated activities and organizational units that compose a value chain. An industry is more than just a segment.[8] It incorporates all actors who serve the demand from a coherent group of segments, or markets, for which one set of participants is the major source of satisfaction.

Looking at examples, we could say that construction toys, such as those manufactured by LEGO, are part of the construction toy segment, which in turn is part of the broader toy industry, as are games, dolls and other toy products. Expensive luxury watches, such as those made by Rolex, are part of the watch industry, as are less expensive models made by companies such as Swatch. Boundaries are not always clear, and judgement must determine what is part of an industry, where one industry stops and the next begins. In our opinion, when a discrete set of players consistently competes in only one part of an industry and not another, a separate industry boundary begins. Tracing product flow, components and technology would show whether we were dealing with a separate value chain.

Industry participant categories

No industry business system is likely to resemble another. Although most consist of several player categories, each has its own categories, labels and flow patterns. Categories we might expect to find include: suppliers, manufacturers, intermediate users (OEMs), wholesalers, retailers, customers and, increasingly, recyclers.

Many supplier categories typically compose one industry, often with a range of different materials or components. In product industries, it is useful to list components that make up a product. In the watch industry, these include watch movement, bracelet, casing, dial and face. For automobiles, we have tyres, glass, electronics, axles, brake systems and lighting systems. Both industries have component flows into the manufacturing/assembly stage. Process industries may have materials rather than components. For paint, we have resins, solvents, pigments and other additives. In either case, components and materials make up the supply stage of an industry.

In the following section, we describe the players to analyse. We will follow later with a list of questions, issues and insights. Rather than adding them at each stage, we will do so for all player categories combined.

- **Upstream component and material suppliers** How far back into the raw material chain to begin analysis depends on whether suppliers serve one group of manufacturers or multiple customers that do not compete.

- **Downstream manufacturers and processors** All steps of an industry value chain, following the entire flow of physical goods or processes.
- **Secondary users or OEMs** In industries where a secondary user step exists (car components such as tyres supplied to auto manufacturers), it must be evaluated with respect to influence both backward and forward.
- **Wholesalers** Part of the macro business system. May also be known as 'distributors'. In some industries, manufacturers wholesale through branch sale points.
- **Retailers** Part of the macro business system. For fast-moving consumer goods (FMCG), supermarkets, discounters and hypermarkets. For automobiles, the car dealer.
- **Consumers and end users** The final stage in most business systems (not to be confused with 'customers' as used to refer to the firms next in line in the business system). Although a firm might view its own direct customer groups as segments, it must also see final users in segment terms and understand their interests.
- **Recyclers** With the emergence of environmental concerns, many products no longer 'end' at the consumption stage. Government regulations in Europe and the US mandate recycling for many industrial products.

Mapping macro business systems

Industry analysis can yield different types of value chains. The analyst must avoid viewing all macro business systems alike. We may identify several prototypes (see Figure 2.2).

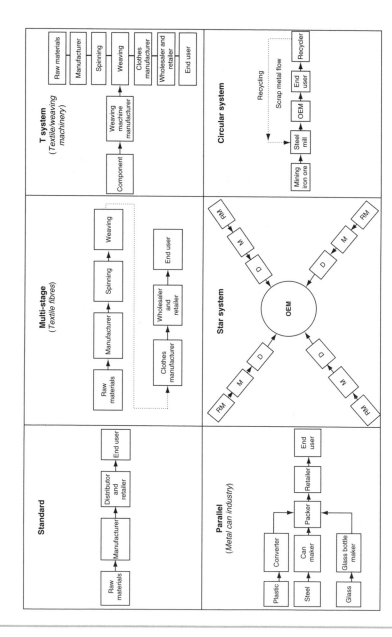

Figure 2.2 Prototypes of industry business systems

The standard business system

This consists of raw material suppliers, manufacturers, distributors and customers/end users. Most industries are more complex and will require the analyst to think creatively about value flow.

The multi-stage business system

In the multi-stage business system, there may be several stages of raw material suppliers as well as several intermediate users. An example is textiles, where raw material (cotton, manmade fibre) travels through multiple value creation steps of industry participants to garment manufacturers and retailers.

The 'T' business system

In some standard and multi-stage business systems, output from a previous stage is consumed at the following stage. This is the case for many materials and consumables. Equipment-based industries are different. Builders of textile-weaving machinery do not see their machines become part of the end product. For weaving-machine manufacturers, business 'ends' with the textile-weaving firms. Likewise, textile weavers do not consider machines as 'raw material'. We may think of the business system as a 'T' with raw material flow on one axis (textiles, cloth, paper) and machinery on the perpendicular axis. It is important, however, to recognize that the business system dynamic comes from the raw material axis, often influencing reality for equipment manufacturers. Industrial equipment marketers must recognize the 'T' business system as different from the traditional business system.

The parallel business system

In circumstances where materials can be substituted, the most insightful way to look at the macro industry is as a parallel business system. Let us use packaging materials as an example. A maker of steel cans supplying a packer of canned food needs to be aware of a parallel industry system of glass, laminates and other packaging materials, all aimed at the same target, the packer, who selects from the materials available. The dynamics of a parallel business system are important to chemicals and materials firms, and also to industrial component suppliers if an OEM can trade technical solutions from two different streams of industry value chains. Here, substitution among parallel business systems governs the competition.

The star business system

One of the most complex business systems is characterized by state-of-the-art configurations of components that need to be integrated. In the case of a factory ('the factory of the future'), this might include components such as machine tools, transfer systems, robots, computer controls and inventory controls. Each of these if analysed would suggest its own industry and could be configured as its own macro business system. Due to the complexity of 'the factory of the future', each business subsystem targets the same manufacturer/client. Each group of participants in the subsystem hopes to become the 'power broker' by assuming control over the decision-making process and the specifications. Whoever controls specifications will be able to 'spec' others in or out and emerge as the *star* with the most power. The dynamics of the star system are different from the others we have identified. The star system is of primary importance to suppliers of complex industrial systems.

The circular business system

We have looked at business systems as a one-way flow from upstream to the downstream end user. In many industries, however, the flow of value added does not stop with the end user. Through recycling we have found a way to reuse materials. Recycling flows are already at a high volume for steel and paper (newsprint in particular). In both industries, recycled material competes directly with material from paper mills and integrated steel mills. It can be expected that the 'take back' portion of other industries will increase and that some will contain a circular system for usage, although in most industries it will not reach the extent of paper and steel.

Developing business systems for service industries

One of the most challenging assignments is to develop a macro business system for service industries. Unlike with product value chains, it is difficult to follow steps and identify players, since there is no physical flow of goods. This does not mean business system analysis is not valid for service industries, only that analysis takes a different form. Its inclusion in a business system follows different rules.

Analysing flows may still be the most appropriate way to draw boundary lines for a service industry. Developing an industry from customer flows may be appropriate for airlines and health care, in which passengers and patients figure on the value chain. For banking and financial services, tracing money flow is a starting point; likewise information flow for credit cards, paper flow for insurance and package flow for courier and transportation industries (see Figure 2.3).

The challenge for service industries is to chart a business system that although different in composition leads to the same analytic goal as for

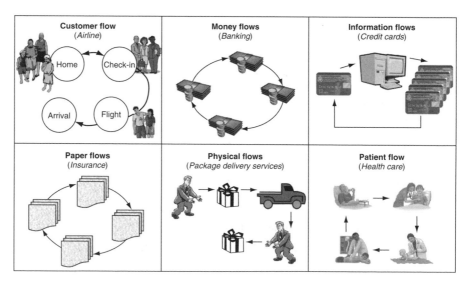

Figure 2.3   Service industry business systems

product industries. We believe the same type of analysis applied to service industries yields as much rich insight. Throughout this book, we therefore apply our concepts to both. However, where the service industry offers particular challenges that require an innovative approach, we note those instances and respond accordingly.

Analysing dynamics of the macro business system

The reason we need to analyse the macro business system a company faces is to understand how industry dynamics impact marketing. If a company wants to create value for customers, it needs to understand industry developments that may change how it markets products and services.

Analysis provides a clear understanding of what will happen to each industry participant in the future and how the complex web of interrelationships will change. For marketing management, we will view this with respect to marketing activity. However, we must first understand key developments and their impact on how business is conducted at each stage of an industry. We will now outline elements for analysis. What follows is not meant as a complete list, but rather as a starting point to uncover industry trends (see Figure 2.4).

Assessing industry developments

Most industries can be described from status quo and, by tracing their business system, we can define the key relationships today. It is much more

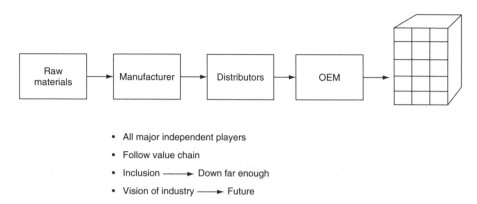

- All major independent players
- Follow value chain
- Inclusion ⟶ Down far enough
- Vision of industry ⟶ Future

Figure 2.4   Strategic mapping

important, however, to anticipate change, which will force all players to adjust their strategy. Looking for changes anticipated in the future, or for a changing business focus, is a point of departure. Change may come from government legislation, environmental requirements, technology break-throughs, emerging market realities or new competitive structures. Macro business system analysis should take into account the important evolutionary factors that may be expected.

The automobile industry provides an excellent example. In the late 1980s, Philips Automotive Entertainment Division, developing car radios and stereo systems, revised how it did business. Historically, automotive companies and customers had expected very little from car radios. Radios tended to look alike, and similar radios were sold to car companies. With the advent of energy-efficient cars, manufacturers were submitting cars to extensive wind-tunnel testing to reduce drag and energy consumption. This resulted in cars looking more and more similar. The dashboard became a differentiating element. Since car radios were mounted in dashboards, their design suddenly became very important. Car manufacturers no longer wanted similar designs, so car radio manufacturers were forced to offer different models to each client. This example illustrates how a particular development, in this case the need to focus on saving energy, rippled through an entire industry and affected the operations of other industry participants.

Identifying industry change is a challenging aspect of developing business strategy. Sometimes change comes slowly as an industry shifts,[9] while at other times abrupt breakpoints may occur.[10] The following section is intended to give structure to any industry analysis.

Identifying industry drivers

The term 'change drivers' refers to factors that have a major effect on an industry and force change in the macro business system. Michael Porter outlines five forces that shape industry dynamics: *industry rivalry*, *new entrants*, *alternative technologies*, *buyer power* and *supplier power*.[11] These forces affect the bargaining power of the players and apply to any stage of the macro business system; a detailed analysis could be performed for any player group.

It is important to understand underlying drivers for an industry. Four sources of drivers can be identified in most industries: technology, economics, changes in customer composition and new entrants.

Technology drivers are perhaps the easiest to understand, though not always easy to spot. The computer industry offers an excellent example of technology change and its effect on all players. Until the early 1980s, large mainframe computers processing vast amounts of information were the lead installations in most firms and corporate EDP departments. In the mid-1970s, they were challenged by mini-computers, which performed the same function but were smaller machines for 'departmental processing'. In the 1980s, the personal computer made possible distributed processing, with microprocessors adding power. The resulting development of client servers that could hold application programs accessed by large numbers of personal computers radically changed the computer industry. The restructuring of IBM and other mainframe suppliers was largely caused by this technology change. Similar technology changes have occurred in other industries, for example the move from mechanical to electronic watches.

Technology change may consist of breakthroughs in design, materials or processes. While design changes tend to be associated most with new patents and products, both material and process changes can have an important impact as well. Many industries associated with chemistry or metals have experienced such changes, for example the development of plastic materials that perform better than steel or aluminium. Processes in some industries can have a major impact, such as the development of better yeast for the beer brewing industry. Information technology changes have greatly affected the structure of many industries, making available cheaper and faster telecommunications.

The technologies of competing industries are often overlooked in industry analysis. Referred to by Porter as 'substitutes' (a concept we shall examine in more detail in Chapter 6), they may become more competitive as a result of technology advances, even when the industry under scrutiny does not face change.[12] Substitutes, which must be analysed for parallel industry business systems, are more difficult to assess because of the 'not-invented-here' syndrome which often makes breakthroughs appear less relevant.

Cost drivers, or industry economics, are of major concern to all players. This term refers to the cost structure both overall and for each player group, as well as the critical mass requirements that lead to ideal unit size. These elements are determined by cost drivers such as economies of scale, learning curve, experience curve and the fixed vs variable cost structure of an industry.

Analysis should yield a complete picture of the value added and its distribution among player groups in the macro system. This step is best approached by asking how much the end user pays for a product or service and by allocating that expenditure among industry participant groups. Once the value added for each group is determined, the analysis must estimate the cost structure for players. It is our understanding that this is not commonly done by market analysts. Estimates must be established for the cost structure of suppliers, manufacturers, distributors, retailers and customers (OEMs). This includes understanding fixed cost, variable cost and scale effects.[13]

Cost dynamics are often analysed inadequately. Scale effects can accrue across an entire company or per plant. For chemical process industries, the relevant scale is the processing plant and its output or tonnage, and company total output is secondary. In car manufacturing, model composition determines profitability. When analysing cost structure, the question to ask is how cost advantages accrue. We need to understand the unit of cost accumulation (plant, model, product line, total output worldwide, segment volume, etc.).

The cost structure of all industry participants needs to be understood. Component suppliers and product manufacturers have a different cost structure from OEMs or distributors, wholesalers and retailers. In the past, marketing has looked at downstream players, at distributors and retailers in consumer goods, at OEMs in industrial marketing and at the cost structure of its own firm. As we will see, this limited view must give way to a broader view of industry economics that includes all other player groups as well.

Cost structure analysis will define critical size, or minimal size for effective competition in an industry. In many industries, minimal size for profitable operation does exist. In the car industry, it is generally believed that an assembly plant requires an output of 200 000 cars annually. Similar measures exist in other industries. Sometimes, the constraint is a function of a key strategy element, such as new generation technology, that occurs in one step. If a company wants to survive, it must expand this element to stay with competitors. Fixed costs may shape minimal size (the required volume a company must have to stay in the game). Analysis of both fixed and variable costs is critical, with reference not only to the cost structure of today but also to that of the future, as some industry trends may be triggered by changing cost structures.

Competitive dynamics of an industry can be shaped by new entrants. Competitors entering an industry can do so at all stages: at the raw material stage, as manufacturers, as distributors, etc. New entrants may be attracted to a highly profitable industry or may enter by introducing new technology. The paint industry has seen considerable technological change from solvent-based to water-based paint and most recently to powder paint. Most competitors in powder were not previously in wet paint and may be considered new. Tracing recent entrants in an industry can help develop a picture or pattern. We need to analyse new entrant impact on operations. Stating that they are present is not sufficient to enhance our understanding of an industry.

Customer dynamics, or changes in customer composition, are another source of *industry* dynamics. These changes come from the structure of users, segments and distribution. Since we will be spending time on segmentation and understanding market structure later in the chapter, we will only mention here that those developments, sometimes in combination with technology, industry economics and new entrants, can create major industry shifts.

Changes in business system configuration

We have addressed developments in each business system group and drivers that may affect players in the macro business system. These developments may result in a different configuration of the business system as players disappear or new categories arise. Reconfiguration may take various forms. One group of industry participants may spawn a new group by splitting in two. A group may disappear through elimination or combination of two industry stages. Finally, the entire industry is affected by any move to integrate either forward or backward.

Splitting of a stage occurs when a new function suddenly arises and a group of companies begins to serve that new function. In the computer industry, emergence of the personal computer generated a new set of distributors and retailers selling PCs. Computers had previously been sold through company-owned branch offices. The PC age gave rise to a new class of industry players, adding a stage in the PC industry business system.

Combination occurs when one stage absorbs another. One player takes over the function of another and, although the same functions are performed, the independent 'box' disappears. In many consumer goods industries, we have seen the disappearance of wholesalers when their role has been absorbed by the FMCGs or by retail chain stores such as Carrefour in France and Aldi in Germany.

Backward and forward integration tends to eliminate stages. However, integration may not include an entire industry. In paint manufacturing, many firms integrated backward into manufacturing resin, an important raw material. Some independent resin manufacturers still sell resins on the open market, mainly to small firms that are not backward integrated, but also to larger firms that require speciality resins. Thus, we may find integration side by side with overlapping business system stages. It is the trends and the evolutionary direction of the industry that are important for analysis.

Developing an industry vision

The analyst must dissect the macro business system in order to understand how the pieces fit together. Managers should try to foresee how a macro business system may configure in the future. Forward-looking business strategies depend on a view of how the industry will evolve, and firms should envision how their industry will look in the years to come. We may refer to the process of anticipating the future as developing an industry vision.

Using concepts and terms introduced by Porter (1985), envisioning a macro business system of the future could begin with the five forces explained earlier.[14] Each business system stage is subject to these five forces. Their impact leads eventually to a new configuration, either by splitting, elimination or separation of stages as discussed above.

Tracking drivers in the macro business system and understanding how each player group influences the other stages, the analyst must determine which stage acts as the power source (drives the other stages). If we conceptualize a drawing of interlocking cog wheels, the drive wheel determines speed and direction. Understanding the location of the industry 'drive wheel' and anticipating changes at that point in the 'interlocking cogs' are the critical aspects of developing an industry vision.

Tracking industry evolution

Marketers need to recognize shifting movements and trends as they lead to changes within the interlocking system described above. Shifts usually result from change in the macro business system. Predicting shifts is a first step in developing market advantage. One approach is to develop industry scenarios.[15]

We may use the pharmaceutical industry as an example. A raw material (a chemical compound) is supplied to pharmaceutical companies, which transform chemicals into drugs. Pharmaceutical companies research, develop, test and market drugs through sales forces to independent physicians or other health-care organizations, depending on the health-care industry structure of a given country. Powerful integrated pharmaceutical firms are the main drivers of this business system.[16]

Changes today in this industry suggest that specialist firms may take over some of the functions of pharmaceutical companies. With the expanding role of biotechnology, new firms have evolved specializing in the drug discovery phase. These small independent start-ups license drugs to large pharmaceutical firms for the rest of the cycle, which includes testing and eventually marketing the product worldwide. If this trend continues, a new stage in the pharmaceutical business system will have been created.

Looking downstream to marketing, we see the testing stage being revolutionized. Pharmaceutical firms now hire independent firms to test drug efficacy, usually through hospitals and research organizations, suggesting yet another step in the value creation process. Evolution may completely restructure the business system for pharmaceuticals in the next decade.

The vision process may feel imprecise to the analytic mind. Our challenge is to envision how industry business systems evolve. We are not doing this in a vacuum. We would like to compare the process to weather forecasting based on a series of satellite photos from outer space, looking down on a particular territory, tracking the clouds (if there are any) over time and projecting the pattern into the near future. The building blocks of our macro business system are constantly updated to reflect industry dynamics. If we are to develop strategies that result in strong market advantage, we must look ahead and develop them for the industry we expect to meet in the future. We would fail if we developed marketing strategies for tomorrow based on yesterday's industry dynamics. Research has shown that rapidly growing companies *have* just such a vision of their industry and its expected course of evolution.[17]

Why marketing managers should be concerned about macro business systems

Analysis alone will not lead to market advantage. A complete understanding of an industry is only the first of several steps to achieving an understanding of the market. Details of the macro business system provide building blocks to understanding an industry and to outlining its key success factors (KSFs). The reason to get involved with these concepts is to gain a deeper understanding of the customers. Let us consider what we mean by key success factors.

Extracting KSFs and industry metrics

KSFs are the basic competitive requirement that a company needs in order to succeed in an industry. They may be an entry ticket for everyone or differentiators among competing firms. KSFs are activities or resources a company needs to bring to the competitive game, and each player category in the macro business system has its own set. They are of strategic importance to each industry player and also to any company desiring to sell products or services to an industry player. The failure of a company to understand KSFs will limit its marketing impact.

KSFs are often expressed as functions, such as marketing, R&D or production. However, such identification is imprecise for most marketing operations, and a company needs to define exactly what the KSFs are, such as a ratio or measurement referenced as an industry metric. Let us review metrics using an example.

A few years ago this author and a colleague assisted a supplier of mass transportation systems (railway) to become more customer-oriented. The supplier arranged a meeting with the operator of a regional transportation system, expecting him to shed light on the relevant KSFs. Before the meeting, we asked the supplier to define what they considered the key metric for rail transportation systems. Led by engineers in the group, they quickly established that the relevant metric was cost per passenger kilometre. The operator then arrived and gave an overview of the operations, the system, the concerns and pressure points. When asked about his key metric, he readily expressed it as cost per train kilometre. He explained that costs were independent of the number of passengers carried and that, once the train had left the depot, costs accumulated regardless of train length or passenger number. Operation on a track with staff in place created a 'train cost' independent of passenger number.

The difference between these two ratios may appear academic to the reader. However, it turned out that under each ratio a very different configuration would be designed. The first required large fast trains; the second cost-effective short trains. A small difference in ratio created a huge difference in design. Only a thorough analysis of the customer's business system and KSFs could yield such insight. In fact, participants from the supplier company dismissed the notion advanced by the operator with the comment, 'He never bought anything from us anyway', only to face major losses and restructuring later. A marketer who ignores the industry metrics in a client's business system does so at his own peril!

Practising value chain marketing

Applying analytic tools to marketing is only useful if we can pattern new marketing approaches accordingly. The following section offers recommendations based on our experience working with many companies. The marketing practices we describe differ significantly from what a typical strategy or business development department in a company might do.

Industry mapping

An important part of value chain marketing is to construct a valid industry map that portrays the target customers. This means outlining the macro business system, identifying its participants and decoding its drivers and participants as explained earlier. Data sources can be found both internally and externally. Internal sources might include the company's business development plans, strategy details and marketing and sales plans. Data collected for a company's own strategy should be distinguished from data on its customers and their industry. Analyst reports and company websites are helpful in piecing together a detailed industry map.

No mapping exercise would be complete without intense debate on its conclusions and their impact on the company. Industry mapping requires an exchange of ideas if it is to achieve an insightful conclusion. The process may then move to the next step.

Understanding the customer

Few marketers would agree that they do not understand their own customers! However, it matters at which level we develop understanding, and with which details. In traditional marketing, we develop expertise in the customer's differentiation and market segments, and in how the customer buys. In value chain marketing, we get into the customer's strategy and business reality as if we were a member of the management team.

We need to become experts at the customer's business, and to do this several value chain steps down, understanding *at each level* what it takes to win. This means understanding the KSFs as the customer sees them, understanding the operating metrics as relevant to the customer and doing all this with a depth that surpasses the customer's own understanding. In our experience, most companies do not push their marketing intelligence far enough to achieve this strategic intimacy.

Exa, the cleaning company mentioned early in this chapter, developed a new chemical agent that can be added to toothpaste. Before meeting with toothpaste manufacturers, the firm went after its own consumer panel, surveys and focus groups. Armed with comprehensive data, it was able to reach a different level of discussion with interested companies.

To achieve this scope, marketers need to apply the tools of value chain analysis at both the macro and micro levels, and to become experts on operational and strategic issues in the client's business. This differs from the practice of 'dropping the products off at the loading dock'. The well-known concept of the customer activity cycle[18] will guide the company to follow the processing stream of products or services and to understand what the customer does with the products or services downstream.

Pooling the customer experience to understand the industry

We often fail to realize that a firm accumulates considerable detail on industry practice based on information gathered through serving a single customer. Firms maintain business relationships with many customers, giving the supplier the advantage of seeing into different operations. The company that manages to pool this information into a generalized body of knowledge can achieve a level of expertise that often exceeds that of its individual customers. The challenge for value chain marketing is to accumulate these individual points of knowledge and to power them up for a deeper understanding with value to all customers. Such industry knowledge, if applied properly, gives a decisive edge over competitors, and this edge is more sustainable than other forms of advantage.

Hendrix, a Dutch animal-feed company, decided to invest in a powerful database that pooled all of its farmer customers' feed operations for pigs and other animals. Combining and drilling across this data, the company was able to extract valuable lessons on how to house animals, which went beyond the nutritional value of its feed. Learning from thousands of farmers, Hendrix could know more than any one farmer alone. The same applies to any company that supplies a large number of customers with shared characteristics, and shows how intelligent data mining can produce deep industry knowledge.

Companies often want to know how far they should take this, or when and where to stop. The insights gained need to add value to the customer's business, with the result that the customer values the insight from the supplier. The marketing company needs to become known for its strategic insight into the customer's business. Only then can the full impact of value chain marketing be harnessed.

Developing value propositions of strategic value

Armed with full understanding of the customer's business, the marketing firm is now in a position to build effective value propositions that impact positively on the customer's strategic realities. Describing products, services or systems in terms of their contribution to a client's strategic issues differs from espousing products based on the customer's buying requirements or expected benefits.

We can illustrate this by going back to one of our examples, the polyurethane company marketing foaming agents to car seat manufacturers. The supplying firm tried to convince car seat manufacturers to switch to a sophisticated foaming system that was more expensive per kilogram than an older type. It ran up against traditional practice and comparison to existing products and their price per kilogram. Even with the argument that fewer kilograms of the material were needed due to the superior cushioning ability of the new foam, car seat manufacturers resisted because of the higher cost. Eventually the polyurethane company managed to turn the discussion to adding strategic value by gaining cabin room, and the customer was finally willing to listen. Although measured in centimetres, this small headroom gain was of such value to the OEMs that they were willing to pay a premium for 'thinner' seats with equal comfort. This strategic understanding was derived from extensive value chain analysis that uncovered needs unmet by existing products. Many clients, we find, do not fully understand their own strategic metric and KSFs. Helping them achieve this is a major contribution and a significant change in marketing practice.

Value propositions based on value chain market analysis differ from the traditional marketing practice of focusing on customer benefit or buying requirements. These traditional ways of viewing customer needs do not yield strategic insight that can be used to turn difficult marketing situations around. Product development needs to be fed with strategic customer insight focused on future trends. The same applies to manufacturing, a function that too often is disconnected from the marketing operation. Value chain marketing can provide important, if not decisive, guidance for non-marketing functions. If used effectively, the additional value created by those functions on the basis of new marketing insight can be exploited by the marketing function to a firm's competitive advantage.

Strategic selling

A firm intending to practise value chain marketing will need to revamp its approach to the sales function. At many companies, the sales function is effective at projecting traditional benefits along the lines of known customer buying criteria. But value chain marketing is unlikely to take hold if the sales force is not brought along. The switch to strategic selling is not to be underestimated, and it challenges most sales professionals. Message content needs to reflect the client's strategic requirements. Firms must train sales staff differently and equip them with a strategic mindset.

The sales force must clarify their firm's contribution to the client's strategic requirements. Too often, the sales force visits on an operational level where strategic interest may not be pronounced and where strategic value propositions may not deliver an impact. The marketing firm should evaluate the customer's buying unit in order to understand where the new strategically focused message may yield best results. This may require contacts outside the narrow user or buyer groups usually visited by sales staff.

This strategic approach is related to but different from the consultative selling practised by many firms. When consultative selling includes a strategic dimension, then it is just a matter of adding new information to existing sales channels and contacts. When consultative selling focuses on customer service or technical problem resolution, the difference is greater.

To operationalize strategic selling, companies rely on key account management teams from local to global approaches.[19] Deloitte, a leading financial services firm, adopted such a system several years ago, empowering an account leader globally and building a team of industry experts in multiple locations around the world. Firms adopting such a system find it brings returns if the account management teams are perceived as contributing strategically to a client's business. Teams are challenged to perform detailed analysis of a client's business to find leverage points on which to build competitive advantage. These teams need to determine client KSFs and metrics by reviewing the business system with the conceptual tools described earlier. Armed with strategic insight, key account management teams can become powerful agents for value chain marketing.

Projecting marketing downstream

As the term value chain marketing implies, companies adopting this approach will be challenged to expand marketing activity up and down the value chain, reaching downstream industry participants that in traditional marketing are rarely approached. The value chain consists of analytical data input as well as active marketing.

We can use one of our earlier examples to show the impact. The agrochemical company with its novel approach to crop protection found it necessary to extend its marketing reach down the value chain to retailers, food processors and restaurant chains. This took the firm beyond its traditional marketing to the farming community through large agricultural distributors. It realized that its traditional customers – farmers and co-op distributors – hesitated to adopt new practices for fear of not being able to sell their crops to food processors. In turn, processors felt at the mercy of retailers who could keep products off the shelf. The agrochemicals company had to learn how to engage the entire downstream channel on issues of product performance and composition. Failing to do that would mean that new ideas languished in the channel, choked by alternatives and unable to provide a return on the investment allocated to development.

Projecting influence downstream is not mere selling of ideas. It requires a company to meet downstream users of its products, even though these are not direct customer accounts. It means meeting with development and marketing professionals in these companies and learning how they address their challenges. It means developing strategic insights into downstream firms in such a way that the upstream marketer is viewed as a strategic asset. Information learned from downstream firms about their own KSFs, metrics and strategic imperatives can be fed back into product development and content for the strategic account management teams who service the clients.

Projecting influence downstream is necessary when a new product, service or system makes change in an industry. New technologies are difficult to introduce if downstream users cannot be convinced. The marketer needs to take this initiative. The entry ticket to these firms is the perceived value added for talking to the marketer. Simply calling up some large firm downstream and asking for a meeting on the basis of 'We would like to find out what is on your mind' is unlikely to result in a positive response. The firm requesting a meeting needs to undertake enough work on its own that the host firm finds it worth its time. Only if the marketing firm has made a significant effort using the value chain tools discussed here can we expect insights to occur.

Projecting downstream influence can mean effective use of communication tools, such as advertising, public relations or other media approaches. We need to point out, however, that downstream marketing activities differ from what is typically referred to as 'pull marketing', when companies use communication tools to stimulate demand to pull products through locked channels. Pull marketing relies almost entirely on mass communication, such as advertising. Value chain marketing uses dialogue and intense involvement with downstream industry participants on issues such as product development, strategic selling and value chain influence.

Organizing for value chain marketing

Knowing how to deploy value chain marketing, and achieving the right insights and messages, does not guarantee success. As most readers will know, unless this new marketing effort is embedded in the day-to-day marketing operations of a firm, its promise will be limited. What can companies do to ensure that they not only conduct value chain marketing but also organize for it? Four elements stand out: *talent*, *mindset*, *process* and *organizational unit*.

Sourcing the talent

A company that wishes to adopt value chain marketing will find this approach requires personnel comfortable with conceptual thinking, strategic analysis and dealing with clients on a senior executive level. The marketer may need to know more about the client's industry than about his or her own. If the client is global, the marketer needs to be able to think globally. This is a tall order for many firms, and even large companies suffer from a scarcity of talent.

Traditional marketing practice often attracts talent that is more action-oriented, operational and tactical. This suggests that moving to value chain marketing may require talent with different abilities unless, as described below, a company finds a development path to grow its own talent.

Two sources offer new talent. First, the firm's own strategy group or business development department may be staffed with people who have mastered conceptual tools, even though they typically focus on the company's own strategy rather than on client strategy. Second, executives from client industries may bring valuable insights. One large multi-national chemical firm recruited recently retired production managers from client firms to refresh its understanding of client requirements, to detail product and process flows and to support discussions on capturing value.

The value chain marketing mindset

Firms may wish to develop their own people into a group that can deploy value chain marketing effectively. This requires a development effort to make large groups of executives, even at lower levels, comfortable using strategic tools. Depending on the level of independence expected, a time commitment of one to two weeks may be enough to bring most people on board. If the group is already conceptually oriented, such as may be the case with engineers, the time may be shorter. DSM, a large Dutch chemical firm marketing to many industries, invested effort instilling the business system and value chain concepts in its own planning process. DSM now uses these same tools to enhance its marketing and business development. The company is undertaking significant effort to expose marketing executives to these concepts.

Firms often underestimate the number of people who would benefit from training. The challenge of building effective training is the need to expose a large number of executives to strategic tools that they were not previously expected to master. If these tools remain the purview of the few, value chain strategic thinking is not likely to take hold. It is imperative for a marketing operation to introduce these concepts to the largest possible number of professionals, and for them to achieve comfort with this approach. The process will involve several administrative levels, from staff who make the first customer contact on up to senior marketing executives.

Embedding value chain marketing in company processes

For value chain marketing to take hold, a process must be adopted that will be consistent over a long period of time. A firm should not view this as a one-time effort, but rather as a part of marketing weaponry that needs to be honed continuously. It requires senior executive support, often from the CEO. Value chain marketing tools should be incorporated into the regular planning cycles, and analysis should over time become 'natural', included in all marketing plans.

To make sure this process becomes second nature, interest expressed by senior management is essential. Since value chain marketing concepts require intensive debate about the customer's industry, senior management must take the lead, engaging dialogue with all know-how holders. This will assure that the conclusions of the exercise are of sufficient impact and stand up under scrutiny. At one large European global chemical firm, all organizational units regularly subject themselves and their managers to analysis, and the company provides a formalized process to ensure quality of output.

Forming dedicated organizational units

Whether or not the process can be entrusted to dedicated organizational units is frequently debated. Although most companies will initially be able to field only a small number of individuals who would be comfortable with value chain marketing, we take the view that eventually this approach must be spread throughout a company. If it is to be adopted widely, many parts of the organization need to participate in data gathering and analysis, as well as in practising value chain marketing. If results are to be used for action in functions other than marketing, it will be difficult for a company to benefit from this new practice if methods for analysing an industry are not shared. This is where a planning or strategy department may help, introducing the analysis more widely and thus helping marketing to adopt value chain marketing.

Managing risk

Firms working with this approach find there are risks involved. Externally, downstream customers might resent efforts to outflank them by directly contacting groups farther down the industry value chain. Obviously this should be handled with care, and sharing insight with customers may be necessary. Internally, the company might be reluctant to get involved due to the fact that value chain marketing tends to create many 'strategists' in a firm. While true, it is precisely this insight-producing strategic mindset that can set a firm apart from those who only dabble.

Summary and management guidelines

- Heightened competition and intensive use of new technologies have led to blocked market access for many firms.
- Blocked market access causes traditional marketing practices to lose their power and effectiveness.
- Value chain marketing is a concept that will allow companies to move beyond traditional marketing practices.
- Value chain marketing makes firms project their marketing activity along the entire value chain or business system.
- Value chain marketing is based on widely used business strategy concepts.
- Value chain marketing requires marketers to acquire deep knowledge of the client's industry.
- Value chain marketing is based on a set of analytic tools including analysis of the macro business system, mapping it and identification of its participants.

- Value chain marketing requires analysis of macro business system dynamics by assessing industry developments and identifying industry drivers.
- Value chain marketing forces companies to search for changes in the business system configuration by developing an industry vision, tracking evolution of the industry and extracting key success factors and industry metrics.
- The practice of value chain marketing consists of industry mapping, understanding the customer, pooling customer experience, developing value propositions to meet customer needs, adoption of strategic selling and projection of marketing activity downstream.
- Value chain marketing goes beyond pull marketing, missionary selling and primary demand stimulation.
- Value chain marketing engages downstream customers across a full range of activity, including product development, research and data mining.
- Firms that wish to organize for value chain marketing need to embed this process deeply by nurturing talent and adopting a specific mindset throughout the company.

References

[1] Kotler, Philip, *Marketing Management*, Harlow: Pearson Education, 2002.

[2] Porter, Michael E., *Competitive Strategy: Techniques for Analyzing Industries and Competitors*, New York: Free Press, 1980.

[3] Porter, Michael E., *Competitive Advantage: Creating and Sustaining Superior Performance*, New York: Free Press, 1985.

[4] Gilbert, Xavier and Strebel, Paul, 'Developing Competitive Advantage', published in Henry Mintzberg and James Brian Quinn, *The Strategy Process*, Upper Saddle River: Prentice Hall, second edition, 1991, pp. 82–93.

[5] Gilbert, Xavier and Strebel, Paul, 'Developing Competitive Advantage', p. 35, Table 2.1.

[6] Gilbert, Xavier and Strebel, Paul, 'Developing Competitive Advantage'.

[7] Abell, Derek F. and Hammond, John S., *Strategic Market Planning: Problems and Analytical Approaches*, Upper Saddle River: Prentice Hall, 1979, p. 9.

[8] Porter, Michael E., *Competitive Advantage*, p. 272.

[9] Gilbert, Xavier and Strebel, Paul, 'Taking Advantage of Industry Shifts', *European Management Journal*, 1989, Vol. 7, No. 4, pp. 398–402.

[10] Strebel, Paul, *Breakpoints: How Managers Exploit Radical Business Change*, Boston: Harvard Business School Press, 1992, pp. 1–6.

[11] Porter, Michael E., *Competitive Advantage*, p. 6, Figure 1.2.

[12] Porter, Michael E., *Competitive Advantage*, pp. 5–6.

[13] Brimson, James A., *Activity Accounting: An Activity-based Costing Approach*, Chichester: John Wiley & Sons Ltd, 1991.

[14] Porter, Michael E., *Competitive Advantage*, pp. 4–11.

[15] Porter, Michael E., *Competitive Advantage*, Chapter 13, pp. 445–481.

[16] Yoshino, Michael and Jeannct, Jean-Pierre, *Case: Ares-Serono*, Harvard Business School, 1995.

[17] Alahuhta, Matti, 'Global Growth Strategies for High Technology Challengers', *Acta Polytechnica Scandinavia*, Electrical Engineering Series No. 66, Helsinki Technical University, Espoo, Finland, 1990.

[18] Vandermerwe, Sandra, *From Tin Soldiers to Russian Dolls: Creating Added Value Through Services*, Oxford: Butterworth-Heinemann, 1994.

[19] Hennessey, David and Jeannet, Jean-Pierre, *Global Account Management*, Chichester: John Wiley & Sons Ltd, 2003.

3
Countering Commoditization: Value-added Strategies and Aligning with Customers

Professor Kamran Kashani

I f the traditional role of marketing was ever to bring about a balanced, value-led relationship between sellers and buyers, then in today's industrial sectors it has failed to live up to that promise. The fact is that some of the market changes highlighted in Chapter 1, namely commoditization, consolidation in customer base and power shift, have combined to give industrial customers more leverage *vis-à-vis* their suppliers, and they are likely to use that leverage to their advantage. While this phenomenon is

---

Parts of this chapter have appeared in an article for the European Business Forum, Spring 2004.

not restricted to any one market, it is particularly pronounced in the industrial, business-to-business (B2B) sectors where, in the zero-sum game of buyer–seller exchange, it's often the latter who pays the bill through ever-present price concessions. In other words, for many of today's industrial vendors the ability to create value is less than matched by the power to capture it, because in commoditized markets the customer is the driver in an unbalanced distribution of bargaining power. The consequences for suppliers can be serious: declining prices and margins, inferior returns on investment, and the risk of falling into a 'commodity trap' where the pressure on profitability leads to reduced investment in product (or service) innovation, which in turn leads to further loss of differentiation and even greater pressure on prices and margins. Few marketers can escape this vicious cycle with their shirts on.

Can industrial companies counter commoditization and avoid falling victim to their ever more powerful, hard-bargaining customers?

The answer for a growing number of companies is an affirmative one. These firms have learned that while core product advantages erode and pressure on prices never lets up, they can still do profitable business by pursuing value-added strategies including aligning themselves with key customers. Put differently, these companies have discovered profitable opportunities in stretching beyond their core products by offering customers compellingly differentiated values. They have thus successfully countered commoditization.

This chapter discusses a number of value-added strategies which can be employed in the battle against commoditization. While they are presented in the context of industrial products and services where the effect of unchecked commoditization can be devastating, these strategies also have the potential of being adapted and applied in other sectors, including consumer products and services.

Value-added strategies

Consider the following examples.

- **SKF, the world's largest ball-bearing manufacturer**, has turned its extensive know-how in rotation technology into value-added services for manufacturing operations. Far from haggling over the price of commodity bearings, the company now helps its productivity-conscious customers, such as pulp and paper factories, to maintain their production machinery, reduce or eliminate downtime and maximize plant yield. Many of these services come with performance guarantees offered on the basis of contracts that ensure continuity of supply and expert advice for plant operators, and long-term retention of accounts for SKF. The company's service business is today the fastest-growing and most profitable division of the company.
- **Raisio Chemicals, a major supplier of chemical compounds** to the global paper industry, recently acquired by Ciba Specialty Chemicals, assists its customers with a range of services, including developing new products, upgrading paper quality and improving printability. The company offers its important customers access to its technical staff and facilities, including a unique pilot coating machine and a newly built printing plant, for testing and experimentation. In the competitive

market for paper chemicals, Raisio Chemical's strategy has led to high customer loyalty and retention rate.

The commoditized markets for bearings and paper chemicals in which SKF and Raisio Chemicals respectively compete represent highly competitive sectors where buyers often have the last word. Unlike many of their rivals, both companies have chosen to refrain from becoming cut-price vendors, a strategy that could probably have won them additional market-share points but at significant erosion in their profitability. Instead, they have invested heavily in becoming knowledgeable about the business of their major customers and used that knowledge to align their own priorities and actions accordingly. SKF has learned, for example, that the top-of-mind concern for its manufacturing customers is not just high-quality or competitively priced ball bearings, but rather operational efficiency. SKF's service offerings were developed precisely to help customers attain that objective. In the case of Raisio Chemicals, the management has come to appreciate the role of new and improved paper grades in helping paper mills to extract a premium in an otherwise price-driven market. Along with chemicals, the company offers its extensive knowledge in paper technology as a value-added service to its chief customers.

Figure 3.1 shows a typical scenario of how the combined effects of commoditization and buyer concentration, common in many industrial sectors, can over time lead to margin erosion. It begins with a steady decline in the differentiation of the core offer. In other words, the firm's customer-value proposition begins to lose its uniqueness and, with it, most or all of its differentiating power. Customers view all competing products alike and dismiss any vendor claims to the contrary. When combined with buyer concentration, i.e. when a growing share of sales is generated from a declining

Figure 3.1 Commoditization: declining differentiation, bargaining power...and returns

number of large customers, the consequences of commoditization can be dramatic: a loss of control on prices (when the seller is no longer a price *setter* but a price *taker*), in addition to losses in supplier identity, customer loyalty and brand equity. The scenario's negative impact on margins and profitability is all too predictable.

Countering commoditization begins with a re-examining of the core business and its customer-value proposition. When all customers appear to look alike and the firm's value offer has a one-size-fits-all quality to it (both features of many commoditized markets), it is time to ask a couple of fundamental questions: beyond the lowest price, what do the customers really value and how could the commoditized offer, product or service, be *re*defined to better reflect the often unarticulated needs of its customers? To illustrate, in its search for what its manufacturing customers found important, SKF management discovered early on that even more important than the price of a ball bearing or its quality was the customers' desire to minimize or eliminate machinery downtime, potentially costing up to tens of thousands of dollars per hour in lost productivity. SKF could offer top-grade engineering know-how to its productivity-conscious customers as an add-on offer and a new source of revenues. In a similar way, Raisio Chemicals discovered that even more important than the price of its chemicals was the papermakers' need to upgrade the quality of their output and reduce expensive waste – two areas where Raisio's expertise could make a difference. Such discoveries are the raw insights that can lead to redefining the vendor's offer in order to provide more value to the customer and greater differentiation and pricing discretion for the supplier – a true win–win scenario.

So what are the strategies that could possibly counter the commoditization scenario cited above? To begin, there are no quick fixes to the pervasive power of commoditization. As a permanent feature of today's marketplace, it will continue to challenge business organizations, even the best managed. The companies surveyed in this chapter, those that have successfully met the challenge, have done so by formulating their own unique solutions, strategies that take into account an in-depth knowledge of their markets and customers and, furthermore, exploit the organization's core skills – what they do best.

Strategic trajectories

Though there is no panacea, we can nevertheless identify three possible strategic trajectories that can bring much-needed differentiation to a commoditized core. These generic strategies are highlighted in the 'value space' of Figure 3.2 and are further explained below.

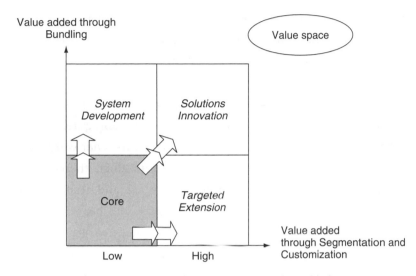

Figure 3.2 Redefining customer-value proposition: value-added strategies

Let us start with the two dimensions of the matrix shown in Figure 3.2: *Segmentation and Customization* and *Bundling*. They reflect the ways in which a company could add value to a non-differentiated core product or service. By moving to the right along the horizontal axis the firm is increasingly segmenting its current and potential customers and, in doing so, customizing its offers around the particular needs of those segments. For example, M-real Corporation, a €7 billion European paper and board company, makes specific grades of paperboard each targeting a different end-user segment of the packaging market – food, pharmaceuticals, cosmetics, tobacco, consumer electronics and so on. The packaging raw material thus produced reflects the specific requirements of each segment in terms of weight, hygiene, colours, printability, etc. At the extreme, a company may choose to produce a special product customized around the specific and unique needs of a single customer. Along the axis, therefore, value is added through better and more effectively meeting the requirements of segments of customers or individual accounts.

By moving up on the vertical axis, on the other hand, a firm is augmenting its value proposition beyond its core product, by 'bundling' related or even unrelated products and services into a single offer. In other words, there is more to the offer than the commoditized core product, thereby allowing greater differentiation. SKF, for example, sells car and truck repair and replacement kits incorporating its core product – ball bearings – encased inside a subassembly such as a water pump, a clutch-release unit or a belt tensioner. In addition, the kits include accessories such as seals, nuts and other tools for sure and rapid installation. Not all the bundled components are produced by SKF; some are outsourced, but the finished kit carries the company's brand and performance guarantees.

Other examples of bundling include add-on services accompanying the core product such as financing, technical support and a general warranty for the total offer. The extra customer value that comes with bundling can be measured in the greater speed and convenience of working with a single supplier, a lower transaction cost and a more complete quality assurance for the augmented offer.

The two value-adding dimensions described above lead to four possible combinations identified in Figure 3.2 as the *Core* and three value-adding strategies: *Targeted Extension*, *System Development* and *Solutions Innovation*. To understand the significance of each of the four quadrants, let us look at them in more detail:

- **Core** This quadrant, low on both value-adding dimensions, is a starting point where the offer lacks sufficient differentiation to avoid becoming a commodity. Customers do not perceive compelling differences between the firm and its rivals in their value propositions. What is offered is not sufficiently adapted to the specific requirements of individual customers or their segments, nor does it have an added 'bundled' value besides the core product. Under this scenario the firm is obliged to look beyond its core for the missing differentiation that comes with added value. Nevertheless the firm could still attempt to bring some measure of vitality into its core offer through a combination of brand building, operational excellence (including quality enhancement) and continuous incremental improvement in product or service.

- **Targeted Extension** This quadrant represents a strategy that aims to add value by extending its core offer to more closely meet the special and possibly unique needs of the market segments or even the individual accounts it serves. The example of M-real applies here. By becoming more insightful about the special requirements of different end-user segments the company is better able to match its offer to customer needs. It may decide to pursue a dual strategy of offering the underadapted core product to some customers and the more targeted ones to others. Or it may decide to leave the low-margin core business altogether and instead focus on developing ever more targeted value-added products. M-real is pursuing the former strategy.

- **System Development** Firms choosing to compete in this quadrant develop a package of products and services that offer the synergistic benefits of a 'system'. In other words, the value added lies in the integration among the system's constituent elements, i.e. the 'bundled' whole is larger than the sum of its parts. The earlier example of SKF repair and replacement kits is a case in point: the user benefits of speed and convenience in installation are directly related to the integrated offer. By *de*bundling the offer, i.e. by procuring the parts from different suppliers and bringing them together at the point of usage, the customer is less likely to get the full value inherent in the kits. As under the previous scenario, a firm may choose to offer the system concept in addition to its core product, or as a replacement for it.

- **Solutions Innovation** What happens when the firm's offer consists of a full set of bundled products and services that are specifically targeted at certain customer segments or individual accounts? This is precisely the strategic scenario of the upper-right quadrant, where value creation takes an ambitious turn away from the core business and addresses specific customer problems with specific solutions – solutions that combine tangible products with highly focused intangible services such as technical advice, training, consulting and the like. To illustrate, M-real supplies its major global consumer goods accounts with printed and ready-to-ship packages anywhere in the world, thereby taking upon itself the tasks of offering not only the right grade of raw packaging material (its core product) but also selection of a network of local carton makers and printers, quality control, warehousing and transportation. For the customer the added value is not only in the savings that come from a single-supplier interface where multitudes existed before, but also from an assurance of the supply of the right packages at the right time anywhere in the world. As the title of this quadrant implies, a firm planning to enter the solutions business needs to 'think outside the box' and reinvent what the industry has traditionally defined as value. Solutions strategy demands innovation in value creation. And it promises attractive margins.

Beyond the core: illustrations

The following examples help illustrate how companies faced with the commoditization of their traditional product offerings have moved beyond the core by adopting all three of the value-added strategies.

The first example is again that of SKF, representing one of the most successful attempts at stretching beyond a core business. As shown in Figure 3.3, the company has extended its product line by offering ball bearings customized around specific end-user applications such as automotive, electrical machinery, industrial and aerospace. Indeed, these segments are recognized

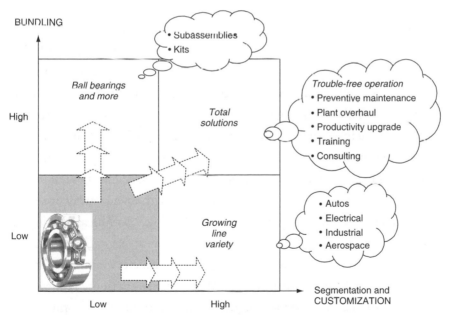

Figure 3.3 SKF

in the organizational structure of the firm, with each having its own semi-independent business unit and management team. Next, SKF has been marketing an increasing volume of value-added subassemblies, including the car and truck repair and replacement kits already referred to. These bundled offerings incorporate some of SKF's best engineering know-how. Finally, the company's solutions business consists of such highly customized engineering services as preventive maintenance, plant overhaul, factory productivity upgrade, and technical training and consulting modules. The solutions activities are marketed under the broad label of SKF's 'Trouble Free Operation' and are among the company's most profitable value-added offerings.

GE Medical Systems' imaging business is the second example. While products such as magnetic resonance imaging or computed tomography scanners do not fit the usual notions of commodities, the fact is that, with these technologies maturing, GE Medical Systems has been active in finding new sources of differentiation and revenues along each of the three value-added trajectories. As shown in Figure 3.4, imaging products have been extended towards increasingly specific medical applications including cardiovascular, neurological, orthopaedic and vascular. Each focused extension consists of products and application programmes targeting the specialists in the medical area. GE has also bundled its product offerings with a wide array of services in the areas of financing, information technology, technical service and training, to name just a few. The product–service package is meant to facilitate the acquisition, commissioning and routine operation of the imaging products by health-care providers. More recently, with the launch of GE Medical Systems' Performance Improvement Solutions, the company has entered the potentially highly lucrative consulting business, targeting

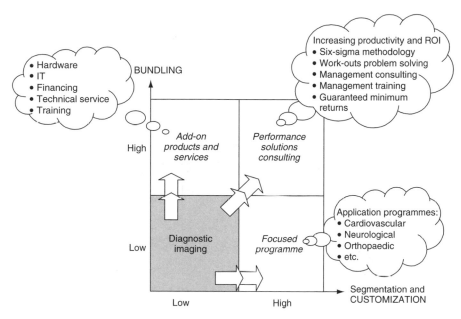

Figure 3.4 GE Medical Systems

health-care organizations such as public hospitals and private clinics. The new offering provides a full range of services aimed at upgrading the productivity and operational efficiency of investments made in medical equipment. Expanding capacity and patient throughput, increasing revenue growth, and improving the return on invested capital all make up the customer-value proposition of GE's solutions business.

The final example shown in Figure 3.5 is that of BASF, a major European-based producer of chemicals and one of the largest global players in the coatings business. BASF Coatings, a unit traditionally concentrating on decorative and industrial paints, has over time stretched out of its historical and increasingly commoditized products into coatings for specialized

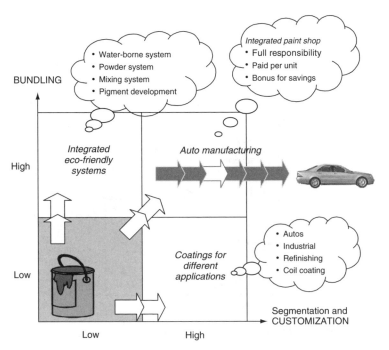

Figure 3.5 BASF Coatings

applications in addition to integrated coating systems and, lately, integrated paint-shop solutions. The company produces coatings for a multitude of application segments such as new car production, auto-repair jobs and industrial usages, including electrical insulation. BASF has also developed value-added coating systems to reduce pollution related to solvents. Among these eco-friendly systems are water-based and powder paints sold with special application programmes. With the integrated paint shop, an innovation in Original Equipment Manufacturer (OEM) auto-coating business, BASF offers to employ its vast know-how in paints to operate a car manufacturer's paint shop, providing all coating products specified by the customer (including those produced by competitors) in addition to technical advice and logistical support. Under this concept, offered to a growing number of car makers including DaimlerChrysler, Volkswagen and Ford, BASF is paid not by the volume of coatings used – the most common practice in the industry – but rather by the number of painted cars passing quality checks. Defects have to be repainted at BASF's expense. At the same time, the company receives a contractually agreed bonus when a customer's stringent cost and quality standards are surpassed. The integrated paint-shop innovation has been a highly profitable addition to BASF Coatings' revenue stream.

Aligning with customers

As one might glean from the above examples, among the three value-added strategies there is a qualitative difference between the Targeted Extension and System Development on the one hand and the Solutions Innovation on the other. While the two former strategies aim to add value by making the offer (extended or bundled) ever more attractive to its intended customers, the latter strategy targets the enhancement of the customer's own perform-ance by solving specific problems. Both SKF's Trouble Free Operation and GE Medical Systems' Performance Improvement Solutions are highly cus-tomized offerings aimed at measurably improving the customer's cost struc-ture and increasing profitability. BASF's integrated paint-shop concept is all about enhancing the customer's competitiveness by reducing the unit cost of a painted vehicle without compromising on quality. BASF's contracts are renewed only when the auto manufacturer realizes savings that are difficult to achieve otherwise. In all three cases the supplier's success with its solutions strategies is closely tied in with enabling its customers to succeed in their businesses.

Figure 3.6 demonstrates the key differences in customer-value propositions between extended or bundled offers on the one hand and solutions on the other. While the former strategies, focusing on broadly defined 'product performance', promise value-added features, advantages and benefits for the customer, the latter offers specific values that enhance the customer's success in its own business – values leading to improved top line, reduced costs and higher profitability.

For the above reasons, success with Solutions Innovation as a strategic trajectory requires tight alignment between a vendor's offer and the customer's business priorities. Alignment, as defined here, enables a supplier's organization to identify and profitably exploit value-added opportunities that enhance a customer's keys to its business success. It should be underscored

Value-added strategies		
Targeted Extension ↓ Customization	System Development ↓ Integrated Bundle	Solutions Innovation ↓ Total Solution

	Value-added strategies		
Customer-value proposition	'Product' performance • Features • Advantages • Benefits		'Customer Success' • Higher sales • Reduced costs • Improved profits

Figure 3.6 Value-added strategies and customer-value proposition

that true alignment is more than a supply-side customer focus. It is a different way of doing business, one that reflects a deeper, more intimate and ultimately more synergistic relationship with customers. In the previous chapter we referred to this as one facet of value chain marketing. Furthermore, as evidenced by the solutions innovations cited earlier, alignment demands supplier–customer collaboration. BASF could not have conceived and offered the paint-shop concept without the close collaboration of its OEM customers. Both sides have invested in the relationship with the promise of mutual gains: profitable customer retention for BASF; reduced costs and enhanced competitiveness for the OEM. Admittedly, collaboration often leads to co-dependency, a condition that limits both parties' degrees of freedom – to liberally switch suppliers or drop customers. That is the price paid by both parties for the benefits of collaboration.

Buyer–seller collaboration can take place along the entire spectrum of business activities, all the way from upstream product development to downstream after-sales service. Figure 3.7 highlights some of the potential benefits from collaboration on each activity for both suppliers and their customers. The benefits represent lower costs, greater speed of action, more effective innovation, reduced uncertainty and new sources of revenues.[1]

Depths of collaboration

Collaborating with customers covers a wide continuum, from little or no collaboration to full-scale strategic partnership. The degree of buyer–seller co-dependency also varies significantly along the continuum. Figure 3.8 shows three typical alignment scenarios, each representing a different depth

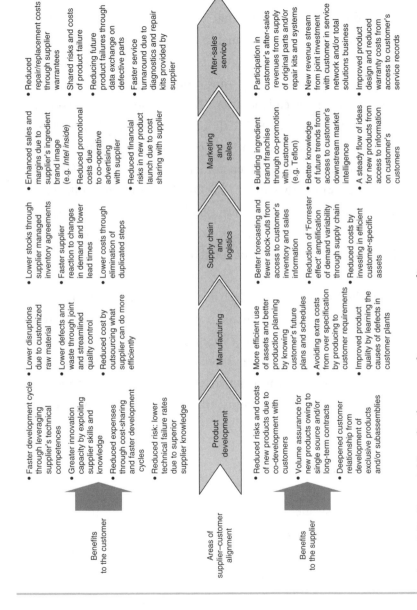

Figure 3.7 Potential benefits from supplier–customer alignment

The author is grateful to Professors Carlos Cordon and Jean-Philippe Deschamps for their inputs in the preparation of this figure

The figure shows "Benefits to the customer" (top) and "Benefits to the supplier" (bottom), organised across the "Areas of supplier–customer alignment": Product development, Manufacturing, Supply chain and logistics, Marketing and sales, After-sales service.

Benefits to the customer

Product development
- Faster development cycle through leveraging supplier's technical competences
- Greater innovation capacity by exploiting supplier skills and knowledge
- Reduced expenses through cost-sharing and faster development cycles
- Reduced risk: lower technical failure rates due to superior supplier knowledge

Manufacturing
- Lower disruptions due to customized raw material
- Lower defects and waste through joint and streamlined quality control
- Reduced cost by outsourcing what supplier can do more efficiently

Supply chain and logistics
- Lower stocks through supplier managed inventory agreements
- Faster supplier reaction to changes in demand and lower lead times
- Lower costs through elimination of duplicated steps

Marketing and sales
- Enhanced sales and margins due to supplier's ingredient brand image (e.g. *Intel inside*)
- Reduced promotional costs due to co-operative advertising with supplier
- Reduced financial risks in new product launch due to cost sharing with supplier

After-sales service
- Reduced repair/replacement costs through supplier warranties
- Shared risks and costs of product failure
- Reducing future product failures through data exchange on defective parts
- Faster service turnaround due to diagnostics and repair kits provided by supplier

Benefits to the supplier

Product development
- Reduced risks and costs of new products due to co-development with customers
- Volume assurance for new products owing to single source and/or long-term contracts
- Deepened customer relationship from development of exclusive products and/or subassemblies

Manufacturing
- More efficient use of assets and better production planning by knowing customer's future plans and schedules
- Avoiding extra costs from over specification by producing to customer requirements
- Improved product quality by learning the causes of defects in customer plants

Supply chain and logistics
- Better forecasting and fewer stock-outs from access to customer's inventory and sales information
- Reduction of 'Forrester effect' amplification of demand variability through supply chain
- Reduced costs by investing in efficient customer-specific assets

Marketing and sales
- Building ingredient brand franchise through co-promotion with customer (e.g. Teflon)
- Better knowledge of future trends from access to customer's downstream market intelligence
- A steady flow of ideas for new products from access to information on customer's customers

After-sales service
- Participation in customer's after-sales revenues from supply of original parts and/or repair kits and systems
- New revenue stream from joint investment with customer in service network and/or total solutions business
- Improved product design and reduced warranty costs from access to customer's service records

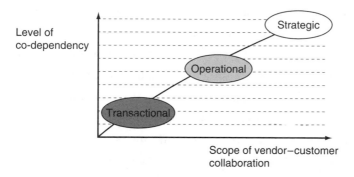

Figure 3.8 Scenarios for customer alignment

of collaboration and mutual dependency. For the purposes of this discussion these scenarios are labelled *Transactional, Operational* and *Strategic*.

- **Transactional** Here collaboration between the supplier and the customer is minimal and is limited to the process of buying and selling well-defined products, or bundles of standard products and services. Collaboration is limited in time and confined to the exchange process: identifying a customer need and matching it to the vendor's offerings, negotiating a price, placing and fulfilling the order. Once the transaction cycle is complete the minimal collaboration comes to an end. Most industrial sales are of a transactional, one-deal-at-a-time nature and are driven by the sales and purchasing people for their respective organizations. Keeping multiple sources of supply is a common practice leading to low vendor loyalty.[2] To encourage repeat purchase, the vendor may offer special privileges for repeat customers. But the relationship remains transactional in its spirit and practice as one or both parties see little value in upgrading it to a higher level of mutual commitment and co-dependency.

- **Operational** Under this scenario vendor–buyer collaboration is focused on specific areas of mutual interest and possibly within well-defined time frames. Alignment is often project-led and meant to solve specific operational problems. Examples include collaboration between a raw material supplier's product engineers and the customer's manufacturing people to reduce production defects and improve finished product quality. Another project might involve joint streamlining of the logistics for reduced inventory and warehousing costs for both parties. Some outsourcing activities, such as design and manufacture of a component or subassembly, would fall under this scenario. Typically, such focused collaborative activities take place alongside the individual buy–sell transactions. But the key differences between this and the earlier scenario are that there is a greater measure of co-dependency and mutual commitment in the supplier–customer relationship and that the interactions between the two organizations are now broader and deeper than those between the buyers and sellers only. The combination of these two factors promotes greater stability in the relationship and far more supplier loyalty.

- **Strategic** The ultimate alignment between vendors and their customers is a strategic one, where senior executives in the two companies together define major areas of collaboration and set long-term goals with mutual interest in mind. Typically, such strategic undertakings require dedicated investments by both parties that can only pay back over time. In the commercial aircraft industry, for example, such strategic collaboration with suppliers often leads to formal alliances for the design and development of new planes, with each supplier taking on a well-defined project the outcome of which will have to be integrated with that of a network of others. In the case of Bombardier Aerospace, the world's third largest aircraft manufacturer and makers of Learjet, the company depends entirely on investments from its many parts suppliers for the creation and launch of a new aeroplane, a complex process that could take years and cost $1 billion. Another example of strategic alignment is the 'hole-in-the-wall' practice of can makers, whereby they install their production facilities literally next door to the filling facilities of major soft-drink customers to ensure a secure and uninterruptible supply of cans on demand. This targeted investment is meant for the benefit of a single customer. By the same token, by integrating the can production lines with its own filling facilities, the soft drink producer is narrowing its packaging supply to a single source. Both organizations are thus putting a great deal of trust in this highly co-dependent long-term alignment. As might be expected, with co-dependency comes entanglement. A failed strategic alignment can cause far more disruption and pain to both organizations than other scenarios.

Alignment with customers can change and grow over time. Starting with pure transactions, vendors might identify opportunities for operational collaboration with a few major accounts. The added knowledge and mutual trust that grows out of success with these projects could lead in some cases to even more ambitious undertakings, including longer-term strategic projects. Within a vendor's customer base, the majority of relationships might well be transactional, but a significant share of the business and profits would be attributed to those accounts further up the alignment curve in Figure 3.7.

A case study: 'Grow me'

For value-adding collaboration to replace the arm-wrestling game of seller–buyer exchange typical of commodities, the benefits must be mutual. The following case study on Tetra Pak's approach to creating such win–win outcomes explains what aligning with customers might entail in practice and how promoting a customer's success can be a powerful boost to the supplier's own performance.

Tetra Pak, the €8 billion company that invented aseptic carton packaging for liquid food, including milk and juices, found itself in the mid-1990s the victim of a number of trends that were reshaping the primary market it serves, the dairy industry:

- **declining milk consumption** due to, among other factors, competition from alternative beverages including soft drinks
- **growth of large food chains** that offered both branded and private-label milk products and increasingly treated the milk aisle as a low-priced traffic builder
- **consolidation among dairy companies** as scale of operation became a critical factor in the fight against erosion of margins and profitability in a declining market dominated by ever-larger retail customers
- **growing price competition** from lesser players in aseptic milk packaging, including both carton and plastic formats.

The combination of consolidation in the value chain, both at the producer and retail levels, and rising competition for a declining carton market, put Tetra Pak's margins and profitability under severe pressure. Also, the company's market leadership was being threatened by an increasing incidence of customer defections. The aggressively low prices and financing terms offered to dairy companies by hungry rivals were hard to match without sacrificing profitability. Tetra Pak's once unique packaging technology was facing the pressures of commoditization. Something had to be done to stop or even reverse the downtrend in the company's performance.

The impetus for major change came after a first-time global customer survey showed serious flaws in the ways in which Tetra Pak and its rivals were serving their markets. The survey revealed that while purchasing managers were concerned about the price of packaging material, the real issues pre-occupying their top management were sales and profit growth. Dairy produc-ers wanted to see both top and bottom lines recover from years of stagnation and decline. The top two factors identified by the survey as most responsible for customer *dis*satisfaction were the operational inefficiency of filling lines and an absence of strategic alignment with packaging suppliers for growth. Simply put, the dairy companies were asking for help in reducing their production costs (and thereby improving margins) and in identifying new growth opportunities inside and outside the dairy industry. The survey revealed that both Tetra Pak and its competitors had failed to be sufficiently attuned to the industry's changing needs. According to the external consult-ants analysing the survey data, the plea from dairy customers could be summarized in six words: 'Hear me, Know me, Grow me.'

This bad news from its customers was a turning point in the recent history of Tetra Pak. Following a short period of soul searching, the top management concluded that its market leadership was unsustainable in the long term without leadership in customer alignment and satisfaction. The poor survey results were, in the words of the CEO, the 'burning platform' the management needed to force it to implement a number of major corporate-wide programmes designed to make Tetra Pak more responsive to customers and better aligned with their management issues and priorities. The initiatives were launched under the internal slogan of making Tetra Pak the 'informed business partner' of its customers, signalling to everyone that a clear shift in the company's strategy towards greater alignment with customers was about to begin.

Significant among the launched initiatives were the Win-Back and Key Account Management (KAM) programmes. With Win-Back Tetra Pak was to take greater responsibility for operational efficiency at customer plants in order to lower production costs. This entailed measures aimed at reducing machine downtime and improving line efficiency, measures that would ultimately 'win back' customer confidence and retention. One major and expensive element of the programme that required active customer co-operation was retrofitting worldwide more than 3300 filling machines at customer plants, an undertaking that alone cost Tetra Pak $50 million. Another component of the Win-Back programme aimed at upgrading the company's technical service and troubleshooting capability at customer premises.

The Key Account Management programme, on the other hand, was launched to bring a closer alignment between Tetra Pak's practices and important customers' business and marketing strategies. High on the list of KAM priorities were joint market analysis for identifying new product opportunities, customer access to Tetra Pak's vast database of product and packaging innovations around the world, active support in developing launch plans for new products, and performance monitoring of customers' portfolios of products. KAM teams, consisting of both commercial and technical experts, worked closely with their counterparts in the customer organization.

Tetra Pak's customer-alignment initiatives have paid back handsomely. Less than five years after the first customer survey and less than four since the launch of the Win-Back programme, Tetra Pak has reduced the total incidence of machine breakdown by 52% and the average downtime per incidence by 75% (from 6 hours to 1.5 hours). Monitoring the results closely, it reports a resulting average increase of 7% in line efficiency, an improvement that can be reliably translated to a general reduction in customers' production costs.

There are also other notable successes from customer collaboration in generating top- and bottom-line growth. A typical example is the case of a major European dairy producer entering the toddlers' milk market at the urging of Tetra Pak. Facing a decline in volumes and market share in its core milk market, the dairy company was advised to shore up its lagging presence among households with young children by introducing an enriched milk product specifically designed for toddlers. After some initial hesitation, the dairy management duly launched the new product with a campaign that was planned in close collaboration with Tetra Pak's KAM team. While the overall decline in the general milk market kept total volumes under pressure, the highly differentiated and premium-priced toddler milk allowed the dairy company to recover more than the lost margins in its core business. Per litre sold the toddler milk was 14 times more profitable than 'plain' milk.

Translating the customers' success stories into its own performance, Tetra Pak points to the following areas where impact has been most notable:

- **a radical reduction in customer defections** (and this against a background of continued price cutting by competition)
- **steady growth in overall sales** in a flat global market for carton packaging
- **significant growth in sales to the important customers** identified as 'crown jewels' – the targets of the company's strategic alignment.

While profitability figures are confidential in this family-owned company, the management signals an unequivocal boost since the adoption of the above-mentioned initiatives.

The challenges of countering commoditization

How typical is Tetra Pak's feat in aligning itself with customers and thus proactively countering the commoditization of its core business?

The disappointing reality is that such outstanding success stories are few and far between. Companies that see a compelling logic in rethinking their tired and often outdated customer-value proposition discover only too soon that the path ahead is strewn with barriers. Among these are misconceptions of what customers would consider meaningful added values with tangible benefits. Other important barriers obstruct customer alignment, including collaboration with key accounts. These involve a company's recent history, its internal workings and the choices it makes in selecting customers for alignment and collaboration. Failing to effectively address these barriers can thrust a company back to the ways of its past, those that no longer serve the organization.

Becoming fully aware of the barriers, many of them internal to the organization, is the first step in countering commoditization. Let us review these obstacles before suggesting ways of overcoming them.

Misplaced added values

Central to value-added strategies is the notion of offering customers incremental values that they consider important and compelling. We have broadly defined these in terms of increased customization, bundled offers and complete solutions. But what are these important and compelling additional values?

The answer lies in an in-depth understanding of customers beyond what they currently purchase. That often means identifying issues and gaps in the way customers buy and use today's products or services and how these weigh on their overall performance. The example of SKF's premium-priced high-quality ball bearings is relevant here. While the extra dimension of quality was of the utmost importance for some application segments, such as planned maintenance in factories, where higher durability meant longer replacement cycles and fewer incidences of machine downtime, for OEM auto manufacturers it only meant additional cost and longer replacement cycles – two factors negatively influencing profits. SKF learned that higher bearing quality *per se* is added value for some, but not for others. Without such important customer insights, added value risks not being perceived as such.

In a similar way, bundled offers without an integrative value fail to impress. A common complaint from suppliers of such offers is that customers prefer to buy the elements of the system separately and thus avoid paying a higher price. Under such a scenario, clearly, the extra value from bundling is either non-existent or poorly communicated. Equally challenging is a related scenario where the added value from a given customer solution is hard to demonstrate and, for pricing purposes, difficult to quantify. While the supplier incurs the added costs of offering a complete solution, it finds it difficult to capture some of the added value in added margins.

Good old products

A company's past success can be a strong hidden obstacle, especially if it has been built on the back of strong product or technology leadership. A track record of winning product breakthroughs or innovative technologies often gets in the way of rethinking the value proposition when it has lost its edge. Management continues to believe in the viability of what worked in the past, even in the face of mounting evidence to the contrary. IBM's decades-long success with its System/360 mainframe platform, a breakthrough for its time, proved a big barrier in lifting the company out of its near-disaster situation in the late 1980s. While every market study showed a clear trend away from the proprietary system on which IBM's mainframe family was built, the management continued to shy away from the UNIX open system increasingly favoured by its customers. One of the early behavioural changes sought for IBM's turnaround, led by the newly appointed CEO, Lou Gerstner Jr., was the 'product out, customer in' notion of viewing the business from the customer's vantage point.[3]

Similarly, Tetra Pak's long success with Tetra Brik Aseptic (TBA), a runaway winner in liquid-food packaging, obscured the growing customer and consumer preferences for differentiated shapes and openings, sizes and types of packaging, including plastic containers. Not surprisingly, this single-minded focus on the winning platform inadvertently opened the door to differentiated products from the competition, causing share erosion in key markets. Combating commoditization with an outdated product line was a non-starter. It took Tetra Pak some years, and more than a few lost customers, before the management could get a clear sight of the changing market and address the increasingly commoditized product portfolio problem.

Good old structure

An organization that represents the management priorities of an earlier era can only stand in the way of a customer-aligned strategy. To illustrate, when M-real revised its business strategy towards 'customer focus and innovative service solutions that enhance customer competitiveness', it soon discovered a major hurdle in its mill-based structure, a relic of a past when mill productivity and operational efficiencies were the primary management preoccupations. The organization had lost its *raison d'être* and was a barrier when it came to serving customers who did business with multiple mills and found the structure confusing. Furthermore, the fragmented management structure obscured a unified view of major customers and the problems the new strategy intended to address. To put the organization on the same footing as the customer-focused strategy, M-real installed a structure mirroring the end-user segments it serves. Thus the Publishing and Commercial Printing divisions concentrates on producers of annual reports, brochures and advertising materials; the Consumer Packaging division focuses on end users and offers total packaging solutions to major accounts; and the Office Papers division aims to serve the users of office paper. The new structure promises an unobstructed view of the customers M-real intends to get close to.

Front- and back-end divergence

When alignment with customers is the objective, it is indispensable to mobilize the supplier's many value-creating activities to help serve the interests of the buying organization. To deliver on that promise means streamlining the front and back end of the supplier organization, including product creation, supply-chain management, logistics, service operations and marketing and sales activities. For example, when sales promises a tailored delivery schedule synchronized to meet a customer's tight production plans, the entire supply chain and its logistics apparatus, including procurement, manufacturing, warehousing and transport functions, must be mobilized for the task. A divergence of priorities between the customer-facing sales function and the supply chain can only lead to unfulfilled promises and frustrations all around. Consequently, when customer alignment is just a front-line concern, it is painfully short-lived. Precisely to avoid such divergence, M-real's recent reorganization has aimed to give the newly created end-user divisions a voice equal to that traditionally enjoyed by the paper mills. Also aiming for greater front- and back-end convergence, at Tetra Pak the development of new packaging is no longer the sole responsibility of R&D working in isolation from the front line. New product concepts, many of them originating from the local units with market knowledge, must now pass a number of customer and consumer tests before being chosen for commercialization. In this process the views of important customers are given priority in developing new value-added products.

Sales orientation

Ironically, among the barriers in countering commoditization via customer alignment may well be the customer interface people, the sales force. They can be the hardest people to win over, as they have come to believe that in tough competitive markets it is their skill in making deals that makes all the difference. Admittedly, this transaction-oriented view of the world is a legacy of years of selling commodities and haggling with their well-prepared and aggressive counterparts in the customer organization, the purchasing managers. But the narrow purchasing-office view of the world can deprive the salespeople of a broader, more strategic knowledge about the customer's business, the one that is essential for formulating new value propositions. The notion of two parties not arm-wrestling over every individual transaction in favour of a broader agreement for collaboration can be a foreign one to many deal-oriented front-line people. They also find unsettling the fact that the keys to success in managing collaborative customer relationships are different from those involved in making deals. For that reason, many salespeople at a medium-sized speciality chemicals company were disqualified from leading key-account relationships because their deal-oriented experience was considered a barrier to learning the new ways of serving customers.

Narrow sales orientation can also be a barrier to another important notion in value added strategies: that not all customers deserve to be treated, in the vernacular of Tetra Pak, as 'crown jewels' – strategic accounts deserving special attention and priority targets for alignment. That idea contradicts some of the deeply felt beliefs held by many salespeople that all customers are special and that sales volume should override all other considerations in assigning priorities. At Tetra Pak there was initially sales force resistance towards a strategy that segmented the company's client base and assigned key-account status to just a small fraction of customers – those that enjoyed progressive and ambitious management teams willing to invest in category development. The size of each account's business, of great importance to the sales force, was just one criterion among others.

Indisposed customers

Customer alignment is impossible if it remains simply a one-sided pitch by the supplier to a sceptical and unwilling buyer organization. It works only when the two act together as collaborators towards well-defined future shared benefits. That said, many potentially qualified customers shy away from any top-level agreement that ties them down to a single supplier and reduces their flexibility to act – to extract the best deal at every buying occasion, to protect the security of their supply line or to shift to substitutes when these become available. The immediate costs of alignment are thus perceived to be higher than any potential future gains. This segment would rather buy the low-priced commodities than consider offers consisting of value-added products, bundled offers or total solutions.

In other cases the same narrow view from the purchasing office described earlier prevails in the upper echelons of the customer organization. For example, when the top management of the Swiss-based engineering company ABB approached one of its large international chemical accounts and made a pitch on the benefits of its newly adopted 'customer-centric' strategy, it put forward the total volume of business done by the customer's subsidiaries around the world to show how centrally co-ordinated global sourcing could lead to tangible benefits for the customer and growth for ABB. But the customer's take-away from the presentation was different. Surprised by the significant size of its consolidated orders, the headquarters management promptly asked for a general price reduction on total purchases before discussing any co-ordinated sourcing. Clearly the chemical customer's agenda was different from ABB's customer-centric strategy. In such cases, by no means rare, the supplier is best advised to look elsewhere and target those in its customer base whose management shares similar visions on the mutuality of benefits from alignment.

Steps to countering commoditization

If countering commoditization is a way out of the growing buyer–seller power imbalance and the source of new value creation and business opportunities, then suppliers must learn how to make it work. The challenge lies in the fact that effective value-adding actions, including alignment with key customers, must ultimately influence everything a company does, from its business strategy to its routine actions.

But how can industrial marketers overcome the barriers highlighted above? To begin, there are no quick-fix recipes: each company must find its own operating model, the one that works best given its strategic objectives, core competences and management culture. Among the companies cited in this chapter, not all attempts at creating and offering differentiated values, including alignment with key customers, have come to fruition. While some have succeeded handsomely, others are still discovering the pathways and dead-end roads.

Not surprisingly, the starting point for almost all the companies studied has been a recognition that the old ways of doing business, the transactional and deal-oriented marketing, can no longer serve their interests. Such realization was in many cases triggered by bad news, a crisis. In the case of IBM, for example, the colossal losses of the early 1990s left the management no option but to cut loose from the ways of its insular past. The 'Operation Bear Hug' that forced the company's top 50 executives to visit a minimum of five clients each to find out what problems they were facing was a first step in learning to align with customers. This unprecedented action led to a new sense of mission that ultimately redirected IBM's focus from its increasingly commoditized computer hardware to enabling customers to succeed in their business. It also helped to reorient the management priorities, from internal processes to doing right by the customer. At ABB, too, the recent struggle for survival has been a key impetus behind its 'customer-centric' strategy of aligning with its major customers. Likewise at Tetra Pak, the first disappointing customer-satisfaction results were the trigger for the top management to embark on a massive change agenda, where virtually every facet of the company's operation came under scrutiny to make Tetra Pak a better informed and more reliable business partner with its key accounts.

Beyond recognizing the need for a clean break and a new beginning, there are a number of steps that a management can take to pave the way towards effective alignment. These steps are:

- redefining customer values
- articulating a value proposition
- reconfiguring the management structure
- segmenting and prioritizing the customer base
- installing a process for customer-relationship management
- following through with targeted actions.

These steps, elaborated below, create a greater force for the desired change when undertaken together than when carried out in isolation.

Redefine customer offer

When BASF Coatings conceived the Integrated Paint Shop business idea, it was redefining the company's offer to auto companies, from traditional paints to cost-effectively painted car bodies. In a similar vein, Tetra Pak's Informed Business Partnership meant a whole new value offer: from selling packaging systems to helping liquid-food companies succeed in marketing a differentiated product line while increasing production efficiency. Both examples demonstrate the critical ingredients as a company searches for opportunities for value-added offers. First and foremost, the supplier organization must educate itself in the segment reality and customer business. The education starts with taking a strategic view of the value chain, or what we referred to in the previous chapter as analysing the 'macro business system'. It also means listening to what customers say about the challenges in their business, observing their overt actions and implicit behaviour and reflecting on what matters the most to their business performance. With that knowledge, the supplier must be able to fully answer a number of fundamental questions: what are the critical factors that impact on segment profitability? What strategy is being pursued by a given key account? How can a supplier add value, beyond its traditional products or services, in ways that can positively impact segment or customer performance? BASF Coatings exploited its in-depth knowledge of the inefficiencies in the OEM in-house auto-paint shops and the customers' increasing willingness to entertain radical supply arrangements that offered added efficiencies. For Tetra Pak, it was its knowledge of the trends in the dairy industry and feedback from major accounts that propelled the management towards alignment with strategic customers.

Second, the redefined customer offer should ideally exploit elements in the company's core skills or know-how. GE Medical Systems' Performance Improvement Solutions, for example, relies heavily on two methodologies developed by the mother company and perfected over the years: GE's Six-Sigma statistical optimization programmes and the 'Work-Out' problem-solving and decision-making process. These two elements, combined with the company's increasingly sophisticated database on best practices, enable GE to promise and deliver tangible improvements. Redeploying a core expertise provides sustainability to the new offer and added protection from 'me-too' rivals.

Finally, the differentiating added value that is at the heart of the redefined offer must be easily communicable and measurable. As mentioned earlier, many potentially promising offers leave the customers cold because they are poorly communicated or their benefits are left ill-defined. To overcome these related issues, GE sells its solutions services using extensive and tailored communication packages that speak the language of health-care providers, addressing their priority problems. It also promises a minimum guaranteed return on its consulting fees, a payback that reassures the customer of the service's tangible and measurable benefits.

Articulate your value proposition

When SKF embarked on its ambitious strategy to develop value-added product and service packages for industrial customers, its 'Trouble Free Operation' mission statement was a clear value proposition that every plant manager could understand and relate to. This outbound promise had the added benefit that it was equally well understood inside SKF's own organization. It signalled to everyone that their company was about to redefine itself in radical ways that were in step with the priorities of its customers. It left little room for ambiguity inside or outside the company as to where SKF was heading.

Similarly, IBM's mission to become a comprehensive provider of integrated business solutions, a key pillar of its turnaround, also had two audiences in mind: its customers and its own employees. Captured in IBM's brand platform of 'Solutions for a Small Planet' was – in the words of its management – an 'outside-in' definition of IBM's new promise, one that spoke the language of its customers around the globe and communicated how the company had grown beyond its past hardware-centred culture. At the same time, through the massive brand campaign, the management was signalling to the rank and file what was expected of them: to better understand and align themselves with what the customers valued – not just computers, but also an increasing portfolio of unconventional services meant to promote customer success in their businesses.

Certainly there are already too many value propositions in business captured by hollow taglines. What distinguishes the above two examples from many others, however, is their compelling customer-centredness, their dual targeting of external–internal audiences and the resolve of the management to see them drive day-to-day management action. They capture the spirit of alignment and, as such, far from being promotional taglines, they constitute effective tools for implementation.

Structure around customers

We have seen how old structures can get in the way of aligning with customers. At IBM, to facilitate the acquisition of the sector knowledge and customer insights needed for its newly adopted solutions strategy, the management redrew the organizational chart to create 12 divisions, each looking after an end-user cluster (banking, government, insurance, distribution, etc.). The new structure replaced a product-based organization that was no longer relevant or comprehensible to its customers. The reorganization was also instrumental in reorienting the company's insular culture from 'do it my way' to 'do it the customer way'.[4] Likewise at M-real, the reorganization along customer and end-user groupings has allowed the development of sector expertise that didn't exist before, or was scattered around the mill-based structure. The company's growing innovative service offerings to its publishing and consumer packaging customers are payoffs from organizing around end-user segments.

Relevant issues to consider in rewiring an organization around customer-focused units include each segment's future volume and growth potential, prospects for new business opportunities from value-added products or services and the extent to which the company's core competences can be stretched to exploit such opportunities. Another factor to consider is the manner and speed with which the old structure is abandoned in favour of the new one. Experience shows how easy it is to underestimate the turbulence a hasty restructuring can provoke inside an organization and how confusing that can be to the customers outside. Companies are well advised to err on the side of overpreparation when redrawing the organizational chart.

Identify the 'crown jewels'

As the ultimate among value-added strategies, getting aligned with customers is a selective process: not all accounts deserve or are suited for alignment. Stated differently, the high cost of aligning and serving the target accounts must be more than compensated for by the additional profit stream directly attributed to the collaborative undertaking. That criterion alone suggests that the current volume of business is probably a less important factor than the future profitability of each target account. In fact experience suggests that customers who have used their high volume of purchases to extract maximum price concessions are less likely to enter into co-dependent buyer–seller alignment. As we saw with Tetra Pak, other criteria must enter into the selection process. These include a fit between the supplier's strategic ambitions and those of the customer, a readiness to invest in joint programmes for shared benefits and a minimum level of mutual trust based on common values as the two companies enter into a long-term relationship with only a fuzzy road-map as their guide. When such stringent criteria are applied, only a fraction of customers qualify as 'crown jewels'. In the case of Raisio Chemicals, out of more than a hundred candidates worldwide only five were designated as global accounts – those with multi-production sites and complex supply needs that demanded dedicated resources and attention. For Tetra Pak, the ratio is higher, but still only 15% of the customer base gets the crown-jewel label.

At ABB, where customer-centric alignment with key accounts is at the centre of the company's turnaround strategy, the selection of strategically most significant 'group accounts' is led by, among other criteria, the customer's readiness to enter into a top-level agreement covering a joint strategy accompanied by joint performance metrics. In the case of Dow Chemicals, a model group account, the global strategy includes goals and objectives covering volume growth, prices and conditions and reduced waste and costs. The performance metrics governing the alignment cover product and service quality, delivery reliability, supply-chain cost reduction, share of electronic transactions and customer-satisfaction scores. ABB's management has staked the company's future on such close collaboration with a select list of its customers.

Lead customer relationships

When Tetra Pak embarked on its customer-alignment strategy, it found that its front-line sales operation was inadequate for the job. Not that the sales force was incompetent: it was one of the best in the business. But building strategic relationships with major accounts, and aligning internal priorities and resources to deliver on the promises of collaboration, was a different job. The company's management also realized that leading such relationships was best done not by a single individual but by a cross-functional team of experts, each representing a different angle of customer interface. If alignment had to be deep and broad, the management concluded, then the team must demonstrate expertise in manufacturing, technical service, marketing, logistics, etc. Only then could the company claim to have under one roof all the internal resources needed for a 360-degree view of the customer's business and all its challenges. Tetra Pak's Key Account Management initiative has proven to be indispensable for aligning with customers.

Similarly at ABB, a previously fragmented structure with business units and country management each pursuing often different objectives, the formalization of customer-relationship management was meant as a necessary instrument to present to each group account a single point of contact with a unified global agenda. To give the newly established account teams the necessary external profile and internal weight, senior executives were assigned to head the teams and lead account interactions from the top.

As the above illustrations indicate, the choice of account management structure and its configuration are important elements in customer alignment. Though different companies have devised different ways of leading customer interactions, the success ingredients include a well-understood charter for account management, active support from important internal stakeholders across the stand-alone divisions or geographic units, and empowerment from the top to navigate inside the organization to marshal the necessary resources and get work done. Another important ingredient is the joint preparation of a strategic account plan in collaboration with senior managers in the customer organization. The document is a business plan that lays out the key premises for collaboration, highlighting the shared objectives and specific deliverables with their key performance indicators. Such a plan, reviewed periodically, should also define the respective roles and contributions of each party to its realization.

Follow-through

If a single variable could explain the difference between success and failure in countering commoditization, between the high hopes and low results, that variable would have to be the leadership qualities of top management in follow-through. As we have seen, it is the top management that defines the logic and sets the strategic agenda behind the alignment; it is the top management that articulates the mission that captures the essence of success through collaboration; and it is the top management that defines the elements of a rewired customer-aligned structure including account-relationship management. But the top management's job doesn't end here. In deciding to refocus the strategic agenda, it has embarked on a major change agenda that will continue to require its active involvement with the entire process for some time to come.

At SKF the division president's personal interest and routine involvement with the 'Trouble Free Operation' programme was a key factor behind getting the idea sold inside the organization. In addition to personal appearances at every possible meeting, he used videos and brochures to spread the strategic logic of aligning with customers.[5] Similarly at Tetra Pak, the 'Informed Business Partnership' concept was on every senior executive's agenda to promote across the company at every opportunity. In all management meetings the results of the company's various initiatives and their impact on customer-satisfaction scores were communicated. In addition, the top management led a revision of the performance-evaluation criteria to better align them with its strategy. The bonuses of country managing directors, for example, were tied to their local implementation of the Win-Back and Key Account Management initiatives, as well as to improvement in their customer-satisfaction scores.

Follow-through, as a top-management task, implies keeping the internal change process on track and energizing it with frequent interventions, to smooth out the inevitable internal hurdles or to communicate encouraging news about the early wins. It also implies top-level interventions with important customers to promote the concept of alignment before sending in the relationship-management team. These are precisely the tasks that cannot be delegated down the organization. They belong to where the whole alignment process must begin, at the very top.

Summary and management guidelines

- The pervasive force of commoditization has changed the buyer–seller balance of bargaining power in favour of the former, thus putting vendor prices under pressure and margins at risk.
- Countering commoditization begins with a re-examination of the core business and its outdated customer-value proposition. Such an exercise can lead to value-added strategies that stretch out of the core and offer customers compelling extra values in one or more of three areas: increased customization, integrated bundles of products and/or services, and total solutions.
- Value-added strategies beyond the core are labelled Targeted Extension, System Development and Solutions Innovation.
- Solutions Innovation requires not only an in-depth knowledge of the buyers and their business, but also 'alignment', enabling the supplier organization to identify and profitably exploit value-added opportunities that enhance a customer's keys to its success.
- Different alignment scenarios imply different depths of collaboration with customers and different degrees of buyer–seller co-dependency.

- Challenges and barriers in countering commoditization include:

  – Misplaced added values that leave customers cold about reformulated value propositions
  – Past success with a core product or service and its increasingly out-dated customer-value proposition
  – Inward-looking organizational structures
  – Divergence between customer-facing front-line priorities and the rest of the organization
  – Narrow sales orientation
  – Poor choice of target customers for alignment and collaboration.

- Management guidelines for effectively countering commoditization include:

  – Create an organization-wide recognition of the need for change, from the ways of the past to customer-centricity and value innovation
  – Become insightful about customers and formulate strategies that promise and deliver compelling added values, those that impact on their business performance in significant ways
  – Articulate and communicate value propositions that are easily understood by target customers externally and by the entire organization internally
  – Structure the organization around segments for the greater intimacy and depth of action that comes from focus
  – Carefully target and select strategic customers for alignment and collaboration
  – Lead important customer relationships with multi-functional account teams that have sufficient organizational weight and credibility to overcome internal obstacles

- Implement the above change agenda with resolve, putting in place management processes that constantly keep the centricity of customers in sight.

References

[1] N. Dawar and M. Vandenbosch have argued that new value creation by suppliers takes the forms of lowering the customers' costs and/or risks of doing business. See Dawar, N. and Vandenbosch, M. 'Beyond Better Products: Capturing Value in Customer Interactions', *Sloan Management Review*, 43 (Summer 2000), pp. 35–42.

[2] Webster was among the first authors to draw attention to the contrasting natures of 'transaction' selling vs 'relationship' marketing. See Webster, Frederick E., Jr., *Market-driven Management*, New York: John Wiley & Sons, Inc., 1994.

[3] The story of IBM's turnaround is documented in various publications but none enjoys the thoroughness of an insider's testimony found in the book by the former CEO. See Gerstner, L.V. Jr., *Who Says Elephants Can't Dance?: Inside IBM's Historic Turnaround*, London: HarperCollins Publishers, 2002.

[4] Gerstner, L.V. Jr., *Who Says Elephants Can't Dance*, p. 206.

[5] For information on the launch of 'Trouble Free Operation', see IMD case studies on SKF (IMD-5 0383 and IMD-5-0384), prepared by Sandra Vandermerwe and Marika Taishoff. For the current scope of SKF service offerings see: http://www.skf.com/portal/skf/home/services

4
The Marketing of Services: How is it Different?

Professor Jacques Horovitz

I n this chapter we will look at the key differences between products and services and how they impact marketing decisions, as well as the extent of responsibility for the marketing function. A special case of the internationalization of services will also be discussed.

So what is different about the marketing of services as opposed to the marketing of products? The short answer is: just about everything.

First of all, products are tangible: you can touch them, test them, try them, feel them before you decide to buy. Services are often intangible. Only when you *experience* them will you know whether or not they are right for you.

You do not need to buy a car to experience it. You do need to have a haircut to know whether the hairdresser is right for you. This difference has big impacts on the way a marketer can attract a customer: what should you say to persuade a customer that this service is right for him or her? How should you say it? And through which channels?

The service marketer has to convince customers of two things if he or she wants them to buy: first the desirability of the service itself, be it a hotel room, a massage, a car inspection, security protection. And second, the ability of the company to deliver on what is promised: will the hotel room be clean and the hotel welcoming; will the massage be done in a professional manner, the car inspection carried out by qualified people, the security guards well trained and well behaved? The customer needs to be assured of the service company's ability to serve before buying or signing a contract.

The next difference is that whereas products are usually produced *before* they are consumed, allowing for quality control before they reach the customer, this is generally not true of services. Also, stock cannot be held in case it doesn't find a customer, as 'production' and 'consumption' of services are often simultaneous. It can be difficult for the supplier either to check quality before the customer does or to know when the customer is going to demand a service, so as to have the appropriate capacity. In addition, the quality is not just dependent on the performance of physical ingredients put together as a product, but on how they are delivered by people – thus incurring more risk of variability in quality. The fact that services cannot wait in the stock room for customers to ask for them makes the management of peaks and troughs in demand more tricky. So how can marketers of services ensure that the quality of the service is uniform? If they cannot, what should they say when they make promises?

Should they underpromise so much that they will not attract anyone, or over-promise and run the risk of causing disappointment? As for peaks and troughs, can they be forecast? Should they be used to adapt pricing to ensure sales even when demand is low? Is there not a risk of customers waiting for the lower prices and making the marketing effort worthless? Can prices for consulting, for instance, vary according to the season or the consultants' workload?

The final major difference between marketing products and marketing services lies in the involvement of the customer. At the international delivery service Federal Express (Fedex), half of the missorting of parcels is caused by customers having made a mistake in specifying the address they want the parcel to be sent to! Every actor will tell you that the performance of a play can be totally different from one night to the next, depending on the reaction of the audience. The same goes for advertising agencies, when work can go from being great to being trash depending on the client. Teachers see sparkles in the eyes of some students and not others; consultants achieve results in certain cases, in others only reports that go in the dustbin, and so on. What can marketers do to make sure that the customer's involvement contributes to quality, which in turn contributes to satisfaction, which in turn contributes to more sales? How can they choose and manage the customer mix in order to maximize their chances of success?

Make the intangible tangible

In the marketing of products, a lot of effort is put into making the product seem different by adding something intangible to its recognized, tangible features. For consumer goods, for instance, the marketer can add value to the product by creating a brand image that says: 'This is for people like me', 'I feel proud to use this product', 'My neighbours are impressed by what I wear or use' or 'I know what I am getting with this product and I am reassured by that.' This is where the brand (which we will discuss in detail in the next chapter) becomes important: it enables the marketer to charge a premium for the product because an intangible difference has been triggered in the customer's mind.

Not so with services. Although there are differences – both in terms of the degree of intangibility of the service and in the intensity of customer involvement – between, for example, getting a loan from a bank, eating in a restaurant, creating an advertising campaign that will work and shipping a parcel across the world, all these businesses need to supply some form of reassurance before the customer will buy: will the loan be adapted to my capacity to repay it, will the food be as good as it sounds on the menu, will the campaign create traffic, will my parcel reach its destination? How can the marketer reassure the customer that all these promises will be fulfilled? The answer lies in making the intangible tangible, and this can be achieved in a number of ways:

- **expressing the service tangibly** in the communication of the brand
- **extending the tangible expressions of the brand** to all contact points between the service provider and the customer
- **providing a service guarantee** to express the intangible in a tangible way
- **packaging the service** – making it look like a product
- **the best of both worlds** – underpromising and overdelivering.

We will look at all these approaches in turn.

Communicating the brand

As far as this author is concerned, Singapore Airlines has had the best service advertising since its inception in 1974. It has managed to express the warmth of its service, the exotic food served, the care you can expect, as well as the new routes and destinations offered, through a single theme varying according to the message expressed: the Singapore girl. Her face conveys care, warmth, humility, tenderness. Her dress says exotic food, her surroundings say London, Sydney, Tokyo, comfortable bed, new and reliable aeroplane. The colours in the picture express calm and serenity; the overall message tells the customer not to worry. A marvel of making the intangible tangible!

This is not an easy thing to achieve. In the past, Club Med's competitive advantage was not about its resorts' quality, nor the destinations available, nor its sports offerings, nor its food. It was about the fact that it offered a totally hassle-free holiday (everything was on site, the customer did not have to organize anything). It was also about learning something new (new sports, new arts or crafts), meeting new people, making new friends and never being pressured to spend more (everything included in the price, friendly organizers whom you did not tip, one price paid in advance). Above all, it was a holiday full of entertainment.

So how do you communicate all that – a hassle-free holiday, making new friends, generous staff with no hidden agenda, enjoying every moment – in one picture in a magazine or in 30 seconds on TV? Because if you don't get those messages across, what the customer is left with is the offer of a mediocre Caribbean hotel or any old beach in Mexico!

A comparison of three Club Med advertising campaigns will show how the company at first emphasized and then lost its unique competitive advantage. The first, which appeared in magazines in the late 1970s, had to do with verbs. It used various situations, each with one picture and one verb – love, eat, play, sleep, taste – so that each ad reinforced the rest. It traded on the brand image that Club Med was for young, fun-loving, friendly people – exactly the message the company wanted to put across. Then, in the early 1980s in the US, 'the antidote to civilization' campaign conveyed Club Med as a different way of spending your holiday: no hurry, no organizing, no crowd, no hassles. However, unlike the first one, which was totally positive and Zen, this one relied on the assumption that people were not happy in 'civilization' and were looking for an alternative. If civilization were to become cool, then the ad would find that it was no longer conveying an appealing message. This problem/solution type of ad is often used for FMCGs – every television advertisement for household cleaning products shows a mother dealing with a stain on her children's clothes; then the miracle of the washing product makes the stain disappear – but may not work so well for services.

The third advertising campaign concentrated on comparing costs. Essentially it provided a checklist of what Club Med offered (room, full board, instruction, sports, music, disco, etc.) and asked the customer to enter the prices of the same items for any other destination, add them up and compare. It certainly helped the customer 'tangibilize' what all-inclusive meant, but inclusivity was an easy feature for other holiday companies to imitate, and the emphasis on cost was not very poetic for customers looking forward to their holiday!

Extending the tangible expressions of the brand

Making the intangible tangible in a 30-second TV spot or a single full-colour page is a challenging exercise. Marketers have to ask themselves:

- What can we convey that relates to our offering?
- How can we ensure that it is not too trivial/boring?
- Can we make it attractive?
- How can we give an impression not just of what the customer will receive but of how he or she will be treated and cared for?

However, there are so many other points of contact between the service provider and the customer that what has to be conveyed briefly and succinctly in advertising can be reinforced vividly and in more detail to underline the tangibility of the intangible. Contacts may be 'physical' (the messages conveyed by the service provider's office, store, reception, trucks, stationery, etc.) or made through interactions with the service provider's staff (waiters, drivers, call-centre employees, consultants ...).

How can encounters like these help make the intangible tangible? How can they converge to reinforce what advertising has started to convey? And, on the other hand, if they are badly used, how can these contact points and people destroy what has been built up or confuse potential customers about what is being offered?

Let us look at an example. Elis is one of Europe's leading linen-rental companies, supplying hospitals, hotels, restaurants and factories. Their trucks are immaculately white: this in itself says, 'We clean your linen.' It is each driver's responsibility to make sure his truck stays white all the time to make the promise of clean linen tangible. In addition, the drivers have the title 'service agents'. Their job is not just to pick up dirty linen and replace it with clean; it is also to keep clients informed of developments in the company's offer (a new service, a new billing system) and get feedback from them (complaints about anything that has gone missing or been mishandled, new needs). By acting as service agents the drivers reinforce every day the caring dimension in the promise in a way that no four-colour leaflet could do on its own.

Let's take another example – this time one with the reverse effect. Pacini, an Italian restaurant chain in Canada, once developed a TV advertising campaign that served two purposes: one, to reassert that Pacini was very generous in its servings; and two, to offer a promotional item – a Caesar salad – to any customer visiting any of its premises over a given period. The tag line was 'more and more', meaning that at Pacini you could have everything you wanted. This author was invited to one of the restaurants by the CEO during the week the campaign was launched. The waitress took my order and of course in addition to what I ordered brought me a Caesar salad. My reaction was: 'Why are you bringing me this? I didn't order it.' She was taken by surprise and did not know what to say. In fact, most of the staff in the restaurants had not seen the TV ad and even those who had seen it had not been trained to transform it into a positive opportunity that would reinforce the promise of generosity with a statement like: 'We are delighted to offer you a Caesar salad on the house. At Pacini we love to give you more.'

So the questions we need to ask the marketer of services are: when, where, how often and how much is your customer meeting your organization? What do those contact points express (physical encounters) or say (interaction encounters)? If, for all those contact points, you communicate the tangibility of your service in a consistent manner, are you not likely to increase confidence in it, and thus transform more potential buyers into buyers?

Guaranteeing the service

As an alternative or a complement to the above, a service guarantee can be a very good way of persuading customers to buy from you. Let us take three examples of guarantees that have proved successful in terms of sales and customer franchise.

BKB is a pest-control service provider: put another way, it eliminates bugs. The company guarantees that if, after it has done its job, you find a pest on your premises, it will reimburse the cost of your annual contract and buy you a contract with one of its competitors. This clearly says that BKB is confident that there are no defects in its service, doesn't it?

Fedex says that if a parcel is not delivered when it is supposed to be, you don't pay for it; you also get your money back if the company cannot track the parcel within an hour. Does this not make the concepts of delivery on time and no loss of parcels tangible?

GrandOptical offers spectacles in one hour through its 250 stores in Europe. The guarantee says:

- If we cannot give them to you in the store within an hour, we will deliver anywhere in the world free of charge.

- If you cannot get used to your lenses, you have 30 days to change your mind (you can either have your money back or be provided with other lenses).
- If you do not like your glasses, you also have 30 days to change your mind (again, refund or exchange).
- If you break your glasses within a year, we will give you a new pair.
- If you do not find the model you want and have seen it somewhere else, we will get it for you within 48 hours.
- If you do not like any of our models, we will produce a custom-made one, just for you.
- If you find the same pair of glasses cheaper somewhere else, we will refund the difference.

This guarantee is posted on a large panel in every store. Does it not make the intangible tangible: one-hour service, advice on the best lenses, aesthetics, right to change your mind, freedom of choice, help in case of accident, personalization and competitive prices?

To be powerful, service guarantees should emphasize what is meaningful to the customer, be unconditional, easy to invoke and easy to understand. Of course, they can cost a lot if the service provider is bad, but they can also express differentiation in a tangible manner, thus persuading more customers to buy.

What role does a marketer play in developing such a guarantee? Should you push for it only when you know that your service delivery is good enough not to cost a fortune in 'paid damages', or is it desirable even if your service is not yet great, as a means to persuade more people to buy – and at the same time encourage better delivery, thus reducing the number of disappointed customers and in turn reducing the effort necessary to replace those who bought, were disappointed and did not buy again?

Packaging the service

Another way to make the intangible tangible is to package the service so that it looks and feels more tangible.

SKF, the leading Scandinavian ball-bearing supplier whose value-added approach we discussed in the previous chapter, did this years ago when it realized that the so-called after-sales market – in this case, the replacement market – was very attractive and not well served. SKF was leaning more towards OEMs (car manufacturers and machine manufacturers) who wanted quality, volume and price. However, when it came to replacement, factories wanted to avoid unplanned downtime with its consequent loss of production, and garages wanted easy-to-mount/dismount bearings for all the makes of car they handled. SKF therefore created a service division which offered preventive maintenance packages to factories and ready-to-use kits for garages. Maintenance packages included bearings, oil, measurement systems and training, while kits contained bearings, tools for mounting and dismounting, and instructions for doing the job quickly and well.

Packaging a service rather than selling each item separately makes it easier for the customer to assess what is in it. Personal health insurance used such a technique, offering 'completa' for all-inclusive care using all medical techniques everywhere as opposed to 'protecta', which provided minimum insurance cover. This approach is also used by financial services to specify the level of risk and return of a particular mutual fund, such as 'new technology' versus 'classic'.

The best of both worlds: underpromise and overdeliver

It may be difficult for the marketer to admit this, but with services it is better to say less and do more; better to reduce the promotional budget and use the savings to improve quality of service. If the measures discussed above have so far failed to produce great campaigns that really make the intangible tangible, easily reliable at all contact points and supported by a service guarantee, it is much better to say less and deliver more than you have promised, rather than the reverse!

Whereas for products, communicating the psychological or intangible benefits adds value to the customer's perception, allowing overpromise ('with Nike shoes on, you will be as great as top athletes'), it is not so with services. The more you promise – especially with intangible benefits – the more you risk disappointing. In the mid-1990s, one airline advertised its new business-class service for short-haul destinations by showing a beautiful leather armchair in the middle of the living room of a castle. It may have appealed to the customer's imagination, but once he or she was on board, they found themselves sitting in the same seat as in economy class, except that it was red instead of blue. (Since then, this airline has improved the offer – all the seats are blue but the middle one is not used in business class.) Apparently, firms often fall into the trap of making the intangible even more intangible, thus overpromising and falling on their face afterwards. Here are two more examples.

Management and IT consultants Capgemini recently put together an international magazine campaign to introduce 'the collaborative business experience'. They took double pages in *Time, Newsweek, Business Week* and so on, and used well-known coaches of stars to express how Capgemini had enhanced the phenomenal capabilities of their protégés. Then the text went on to say that Capgemini would be a nice partner on which to count every day. But what is new about that? Isn't it what every consultant would say? If Capgemini had said that if they failed, they would cut their fees by half, their claims would have become more tangible and therefore more credible. Would it not be better for Capgemini to spend more time with its customers delivering obvious, measurable, observable results?

For a number of years, the Paris metro spent a fortune on an advertising campaign called *'ticket chic, ticket choc'* (chic ticket, shock ticket). The intention was to make customers believe that it was chic, upbeat, to ride the underground and that the price was 'shockingly' reasonable. Probably the people who wrote the campaign and those who approved it never took the metro: if they had, they would have realized that what customers cared about were crowds, perspiration, noise, the feeling of insecurity, beggars, dark tunnels. So what happened? A new advertising campaign emphasized the progress that had been made towards increased safety, comfort and cleanliness.

So if in doubt, or when it is not easy to describe tangibly all the facets of a service, it is better to say less and do more – then you avoid the risk of disappointment.

Selling the service and the ability to serve

Even if communication is able to 'tangibilize' the service on offer, is this enough to make a risk-averse customer buy something he cannot test or try? When you are considering buying a product, the specs are quite well defined, allowing you to assess whether or not it is what you want. If you buy it and find that it doesn't do what it is supposed to do, you can return it or exchange it. But when you buy a service, you are buying a promise that the service provider has the ability to serve. Granted, some services are more 'physical' than others, thus more 'touchable' and tryable. You can, up to a point, check a hotel bedroom before trying it (even if you are a long way away, a picture in a brochure or on the Internet will be of some help). But how about a hairdresser – can you return the wrong haircut? Will half the head do it? And a lawyer? How do you know if he will be any good?

One of the key challenges for the service marketer is to convey not just what the service is all about – the service value proposition – but also that the company has the ability to deliver the promised service. Whereas making the intangible tangible arouses interest from customers, demonstrating the ability to serve can make the customer decide to buy.

Judging a service from peripheral cues

Since it is difficult to assess directly whether a hairdresser will have the ability to cut your hair properly, how do you decide to go to a particular hairdressing salon in a new city? The shop itself, the hairdresser, the pictures on the wall? These cues do not tell you directly whether you will have a haircut that suits you, but will probably give you some indication of the hairdresser's ability to do a good job. We often judge whether or not to go for a service provider by these indications, which are called peripheral cues. For example, staff at Fedex answer 99% of phone calls on the first ring. This is a good indication of the speed of their service, even if that service actually involves delivering a parcel rather than answering the phone quickly.

Peripheral cues are multiple since, as the name says, they are peripheral. What is key is to identify them in our physical encounters – on our documentation, in our proposals, in the words we use – so that the cues converge in such a manner that the customer says: 'They seem to have the ability to serve; I will buy from them.'

This author's book *Service Strategy*[1] describes these peripheral cues and how one might want to look at them. 'Peripheral cues are those physical

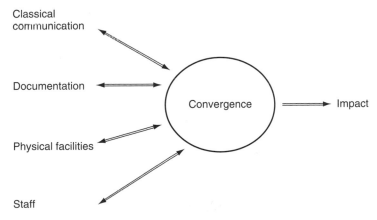

Figure 4.1 Do your cues send the right message?

communication processes that will reinforce the demonstration of your ability to serve before the customer is served. When Otis checks an elevator, you see the signature of the repair operative in the elevator; Decaux, a company which manages bus shelters and their advertising throughout Europe, has white trucks to show its ability to carry out a clean and efficient job!' The example quoted earlier of the linen service company Elis and its insistence on immaculate white trucks makes the same point. Figure 4.1 shows one way for marketers to assess whether their cues are converging.

Indirect marketing methods can be better than direct ones

It is not easy to convey the message 'I am a good lawyer/doctor/maintenance company/holiday resort/restaurant', because boasting that is not supported by evidence can create suspicion rather than attract potential customers. An alternative, external source of information has more impact. In other words, it is much easier to gain credibility if someone else says your service is great! Restaurants recognize this when they show pictures of famous people having dined there with a few words from them. Consultants always put the name of referees in their proposals ('See, I have already done it with so and so'), while health-care organizations use patients for their testimonials.

Indirect marketing methods include the heavy use of others speaking about your services rather than you being your own spokesperson.

- **References** attest that others have used the service to their satisfaction. Well-known names of companies or people add credibility to your claims about your ability to serve.
- **Testimonials** go one step further by having past users tell about their experiences, adding reassurance to credibility.
- **Co-marketing** with clients/customers (or with suppliers), be it through joint publications, joint conferences, joint appearances at exhibitions, joint events or users' clubs, can also reinforce the credibility of a service provider.
- **Public relations** must always be preferred to direct advertising. When Virgin Atlantic Airways was launched, its founder, Richard Branson (whose leadership style we will discuss in more detail in the next chapter), used both media events and open attacks on British Airways, the existing 'dinosaur', to convey to the public that Virgin Atlantic was the new kid on the block, the underdog, the fighter against the sleeping giant, the rebel sitting on the customer's side to make air transport more service oriented, more fun, more comfortable, more innovative and cheaper. Not only did Branson's quite vociferously expressed stance against 'Goliath' give him a lot of media value (Virgin Atlantic did not advertise), but the fact that the press talked about the young airline gave it seriousness. In addition, by hiring experienced pilots from British Airways – a peripheral cue – Branson conveyed the message that the airline was safe.

Of course, public relations efforts pay in terms of the buzz they create and the amount of media coverage they get only if you have something to say! Virgin Atlantic was always the first to introduce a new service on board or on the ground. It also used customer advocacy ('We fight for you against Goliath') to get attention. In another segment of the same market – the low-cost, short-haul destinations – easyJet used the same tactics to make themselves heard. Out go the expensive tickets, unaffordable prices, heavy commissions to intermediaries. Here comes direct, cheap, affordable transport to help you reach your family, your holiday spot. easyJet received the same type of media coverage through customer advocacy.

Which indirect method – references, testimonials, co-marketing with customers or PR – works best depends of course on the type of service provided, its newness and the speed with which a company needs to reach all its potential customers in order to achieve volume.

Simultaneous production and consumption: impact on prices and prevention

In the previous two sections, we have emphasized the need to make the intangible tangible in order to arouse customers' awareness and interest so that they consider buying; and the need to sell both the service and the ability to serve to make the customer *decide* to buy, to help convince customers better and faster about a service offer.

However, as we have seen, services are inherently different from products in the way they are produced: no inventory can be taken to allow for additional capacity if demand is high or to keep and sell tomorrow something not sold today. In addition, quality is more difficult to control as the 'quality controller' is often the customer. This has three impacts on the marketer:

- pricing for peaks and troughs
- extending the role of marketing to service delivery

- less use of indirect channels of distribution to minimize variability in quality.

Pricing for peaks and troughs vs being equipped for peaks – two different philosophies of service

Why are lastminute.com and travelocity.com so successful? Because they have understood that unsold capacity in the travel industry, which is essentially a fixed-cost business, can be very damaging to travel operators. By offering bargain prices for the unsold capacity, not only do they attract bargain hunters, they also help operators fill their beds or seats.

Yield management has become common for companies that need to fill their service space to maximum occupancy. Early bookings, advance orders or last-minute deals can help. In that mode, the marketer needs the help of sophisticated forecasting techniques so that he can constantly adjust his prices to suit varying demand. He has the choice of selling capacity early (as low-cost airlines do) or making it cheap to buy last minute in order to cover fixed capacity (as cruise ships or hotels do). Both methods attempt to shift customer behaviour, either to book early or to buy on impulse. If they are too successful, i.e. if all customers change their behaviour in the way the service provider wanted them to, the marketing effort defeats its purpose. This is particularly true with the second method – cutting prices at the last minute, which can lead to late bookings and in the long term reduce sales. In contrast, offering cheaper prices for early bookings is a promotion that can be switched off if it is too successful: the customer can be told that there are no more seats, no more time, no more beds . . .

In order to avoid falling into the commodity volume trap, for early price cuts the marketer needs tools to know at which point he must increase prices; and for late price cuts at which point he must start decreasing them. Last-minute price cuts can, however, be devastating to the image of a company, as well as to its profitability.

Recently, large hotel chains such as Hyatt or Hilton stopped using dot.com last-minute intermediaries, because they realized that their offers had become a commodity; that about 25% of sales were last minute; that they had no control of who booked where at low value; and that they depended heavily on one or two Internet travel agencies, with customers starting to pursue bargains and not wanting to pay a price nobody else in their circles paid. Instead, the hotel chains introduced direct offers to loyal customers via their own websites. (We will look further at the effect of last-minute on-line offers on differential pricing in Chapter 7.)

Whereas early booking of service capacity can have a boosting effect on sales while limiting risks of margin destruction, last-minute price cutting should only be used if the total price the customer will eventually pay is higher than the face value of the service. For instance, cruise lines do offer last-minute deals, because they know that one additional passenger on board means one additional player in the casino, one additional customer at the boutique or hairdresser, so they can expect to recoup the discount given on the cruise when the customer spends on other things.

Pricing can also be adapted not to early or late 'booking' but to low and high demand times. Mobile phone operators have a fixed network with a certain capacity level. They offer cheaper rates at night or at weekends in the hope of reducing utilization during the day and thus avoiding network congestion, which would lead to a deterioration in the quality of service and force the companies to invest further in capacity.

In total contrast to the price adjustments described above, there is an alternative approach which consists of being fully equipped for peaks in terms of demand (for handling claims, serving customers or whatever the case might be).

Take the example of GrandOptical, the high-street supplier of spectacles discussed earlier. Everyone in retail knows that 50% of sales are made on Saturdays. GrandOptical has chosen to equip all its stores with minilabs that can cope with Saturday's traffic. However, lab equipment would not be enough to serve all customers in one hour (a key factor in Grand-Optical's offer) on peak days. Staff must be there too. In addition to arranging schedules that allow for all teams to be present on Saturday and rotate days off during the rest of the week, all staff are cross-trained so that they can both serve customers and operate the machines, thus increasing capacity.

Being equipped for peaks is the better alternative when prices will not cause a major shift in customer behaviour. To continue with the GrandOptical example, no matter how much cheaper the company made its products during the week, there would not be appreciably more people taking time off work and going to shopping malls on a weekday to buy a pair of glasses!

The two approaches are summarized in Table 4.1.

Table 4.1   Price management vs coping with peaks and troughs

Use of prices	Managing for peaks
Lower gross margin	Higher gross margins
Higher investment in capacity	Lower investment in capacity
Price changes influence customer behaviour easily	Price changes do not help change behaviour
Additional sales help recuperate part of loss	Additional sales not possible

Quality of delivery: is the marketer involved?

Usually the people responsible for the quality of products are those who design them and produce them. If a product is defective, it is either reworked, thrown away or exchanged. Because of the simultaneity of production and consumption, this is not the case with services. Redoing an ill-performed surgical operation is not well received. Throwing away a wasted vacation is not possible, reworking an underperforming portfolio of stocks may be too late, exchanging a badly repaired elevator too costly and so on.

So what is the alternative? The answer sounds simple but can be very difficult to achieve. It is prevention. Doing it right the first time.

Marketers have a big role to play here: in designing the training of sales-people as well as those delivering the service; in putting together the tools that will help the salespeople sell the right service for the right need and provide support after the sale is done.

Let us take two examples which show the important responsibility of the marketing organization in minimizing variability of quality.

Mobile phone operators are very quick to invent new 'products' in the form of price plans packaged with a mobile, a series of services included in the price, additional charges for going beyond what is included, a free trial period that expires in two months and will be automatically transformed into a contract unless the customer voices his refusal two weeks prior to the expiration of the trial period, etc. Needless to say, all those not-so-transparent, tactical packages create a lot of calls to the company's call centre from irritated or confused customers wanting to know why their bill is so high or so complicated, why they have received a service they did not ask for and so on.

The smart minds who invented these packages can either extend their role into the call centre or leave it to another department, even subcontract it. At Bouygues Telecom, a French mobile operator, the call centres used to report to the director of sales and distribution while the people designing the packages reported to the director of marketing and communication. This resulted in internal conflicts between the two divisions ('You can't explain anything', 'Your package design is crazy') until they were integrated into a single unit with marketers becoming responsible not just for attracting, but also for satisfying and retaining customers. Today the marketers are much more responsive to customer complaints and support call-centre staff with adequate answers to questions.

Châteauform is one of the leading European conference centres. Its marketing department, which it calls customer relationships, is divided into five sections:

- **marketing**, responsible for communication and customer events such as open days
- **sales and reservations**, responsible for bookings
- **campus**, responsible for companies who use Châteauform's premises and facilities as their own 'corporate university' year round (other companies might call this department 'key account management')
- **customer liaison**, responsible for knowing participants' needs and special requests so that these can be passed on to the sites; also responsible for obtaining and acting on customer feedback
- **nannies**, responsible for helping the customer to prepare for the trip once the booking is made.

The fact that the nannies are part of the marketing department is a deliberate choice. It ensures that customers are not left to themselves once they have made a booking. The nannies brief the site on particular requests, prepare invitations for participants, special events and welcome presents, organize transportation to and from airports, etc. One could argue that they should report to the head of operations or be attached to the sites. Not so. Keeping them in the marketing organization signals that the job of marketing is not finished once a sale is done. Châteauform's marketing department must support clients to the point of arrival on site. Keeping the nannies separate from operations reduces the risk of compromises. If the two functions were separated, a situation might arise where marketing had sold, the nannies received a request, the site said it was not possible, the customer was punished – and disappointed.

How far marketers should go in supporting their marketing and sales effort is of particular importance in services. Spending money on marketing that attracts customers only to disappoint them is like pouring water into a bucket full of holes! This is why we say that in services it is not only better to underpromise and overdeliver but it is also better to put more resources into satisfying than into attracting customers.

Managing the customer mix and customer involvement

Of the many ways used to classify services, one very useful one is to measure the degree of customer involvement in the quality of delivery (see Figure 4.2).

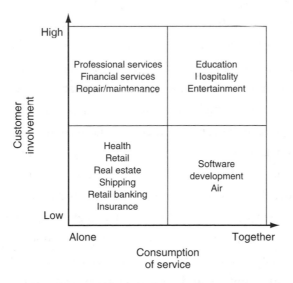

Figure 4.2 Examples of types of services according to the degree of customer involvement

Some services are quite involving for the customer, others less so. Some are consumed in the presence of other customers, some 'alone'. The degree of involvement and intensity of 'communal' consumption has an impact on marketing on several counts.

Customers who use a service together interact with each other and also interact with the service provider, either to exchange information or to voice pleasure or discontent. In these services the involvement of the customer with the service provider can contribute to the quality of the service.

- **Exchange of information** leads to a greater need for transparency and fairness in sales conditions and pricing (of airline tickets or holidays, for example). Otherwise customers will quickly learn that their neighbours paid less or got a special deal and will be angry with the provider.
- **Voicing pleasure or discontent as a crowd** can add to the motivation or the burden of the service provider to ensure that the quality of the service provided has no weak link that can make everyone angry (a badly made shoe, a poor meal in a restaurant), or conversely to ensure that what triggers pleasure is emphasized so as to mask any weak point. For instance, as discussed earlier, Club Med was designed with an emphasis on such 'soft factors' as celebration, generosity and informality to compensate for fairly average hotel facilities. At some point, the policy and culture changed in such a way that the soft factors disappeared and customers were left with nothing more than the unexciting 'physical' facilities. Without the attractive features that had compensated for these, customers defected en masse to the better facilities offered by other providers.
- **Customer involvement and togetherness** in consuming a service also pose the question of managing the *customer mix*. No matter how good

the facilities of a hotel resort may be, if people who come there do not consider that they belong to the same crowd as the others, or have different tastes, they will be dissatisfied and this will lead to negative word of mouth. Coming back to the Club Med example, the company once tried to attract customers from Minneapolis, in the American Midwest. These clients expected professional shows of the kind they had seen in Las Vegas, not shows performed by staff; they expected room service, not self-service, and overall did not fit in with the Club Med ethos or the rest of the Club Med customers.

To take another example, everyone who teaches in executive education knows that the quality of a session depends in great part on the interaction between the participants themselves and between the participants and the teacher, and on the participants' interest in the topic. The more intensive the contribution of each participant to a session, the better the quality of delivery will be. In this case, it is the role of the marketer to attract customers who offer the diversity that will promote richness of discussion while at the same time making sure that everyone is interested in the topic, has something to learn and, even more, recognizes in his peers people worth being around.

Successful fashionable restaurants and discos know how to manage their customer mix: a proportion of their customers must be opinion leaders, people 'in the know' and people 'who are known'. Others must be people who aspire to be like the first group but do not scare them away! The marketer's job is to make sure everyone knows who is there, who is allowed in, who is not. The same goes for users' clubs in industrial services, business clubs, multi-client studies in consulting or private banking seminars for clients. If customers do not feel they belong, they will stop coming.

To summarize, the more involved customers are in using a service and the more they consume it together, the more effort the marketer should put into managing the customer mix, providing information and expectations, being transparent and managing feedback.

Different services require different emphasis

All of the above are general rules on how to adapt marketing to services. However, there is a different intensity to this adaptation depending on the type of service offered. When moving from a pure 'product' type of service to a skills-based service (by adding more experience, more interaction to the basic offer to avoid the commodity trap), the above discussion will still apply in many cases, though perhaps to a lesser degree. For instance, it makes more sense to try to make the tangible intangible (like a product) for a product-based service (like a restaurant) than it does for a purely knowledge-based service (like Capgemini). McDonald's brings a lot of 'imagery' to what is 'only' fast food, for example. Standardization of packaging, and assuring consistency of quality are also easier for product-based services. We have classified different services into three categories, as shown in Table 4.2.

Product-based services are the most tangible of all. They can easily be packaged. They rely more on physical and transactional encounters ('hard factors') to be successful. Technology plays a big part. The more you move to skills-based or knowledge-based services, the more important soft factors, including interactions with people, become. This classification has an impact on marketing as depicted in Figure 4.3. Of course this only shows

Table 4.2 Different service types

Product-based services	Skill-based services	Knowledge-based services
Hotels	Hairdressers	Professional services
Restaurants	Doctors	Education
Retail	Garages	Research labs
Insurance	Hospitals	Investment banking
Retail banking	Maintenance	Engineering
Air travel	Fire fighting	
Shipping	Entertainment	
Real estate	Freight forwarding	

From product-based services	To skill-based services	To knowledge-based services
More tangible	⟶	More intangible
More amenable to standardization	⟶	Customization
Easier to package	⟶	A la carte
Easier to communicate the service	⟶	Must demonstrate the ability to serve
Indirect distribution possible	⟶	More direct distribution
Low customer involvement	⟶	High customer involvement
Customers consuming alone	⟶	Managing the customer mix more important
Some peripheral cues needed	⟶	A lot more peripheral cues needed to judge before buying
Standard quality possible	⟶	Higher risk of variability in quality
More resource allocation in attraction	⟶	More resource allocation in satisfaction and retention

Figure 4.3 Refine service marketing to suit different types of services

trends, and since many product-based services try to differentiate by adding skills and interaction to their basic offer (becoming skill-based services) in order to avoid the commodity trap, the degree of application of the above discussion must still be assessed to suit individual cases.

Resource allocation and the marketing organization

The above key differences between marketing products and marketing services impact on how marketing money is spent and how far the responsibilities of the marketer go.

- **More money should be spent on satisfaction and retention, less on attraction** If we admit that the role of marketing generally is to attract, satisfy and retain customers, for services there is a need to put more emphasis on the latter. To avoid filling a bucket full of holes with water, we must make sure the delivery is there before putting more money into attracting new customers, as services sales growth relies heavily on 'experiencing' the service.
- **More money in other parts of the promotion and communication mix** than advertising is also required. Because of the need to educate customers who do not understand the intangible, to make sure that sales people are also involved in managing the customer mix, in sales support, even in after-sales service, more resources need to be allocated to non-advertising communication such as peripheral cues and documentation. (The term 'documentation' covers everything that customers receive on paper or through the Internet: brochures, proposals, stationery, contracts, bills, notices, maintenance manuals, etc. The clarity of these documents, the type of paper chosen, the language used can say a lot about how easy it is to do business with a specific firm.)
- **The marketing organization should take more responsibility** for the *whole cycle* of marketing: attracting, satisfying, retaining. Whereas for

products, the task of marketing is often limited to attracting customers, leaving to production and after-sales service the roles of satisfaction and retention, our suggested approach would make marketing responsible for after-sales service (as in the call centre for mobile phone operators described earlier, or in e-commerce companies), even for measuring customer satisfaction. It follows that service marketers should be incentivized on satisfaction and retention, not just on attraction. Otherwise, they may be tempted to promise the moon and end up disappointing everyone.

- **The role of distributors in providing service becomes less obvious**, unless the service is well packaged. Distribution cannot change a product's nature, its specifications or its contours. With a service – especially if it involves a lot of soft ingredients such as skills and knowledge – a distributor can destroy the integrity of the service offered. Thus, the use of distributors in services requires much more education, surveillance and co-marketing to keep the quality of sales and delivery intact. It can be facilitated by packaging the services, for instance in using third-party maintenance companies or value-added resellers for IT solutions. The service provider packages its services, which include products such as spare parts, or software and services such as information, tools, methodologies as well as a performance level to be achieved (say 95% or 99% uptime). Packaging the service can help the distributor distribute, be clear about his margin and his role and put a safety net on the quality level achieved in delivering the service.

- **Marketing performance for services requires new measurements**. As it is difficult for customers to assess services before using them, it follows that the performance of marketers in services should move away from pure sales or image figures to customer satisfaction, word of mouth and customer retention. Salespeople who usually report to marketing departments should in turn be assessed not just on their ability to bring in new volume but on increasing volume for a given customer and resolving complaints to the customer's satisfaction.

Specific issues in the internationalization of services

Internationalizing the marketing and sales of products follows four clear stages if a company wants to do this itself. It starts with exporting the product directly to key clients or through distributors. As sales develop, companies set up sales and marketing subsidiaries abroad whose job is to market the products on demand, either directly or through distributors. Production subsidiaries follow; then, at a later stage, complete international centres of competence develop worldwide with their own R&D, production, logistics, marketing and sales functions.

For services, it is quite different: there is no 'physical' flow of products to start expanding abroad. You either go or don't go yourself – and results do not always follow. Take AXA, one of the biggest insurance companies in the world, born in France. Today France represents 25% of AXA's sales but 70% of profit. Zurich Financial Services, who decided to go worldwide a few years ago, got into deep financial troubles even though it took the acquisition route in the UK, US and Australia in order to speed up the internationalization process. Club Med has been in the US since the late 1970s, but has never been able to top its mid-1980s North American customer base of 180 000 customers per year.

Disney theme parks, so successful in the US, approached disaster in Europe. In 2004, 12 years after opening, they are not yet making money in Paris. Zara, the Spanish international retailer, still reaps most of its sales and profits from its Spanish stores, although foreign stores are in the majority. Supermarket giant Carrefour had to give up on many countries in which it tried to establish itself, and even Wal-Mart decided it was better to buy UK or German companies rather than setting up shops in some foreign markets (with yet undetermined outcome). Egg, a very successful British Internet retail bank, fell flat on its face when it entered the French market, and had to sell its subsidiary after heavy losses. Lift manufacturers Otis and Schindler have learned the hard way that when they move abroad, their biggest competitors for the profit-making after-sales service activity are local companies.

So what are the reasons for these failures, and what must marketers do to overcome poor performance in international markets?

Probably the most important reason has to do with the intangibility of services. When internationalizing the intangible, there is a tendency to become blind and deaf, to forget that the familiar approach that has succeeded domestically will not necessarily work internationally. The intangible is more 'culture bound' than the tangible, requiring a totally new learning curve or at least a very careful assessment of the universality of a concept.

Let us take Disney. It sent its best senior executives from Orlando to start Disneyland Paris. They applied what they knew best and what worked best in the US: authentic New York steaks shipped from New York to be served in the New York Hotel in Paris; no wine, no beer in the park; 0.48 seats per bedroom in the restaurants of hotels for breakfast, lunch and dinner, since

American customers snack all day; price promotions for those eating before noon or 7 p.m. to reduce bottlenecks in restaurants in the park; direct pull marketing to consumers rather than push marketing to bus operators, tour operators and other distributors, as the brand was strong; a central reservation system that favoured early bookers – but these turned out to be mostly Nordic Europeans, who unfortunately spent less in the park than the late-booking Italians and Spaniards, who loved to spend and stayed longer in the best hotels! Those are some examples of what led to a financial disaster still not resolved in 2004, with a second renegotiation of the debt with banks to avoid bankruptcy. What went wrong? In a few words, lack of local adaptation. Senior executives, ingrained in their past US success, were not open enough to see that French people don't snack, that Germans travel by coach, Italians are last-minute purchasers with a lot of cash to spend and so on.

Does this mean that all services should be adapted locally both from a 'product' viewpoint and from a marketing techniques viewpoint with local teams? Not necessarily.

Take Carrefour in Greece. It has opened several hypermarkets successfully in the space of five years and now employs close to 5000 people there. Yet the team of 16 executives sent to open up were all 'Carrefour people' who had at least ten years of Carrefour experience in other countries. So what makes the difference? Four aspects need to be assessed carefully by the international marketer of services:

- universality of the concept
- amount of local adaptation

- leads and lags in market development
- degree to which one can follow one's clients.

Universality of the concept

If the service concept is universal, then what is required is the 'transfer of formula'. In turn, this requires formalization of the formula, transfer of the know-how by people who know it by heart. This was the Carrefour way.

Amount of local adaptation

If the service concept requires a lot of local adaptation, then blindly transferring a winning formula will lead to disaster. The best way forward here is to recruit local people or at least to send people who know the mother company service concept but are young enough to adapt to local requirements. Had Disney sent 'Disney people' who were less than 35 years old to open Disneyland Paris, they would probably not have failed. Those younger executives would have known about Disney ways, Disney show-quality standards, Disney marketing methods, but they would have been young enough to listen to what the local managers kept telling them.

Leads and lags in international marketing

When Club Med was an established business in France, it was a start-up in Singapore, Hong Kong and Malaysia. Whereas in France it used mass-marketing methods (advertising, direct mail to past customers), in Kuala Lumpur what

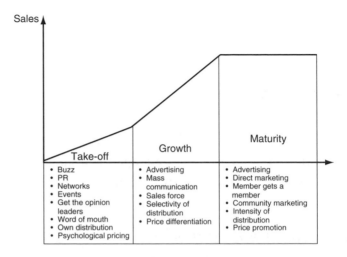

Figure 4.4   Market lifecycle and marketing tools

worked best were public relations events to create the buzz and attract opinion leaders, 'people in the know'. By avoiding centralizing its marketing worldwide, Club Med let local marketing managers adapt their marketing tools to the stage of development of the market as depicted in Figure 4.4.

As service organizations move abroad, they must refrain from taking the approach that works for them in mature markets and applying it blindly to take-off and growing ones. This is a challenge for several reasons:

- **The domestic market dominates** both in terms of sales and profit. Its people want to have a say in what is going on internationally.
- **If the domestic market has reached maturity**, it has also reached success in terms of sales volume. The people in charge there are powerful because they are successful and they don't necessarily remember how it was when the domestic market was at the start-up stage, either because their mem-

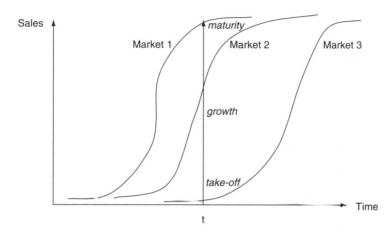

Figure 4.5 Leads and lags in international markets

ory has lapsed after 10 to 20 years or because those who manage the big volume today are not those who marketed the start-up or even the growth phase. They don't know how to operate in such different market conditions as depicted in Figure 4.5. At t, Market 1 is at maturity, whereas 2 is at growth stage and 3 at take-off stage, requiring different marketing tools.

This is probably what happened to Disney when it sent its senior managers to France. They thought they just had to replicate Orlando as it was then – in 1992, with 20 years of business behind it – and not as it had been in 1972, when it opened.

Follow your clients: they will do the job for you!

One of the easier ways of becoming international in services and avoid having to deal with the previous three questions (universality, local adaptation, leads and lags) is to follow your clients, accompanying your existing domestic customers when they go international and serving their needs in other countries. This is how a number of big US-based accounting firms first developed, and it is done in merchant banking, reassurance, shipping and professional services. For the service provider, this delays the need to learn to adapt locally, as this is done by the clients. On the other hand, it helps develop sales internationally, thus complementing mature domestic sales. What is required here is a fair amount of mobility, cross-fertilization of ideas, knowledge and skills that will serve well everywhere. Expansion beyond the existing clients can then become smoother as time goes by.

Summary and management guidelines

* Services are marked by three essential differences with products.

    – They are intangible. The challenge is to make them tangible so that the customer will buy.
    – Because of the lack of 'physical' evidence of a service that would be present in a product, the customer needs to be reassured not just about the service itself, but also about the ability of the service provider to serve.
    – Consumption and production of services are simultaneous, making it harder to provide consistent quality and almost impossible to 'stock' a service for later sale. This, in turn, forces the service marketer to be more sensitive and to take a bigger role in the quality of service delivery, to optimize demand and supply through

pricing (for peaks or troughs), as well as managing the mix of customers targeted.

- So, what guidelines should those characteristics give to the service marketer? They can be regrouped into the following points:

  - A careful selection of customers to avoid destroying the quality of the service by too heterogeneous a customer mix.
  - A communication strategy that can reassure customers to buy, using all the contact points – be they physical or through staff – that can 'tangibilize' the offer, as well as prove – directly or indirectly – that the service provider has the ability to serve.
  - A pricing and/or a capacity strategy that recognizes peaks and troughs, i.e. adapts to heavy or low demand.
  - A packaging strategy that reinforces reassurance *vis à vis* the customer that he is making the right choice and makes it easy for him to choose a service.
  - More direct distribution channels, especially when the service sold needs a lot of explanation, education and concrete proof before customers will buy.
  - A higher involvement and responsibility of the service marketer in assuring quality of service: a sales force that does not stop its contribution once the deal has been done, but is also involved in sales support; performance measurements or customer satisfaction which are included in the service marketer's incentives.
  - Allocation of resources that favour a higher share of marketing investment in customer satisfaction than in customer attraction to avoid having disappointed customers.

- Careful selection of the marketing team to avoid profiles of pure 'product marketers' who are going to use classical tools to the detriment of focus on service marketing.

- As far as internationalization of services is concerned, three issues should be looked at:

  - Amount of local adaptation
  - Adapting the marketing mix to the degree of market development
  - And to be on the safe side – especially for the more intangible skills or knowledge-based services – to initially follow clients abroad to start business there.

- Guidelines for management can be summarized as follows:

  - Try to make the intangible tangible in your communication
  - Extend this communication beyond advertising to embrace all contact points
  - Manage your peripheral cues to convey better what you are all about
  - Consider a service guarantee to make your service offer more powerful
  - Use indirect as well as direct methods to persuade your customers of your ability to serve
  - Systematically underpromise and overdeliver
  - Minimize the number of fast-moving consumer goods marketers in your team
  - Make sure you are equipped for peaks, troughs or in between
  - Consciously manage your customer mix
  - When moving abroad, consider how universal your service concept is. If it is, formalize the formula and the way it will be transferred. If not, make sure you listen to your local managers.

- Consciously manage leads and lags in international markets
- Make your marketing department responsible for customer satisfaction and retention, and base incentives for your marketing people on this as much as on sales
- Make sure your sales people go beyond selling to provide customer support.

References

[1] *Service Strategy*, 2nd edition, Harlow: Pearson Education Ltd, 2004.

5
The Missing 'P' in the Marketing Mix: Putting Passion into Brands

Professor Dominique Turpin

B rand management is one of the hottest topics in marketing today. More and more companies are committed to investing in communicating the benefits of their brands externally. However, few firms have yet gone the extra mile to manage the 'P' in their marketing mix: turning strong brands into 'passion brands'.

In this chapter, we will argue that products/services and people make a single complete unit. Building and managing passion brands is not only about external communications; it is also about communicating effectively internally and making sure that employees become the best brand ambassadors by creating a strong emotional link between the company and the market. Only then can executives expect to dramatically differentiate their products and services from those of their competitors. Building on the experience of companies such as Starbucks, Nike, Virgin and Ducati, this chapter suggests why internal branding is a worthwhile exercise, what an appropriate internal marketing strategy might be and what tools are necessary to motivate employees to achieve better results.

Brands as the ultimate differentiation factor

While an increasing number of executives are facing the challenges of how to develop strong brands and/or how to better leverage the power of existing well-established names, many still have to deal with sceptical colleagues asking questions such as: 'Is brand management another of these "fashionable" business subjects that regularly come and go?' or 'Is it really worth investing in building brands when we could use scarce financial resources on other projects?' We believe that brand management is – and will remain for many years to come – a key marketing issue. The reason is simple: it is increasingly difficult today to differentiate your products from those of your competitors. Building passion brands is one of the answers to this critical challenge, since brands have become the ultimate differentiation factor for many companies, provided of course that they are managed properly.

Differentiation has always been one of the key words in strategic marketing. Imagine for a moment that your company has the world monopoly on a particular product or service. Do you really need a marketing strategy? It would probably be nice to have one, but not an absolute necessity to your survival in the short and mid-term. However, as soon as your company faces a number of competitors, it becomes crucial to define differentiation factors, to make sure that potential and existing customers pick up your product rather than the competition's.

Differentiation – the key to sustainable competitive advantage

Over decades, companies have worked on three major dimensions in order to differentiate products from their competition and create perceived value in the minds of their customers: *innovation*, *quality* and *customer service*. The challenge is that in the competitive world of the twenty-first century, it is becoming increasingly difficult to build a sustainable competitive advantage on any one of the three dimensions.

- **Innovations** are more and more difficult to protect as information flows faster and faster from one market to another. Consequently, many companies such as Motorola and Xerox have recently decided not to bother patenting some of their new ideas, since they may be copied the next day in another part of the world.
- **Quality** was a key factor of differentiation back in the 1980s, when Japanese companies were taking market after market away from their Western competitors. However, quality is now taken for granted by many customers. Western corporations have in many cases caught up with Japan in this dimension in industries as diverse as semiconductors or automotives. Quality has become a qualifying criterion for any company wanting to participate in the competitive race; and the movement

of the early 1990s to refocus management attention on quality with International Standards Organization (ISO) certification campaigns has run out of steam. Every factory in the world is now ISO certified. Even Chinese factories that lagged behind Western standards a decade ago have reached levels of quality that rival those in Western and Japanese markets.[1] Encouraged by a combination of good manufacturing quality and cheap labour, a growing number of companies are now outsourcing their production to China, leaving people at home to focus on R&D and marketing issues.

- **Customer orientation** is another element of differentiation more and more taken for granted by today's customers. Although many companies are still struggling to be market oriented, customer orientation is a must, an obvious necessity in any competitive market and not really a factor of differentiation. Nowadays, if your company does not have a minimum of customer-orientation focus, it is likely to be left behind by its competition. Customers' expectations have reached such a high level that every company – including public corporations – has made major efforts to boost both customer satisfaction and customer loyalty.

So what is left to differentiate your company from the rest of the pack? Of course, companies should continue to innovate and produce high-quality products and services, as the more elements of differentiation a brand possesses, the more competitive it will be. However, products and technologies can be copied but brands are yours and only yours. As one senior marketing executive puts it: 'Brands are increasingly being recognized as the most important assets and the primary source of competitive advantage companies can have. Today, it is probably more important to own markets than factories. And the only way to own markets is to own market-dominant brands!'[2]

So what exactly is a brand?

Branding is truly the art and cornerstone of marketing. Academics and executives have both offered definitions of what brands are all about. Some executives talk about them as the essential tools with which to develop trust and a personal relationship with customers. The American Marketing Association defines a brand as 'a name, term, sign, symbol or design, or a combination of them, intended to identify the goods or services of one seller or group of sellers and to differentiate them from those of competitors'.[3] And Pavel Lhotka, Vice President for Northern Europe at Danone, the leading French food company, explains: 'You can argue that water is water is water ... Unless that water happened to be Evian, one of our brands that most consumers around the world know, trust and are ready to pay a premium for. Our experience illustrates the old adage that there is no such thing as a commodity and that any product on earth can be differentiated provided the brand is managed well!'

Jean-Noel Kapferer, a pioneer in strategic brand management, has suggested that a brand is a complex symbol that can convey up to six levels of meaning:[4]

- **Attributes** A brand brings certain functional and emotional attributes to mind. For example, Mercedes-Benz suggests expensive, well-built, well-engineered, durable and high-prestige cars.

- **Benefits** Attributes must be translated into functional and emotional benefits for customers. For example, the attribute 'expensive' translates into the emotional benefit 'the car makes me feel socially important'.
- **Values** The brand also suggests something about the manufacturer's values, what the company really stands for: Mercedes-Benz means high performance, safety and prestige.
- **Culture** The brand may represent a particular culture: Mercedes-Benz symbolizes elements that are widely perceived as part of the German culture – seriousness, quality and hard work.
- **Personality** The brand can project a certain personality. Mercedes-Benz suggests affluence, prestige and conservatism.
- **User** The brand suggests the kind of customer who is most likely to buy and use the product. In the case of Mercedes-Benz, we tend to envisage business people at the wheel rather than students.

Over the last decade, academics and communications consultants have suggested many other alternative and additional dimensions to explain how customers make decisions regarding brands.[5] However, trying to interpret the complexity of the human mind when it comes to brand decisions is challenging, as customers form both rational and irrational thoughts about products and brands. We suggest that a simple and pragmatic tool for managers to evaluate the power of a brand is to focus on three key dimensions:[6] the brand values (from whom?), the brand target (for whom?) and the brand purpose (for what?) – see Figure 5.1.

- **Brand values** suggest to customers what your company stands for, e.g. Apple stands for intelligent, creative and cool.
- **Brand target** suggests the kind of core customers your firm is targeting – young and autonomous in the case of Apple.

- **Brand purpose** suggests the kind of benefits, real and emotional, that customers will experience with your products – Apple stands for user-friendliness, self-enhancement and entertainment purposes.

As a practical exercise, we suggest that you and your management team try to answer these three key questions for your own brands as well as for your main competitors. The answers for your own brand should be consistent. If they are not, you cannot expect your customers to have a clear idea of what your brand really stands for. Your answers should also be different from the answers you give for your competitors' brands. If not, your brand is not differentiated enough from those of the competition!

The benefits of building strong brands

It is not rare to find marketing managers frustrated by the lack of understanding implicit in thcir colleagues' questioning of the necessity

Figure 5.1 The three components of a brand (Source: Professor Nirmalya Kumar, IMD)

to invest in brand building. Typically, they have to deal with the following arguments:

- 'Customers don't care about brands, price is the only thing that enables the business to grow'
- 'Half the money we invest in brand is wasted'
- 'I'm not sure there is any emotion in what we sell'
- 'Our technological edge will make the difference'

If indeed it is not always easy to directly measure the return on investment of the money spent on building brands, building strong brands does undeniably offer several benefits. Among others:

- **Brands that come top in customers' minds** typically enjoy customer preference as well as higher repeat purchases. Even if your company deals with so-called commodity products such as steel, glass or oil, being top in your customers' minds means that you will at least have a chance of being called to participate in a tender.
- **A strong brand usually enables you to charge a premium** *vis-à-vis* the competition. For example, although Sony's flat-screen televisions are mostly made with technology developed in conjunction with a Korean competitor, Sony can still sell its sets at a premium simply because its brand equity is perceived as superior to that of Korean brands in many markets. (This is true at least for a certain segment, typically consumers over 45 years old who remember the times back in the 1970s when 'made in Korea' meant low quality.)
- **Strong brands provide leverage *vis-à-vis* the trade**. It is easier for a company with a stronger brand name than one with a less well-known name to introduce new products. For example, it has been relatively easy

for the German pen manufacturer Mont Blanc to move into watches and cosmetics in comparison with another brand less associated with prestige and luxury.

From products to brands to great brands to passion brands

Brands differ from products in several aspects (see Table 5.1). The most critical dimension of brands is the emotional factor. While products are made in the factory, brands are made in the consumers' minds.

Brands can be classified on a ladder made of five key steps: *awareness*, *acquaintance*, *relationship*, *emotions* and *passion brands* (see Figure 5.2). Passion brands therefore represent the ultimate stage of brand recognition when customers show exceptional attachment, loyalty and engagement. Broadly defined, passion brands can be described as a collection of functional and exceptionally strong emotional values supporting promises about very special and truly unique experiences. The more marketers build emotional

Table 5.1 A brand is more than a product (Source: Nestlé)

Products	Brands
Made in the factory	Made in consumers' mind
Can be copied	Are unique and proprietary
Have functional value	Have both functional and emotional value
Can become outdated	Can become timeless

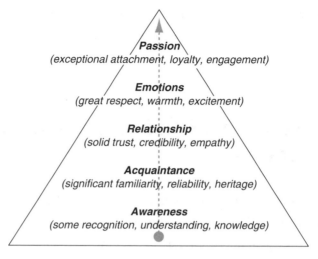

Figure 5.2 The brand ladder (Source: © Dominique Turpin, IMD 2004)

elements around special and unique experiences, the faster the brand will move up the ladder. Typically, special and unique experiences are built around superb innovations (e.g. Starbucks); superior performance (Ferrari); a historical, almost mythical heritage (Ducati); great storytelling (Harley Davidson); and superb leadership! As Scott Bedbury, an advertising executive who works with both Nike and Starbucks, puts it: 'A great brand taps into emotions ... Emotions drive most, if not all, of our decisions. A brand reaches out with a powerful connecting experience. It's an emotional connecting point that transcends the product.'[7]

Nike has been particularly successful at building lots of emotions around its brand thanks to constant product innovations (e.g. the wedged heel, the cushioned mid-sole and nylon uppers), sponsorships (the Olympic Games), endorsements by leading athletes (Michael Jordan, Tiger Woods), flagship stores (NikeTown), creative communications (the 'swoosh' logo) and a constant flow of new designs (Air Jordan), as well as outstanding leadership. CEO Phil Knight communicates and lives the story of the brand on a daily basis. He and many fans have been so passionate about Nike that they have even had the 'swoosh' logo tattooed on their bodies. That must be the ultimate test of a passion brand!

Putting passion into brands

Obviously, the tattoo example given above is a bit extreme. Only a handful of brands can meet the challenge of the 'tattoo test' (Harley Davidson, Ferrari, Ducati and a few others). Nevertheless, you may be surprised by the kind of 'corporate brand tattoos' examples that can be found by simply surfing on the Internet (Lego, Absolut Vodka and Coca Cola, to name just a few).

However, it is possible to instil great passion into brands just by paying more attention to people, both inside and outside your company, and to leadership factors. Today, many firms spend large advertising budgets on creating or reinforcing awareness of their companies, expressing the values they stand for and communicating the benefits of their products and services in order to further differentiate themselves from the competition. However, brand management is much more than just external communications. It is also about understanding how consumers perceive every aspect of what the organization does. In particular, brand management means communicating the values of brands to your own people; making sure that employees understand these values and leading them to become the best ambassadors of your company and products. Only then can you expect to develop passion brands and dramatically differentiate your company from all other competitors in the eyes of your customers. As Luca di Montezemolo, chairman of Ferrari, puts it: 'The real secret of our success is enthusiasm for the brand, shared by our own people and our partners. Enthusiasm is the sparkle in their eyes, the swing in their gait, the grip in their handshakes.'[8]

Employees are an essential factor in shaping customers' perceptions of brands, as they are ultimately responsible for delivering products and services to customers. As such, they need a clear and shared understanding of the company's brand and other marketing values. It is important for employees dealing with customers to be well informed and to behave appropriately. This is usually done through training programmes during which senior executives share with employees the value of the brand, using concrete examples to explain how they have experienced and lived brand leadership. Organizations such as McDonald's, Philip Morris, Disney, Samsung and others are particularly dedicated to this practice. These training programmes are often followed by 'mystery shopping exercises', in which, for example, the McDonald's QSC (Quality, Service, Cleanliness) standards are measured by mystery shoppers who use a checklist to verify the consistency between the desired and actual quality of service and staff behaviour.[9] Other companies have members of staff call their own offices as if they were customers in order to verify that phone calls are being answered properly. As a senior executive from a leading domestic-appliance company that is using this technique explains: 'This is a powerful tool to make people realize for themselves how badly some customers can be treated over the phone. We then usually have no problem getting these people to implement the right corrective measures.'

Brand building is more than just advertising

Branding is often the most misunderstood element of marketing strategy. It is still perceived by too many managers as 'advertising' to create an image for their products and services. In reality, brand management includes every aspect of communications, and every aspect of what the organization does influences it. Branding is not only about your products and the other elements of the marketing mix (price, distribution, communications); it encompasses the whole enterprise, and first of all people. To quote a Nestlé executive: 'A strong brand is simply the reward offered by the market for implementing an overall good business management.'

And just like any other aspect of strategy, brand management can only be effective if properly implemented through people. Every single interaction that takes place between your customers and your employees (or your partners' employees) before, during and after sales is an opportunity for the customer to test and judge not only the quality of your products but also the corporate brand equity. Consequently, all employees – in particular those closest to the customer – need to understand that they are the key ambassadors of your brands.

Internal brand management

Not all companies and brands have the same internal/people challenges. In the service industry, for example, where the customer faces the 'product', every employee's action is a brand action. Every interaction between employees and the customer is a 'moment of truth',[10] an opportunity for the customer to judge whether a company is genuinely practising what it claims. Every second wasted by a customer waiting for a call to be answered or lost to repeated dialling when your office phones are busy tarnishes the goodwill and credibility of your company. It may even result in lost business.

Internal branding in service industries

In the service sector, great brands typically tap into both staff and customers' emotions, since the nature of the business involves many such 'touch points' (situations where the consumer comes in direct contact with or is directly affected by the employees' actions and behaviour). In 'high-touch' industries, such as airlines, consulting or hotels, emotions drive most of the customers' brand perceptions. Therefore in the service industry, internal brand management is priority number one.

As exemplified by the phenomenal success of Starbucks, mass advertising can help build brands, but authenticity 'through a people experience' is what makes a brand strong and durable. When contrasting Starbucks' brand strategy with that of its competitors, we found that the striking difference was the exceptional emphasis that Starbucks put on the human factor. In fact, the company decided to invest in mass advertising only a few years ago, once it had its internal communications right. Until recently, it was mainly investing in products and staff. And even today, it continues this policy by building strong emotional links between the company values (from friendly service to increasing emphasis on 'fair trade' practices), the products' benefits and the customers' experience.[11] The emotional connection transcends the product thanks to human actions and behaviours. As a Starbuck executive explains: 'We are not in the coffee business serving people, we are in the *people* business serving coffee!'

Internal branding in fast-moving consumer goods industries

In 'low-touch' industries, too, branding can be a significant source of competitive advantage. When we compare the 'high-touch' brand management of Starbucks with that of Nescafé, one of the 7000 brands marketed by Nestlé; it may be more difficult to argue that the actions of staff and management have a direct impact on the image of the product. In fact, the retailers who are distributing the product probably have more influence on the Nescafé brand equity at the consumer level than the Nestlé employees themselves. Companies like this have to rely on other means of building their brands. For example, a few years ago, Nestlé UK ran a phenomenally successful television advertising campaign for its Nescafé Gold Blend instant coffee, which still features regularly in any round-up of the British public's favourite commercial. In the first of the adverts, two attractive young neighbours meeting for the first time were attracted to each other by a shared liking for this particular brand of coffee. As the series progressed the two neighbours got to know each other better, shared many cups of coffee, and romance blossomed. Nestlé saw sales of Gold Blend grow significantly with consumers who presumably believed that drinking this brand would enhance their social lives.

Like Nestlé, Shell delivers service to millions of customers through agents who are not directly on the oil company's payroll. Its products are sold through thousands of petrol stations franchised to independent garages. But for the average motorist, every petrol-station employee with the Shell logo on his or her cap or shirt is an 'ambassador' of the brand. Reaching out and educating 'ambassadors' such as these in different parts of the world on what the brand stands for represents new challenges for marketers. As Venetia Howes, Global Brands Strategy Manager for Shell International, explains: 'One of the biggest challenges facing Shell is to continue the transition from a company which is comfortable with wells, drills, refineries, tanks, pipes and other bits of hardware, to one which still does these things well and excels at customer understanding and service ... What is key to these intangible benefits of service and brand? The daily behaviour of our staff and all who represent the face of Shell to customers and other stakeholders.'

Increasingly aware that direct contact with end users is key to the image of their brands, companies such as Harley Davidson, Lacoste, Nespresso, Nike, Swatch and others have decided to control their own distribution channels. Having established a network of franchised distribution outlets across the world, these firms are better in touch with their end customers and benefit from extensive feedback on what the market is looking for. The rationale is that a well-trained staff, truly passionate about its products, can provide a superior shopping experience, unmatched by the competition or limited by the conflicting needs of other retailers. Obviously, being in control of their distribution channels is a more powerful proposition for Nespresso (a subsidiary of Nestlé that markets a range of espresso machines and supplies) than for the rest of the Nestlé Group. But even for companies such as Nestlé that still rely on independent distributors to sell their products to end consumers, the behaviour of sales reps, truck drivers and call-centre people and all other interactions between the manufacturers' staff and the trade help reinforce the brand perception by bringing congruence between the external corporate communication message and what the staff does and says. In any case, motivating employees to support the corporate brand never hurts! As Allan Stefl of Nestlé explains: 'Our branding effort has increased the quality of our product and processes. Quality and loyalty are the key outcomes and they are both measurable in terms of turnover, product and everything else we do.'[12]

The public's reaction to a brand can, however, extend further than its response to its 'ambassadors' or its advertising. When multinational corporations fail to act as stewards of public health, workers or the environment, some consumers are likely to vote with their chequebooks by boycotting their products. Examples such as Nestlé's infant-formula mismanagement in Africa in the 1980s, Union Carbide's Bhopal gas tragedy in India in 1984, Shell's plan to sink its Brent Spar oil rig in the North Sea and the protests at its Nigerian facilities in 1995 are still having an impact on both the brand and the behaviour of certain consumers.[13]

Internal branding in B2B industries

Even in the industrial world, where rational purchasing decisions tend to be the rule, internal branding can play a critical role in differentiating your products/services from those of the competition. Even if your company sells so-called 'commodities', the human factor is still often an unexploited element which could strengthen your competitive advantage. At the end of the day, all business transactions involve people selling solutions to other people's problems. More and more industrial firms are realizing that they need to differentiate themselves, not only through the technical performance of their products, but also through the services they offer (logistics, invoicing, product claims and other after-sales services) and consequently through the behaviour of their own people. In Japan, for example, Canon insists that its repair people wear a white shirt and a tie. The white shirt helps to reinforce the perception that Canon's photocopiers are truly user-friendly and easy to service. Canon's senior management believes that employees are critical to the customer's brand experience and that no one will sound as convincing as a sales or repair person who is truly passionate about his or her company's products. As a senior executive at medical technology giant Medtronic Europe likes to emphasize: 'All employees are salespeople, not just those in the front line.'

Employees' attitudes (both in the front line and in the back office) play a role in influencing customer trust and corporate reputation. For instance, at Hitachi Metals, senior management considers that answering phone calls from customers promptly and nurturing a knowledgeable and courteous staff are as important as turning out flawless products from the steel mills. As a senior executive in this Japanese company explains: 'Every single employee is an ambassador of our corporate brand. Their actions and behaviours directly and indirectly affect our reputation in the whole business chain.'

A similar customer philosophy is shared at an increasing number of B2B companies such as DHL, BASF and DSM. Senior management in these organizations also sees the involvement of the back-office staff as critical in improving the company's overall offer. 'A customer receiving the wrong invoice or being transferred over the phone from one department to another is likely to be upset and this may reflect on the overall reputation of the company, namely our corporate brand', suggests the Marketing Manager Human Nutrition & Health of DSM Nutritional Products in the Netherlands.

At Tetra Pak Belgium, a company whose successful approach to customer alignment we considered in Chapter 3, the receptionist is now a full member of the 'key account management' team. Managing director Elisabeth Mox explains: 'The receptionist is the first contact of our company with the customers. If you have an unfriendly person on the phone, you are already irritated before you come to the essence of your call . . . So it's very important that everybody feels involved, that everybody knows they are playing a very crucial role for the customer in the whole process. As result, the staff feel much more involved. Our people are more motivated. Our customer is their customer. They care more. For the technicians on the floor, it's their customer. They are proud of it, they take care of them . . . and the feedback that they get is really very useful. Very minor things can mean a lot to customers. The more the team gets closer to them, the better they can work with them!'[14]

Passion brands and the leadership factor

Internal passion for the brand does not happen without great leadership. The marketing vision must be clearly articulated and communicated relentlessly and consistently by senior executives. However, as we all know, little happens unless the vision and strategy are properly executed. The culture of a company lies in the behaviour of its leaders. Therefore, both the marketer and the CEO must 'walk the talk' in an honest way. In other words, they must lead by example – live the brand and demonstrate real passion and commitment for the customer. They must also put in place the necessary mechanisms to break the functional silos, facilitate communications between employees, encourage, support and reward the right actions. Enthusiastic marketing leaders who do not pay lip service to customer orientation but truly live the passion for the customer characterize great market-oriented organizations. Their enthusiasm is both a magnet and a major motivation factor for their employees, which is what marketing leadership in action is all about.

It is not by accident that passion brands are led by exceptional (and sometimes controversial) leaders genuinely passionate about their company and their products. Think about Akio Morita at Sony, Phil Knight at Nike, Luca di Montezemolo at Ferrari, Nicolas Hayek at Swatch or Richard Branson at Virgin Airlines, just to mention a few. These great 'marketers' live and breathe their products and their brands 24 hours a day, 365 days a year. As a result, their personal enthusiasm has infected all their employees.

Obviously, not every CEO can be or wishes to be as controversial as Sir Richard Branson, who never misses an opportunity to cause a sensation, wearing a Virgin Atlantic stewardess's uniform, posing in a bikini on board a yacht or letting himself be photographed in his bath.[15] However, low-profile entrepreneurs and 'quiet leaders' such as Ingvar Kamprad of Ikea in Sweden or Masatoshi Ito, founder of Ito Yokado in Japan (and owner of Seven-Eleven), have a lot in common with the most outspoken business leaders when it comes to brand management.

'I prefer the words "corporate reputation" to "brand management", but we probably mean the same thing', says Mr Ito. 'We seem to share a common philosophy that is based on a great deal of common sense. Typically, we believe in simple but challenging ideas. We do the obvious and apply the basics. We love to put ourselves in the shoes of our customers and our employees. Even in mature markets, we look for differentiation and we want to give consumers more value for their money.'

For these business leaders, brand success through change is a journey, a constant challenge. They know that the ideal employee is informal but caring, vibrant, interested, courteous and willing to go out of his or her way to help customers. Richard Branson explains: 'We aren't interested in having just happy employees. We want employees who feel involved and prepared to express dissatisfaction when needed. In fact, we think that the constructively dissatisfied employee is an asset we should encourage and we need an organization that allows us to do this – and that encourages employees to take responsibility, since I don't believe it is enough for us simply to give it.'[16]

Richard Branson believes that staff involvement is key to superior results: 'I want employees in the airline to feel that it is they who can make the difference and influence what passengers get', he stresses. He writes to employees regularly to seek their ideas and to ensure that relevant news is communicated to them. His phone number is even given to all staff, who can call him at any time with suggestions or complaints![17] How many CEOs are truly following this example?

What is even more important is that these executives make sure that their example is followed at every level of the organization. Stelios Haji-Iaonnou, founder and chairman of easyJet, the leading European low-cost airline, wants to provide the best possible service while remaining low cost and yet original, spontaneous and informal. As a result, easyJet's management flies regularly, interviewing passengers informally and getting feedback. Stelios Haji-Iaonnou himself takes every opportunity to fly in his own planes, welcome passengers on board, chat with customers. Ingvar Kamprad and Masatoshi Ito still take pride in visiting their stores regularly to 'get the customer's pulse', as Mr Ito puts it.[18] Although officially retired, both retailers – respectively in their late seventies and early eighties – still continue to stroll through the back and front office to make sure that the corporate values are shared internally and remain intact. Both are particularly aware of the dangers of complacency. Mr Ito likes to repeat to his directors that 'a store manager must never allow his attention to be taken up entirely by the voices of the customers who do come. He must also find creative ways to listen to the customers who do not come.' The challenge is to keep the corporate brand fresh and strong by maintaining both customer interest and employee loyalty. 'Customers want to receive good service that comes from the heart', Mr Kamprad says.[19]

Putting passion into the brand: the case of Ducati[20]

The recent history of Italian motorcycle manufacturer Ducati Motor SpA offers an interesting example of successfully instilling passion into a brand. This case study describes in more detail many of the elements highlighted earlier in this chapter.

Back in mid-1996 Ducati's glamour was quickly fading away. The company was experiencing serious cash-flow problems and was close to bankruptcy when American venture capitalists Texas Pacific Group (TPG) acquired it and appointed Federico Minoli as the new CEO. As a management consultant from Bain & Co., Minoli, an Italian national, had been involved in the due diligence for the acquisition and had found plenty of daunting challenges: the quality of Ducati motorbikes had deteriorated and warranty costs were soaring; the company had no marketing strategy; sales and distribution were in disarray; the 'artisan' production set-up at the company's single factory in Bologna was terribly inefficient; suppliers were threatening to stop delivery of parts unless they were paid in advance; the factory roof was leaking; and overall morale was going down day by day.

Despite all these difficulties, Minoli believed that Ducati had several important assets that made it an attractive investment opportunity for TPG: top-notch engineers and sophisticated engine technology; stylish bike design; a racing team that had achieved numerous victories and much media attention; and a strong Italian heritage. Part of that heritage was the desmodromic engine invented and refined in the 1950s by one of Ducati's leading engineers, Dr Fabio Taglioni. The 'desmo' engine was fitted on every bike and its deep pulsing resonance came to be identified as the signature sound of a Ducati.[21]

At the time when Minoli took over, Ducati, unlike its more mass-market Japanese competitors (Honda, Yamaha, Suzuki and Kawasaki), focused on the sport subsegment, a special niche of the motorcycle business, targeting young, mainly male, fast riders, who dreamed of 'knee sliding' on the curves. In 1995 Ducati sold 20 000 motorbikes worldwide. Europe accounted for about 80% of sales, with key markets in Italy, Germany,

France and the UK. Only 12% of total sales were to the US. Most of the staff had started working for Ducati immediately after graduation and were in their forties. They were frustrated by the poor state of the company, but shared a status-quo mentality that was not compatible with Minoli's vision for the future.

The first thing the new CEO had to do was to form his management team. He hired an American international corporate attorney specializing in mergers and acquisitions to be responsible for strategy development; another American, who had worked at an external design studio for Ducati and was obsessed with motorbikes, to be responsible for design and engineering; and an Italian former colleague at Bain & Co., who had been involved in the due diligence for the Ducati acquisition, to be responsible for product development.

Minoli also brought in other high achievers with diverse backgrounds from the US, some of them from Ford Motors. He commented: 'Although none of these young talents spoke Italian or had worked in the motorcycle industry, I preferred them because they were visionary, driving, passionate and not afraid of change and risks. However, I knew that bringing people from Detroit with thinking and habits different from Italians was a potential recipe for disaster.' One of the new team's first tasks on a long 'to do' list was to let go a number of unreliable or incompetent employees.

What Minoli wanted to do was turn Ducati from 'a metal-mechanical organization' to 'an entertainment company based on a passionate brand'. He believed that building the brand should be the top priority; rationalizing the factory and refocusing on R&D could come later.

Building the passion

Minoli described the importance of forming a passionate team to turn Ducati around: 'It was difficult to build a new culture at the beginning. I tried to find the common ground between my American and Italian staff, and then I realized that the passion for Ducati was the glue. The turnaround will be successful only if everybody wants to be part of it ... When I first came here, I saw a parking lot reserved for top managers in front of the main building. Everybody else parked far away. I granted the employees who own Ducati bikes the privilege of parking their bikes there, while the parking spaces for top managers were moved further away ... I made every employee go to motorbike school. We organized buses to take us to watch races together. I also allowed employees to use our bikes for going to Ducati events over weekends. And I offered discounts to staff who wanted to buy Ducati bikes.'

When Minoli took over, Ducati's product positioning was in the quadrant of 'Performance and Function' according to the company's own assessment of the marketplace (see Figure 5.3). Its Japanese competitors covered every segment of the motorbike industry, while other bike manufacturers such as Harley Davidson and BMW pursued their own clearly defined market sectors. While maintaining its existing positioning, Ducati decided to push the boundaries of its niche toward comfort and lifestyle in order to broaden its fan base and increase repeat purchases. It thus entered a new (to it) category of the sport subsegment – sport touring – to target racing fans who were over 30 and looking for comfort in long-distance travel. It introduced special models known as the Monster line to satisfy racing fans with

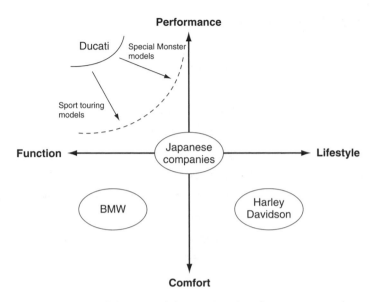

Figure 5.3   The sectors of the motorbike marketplace (Source: Ducati)

a taste for lifestyle, and aggressively targeted female customers, establishing a riding school for women, introducing apparel for them and including them in its marketing communication.

Ducati also focused on building up its fan base. Minoli commented: 'I realized that we don't actually have customers. All we have are passionate fans – *Ducatisti*! When I look at our fans, I cannot find any good ways of segmentation. Maybe the only thing they have in common is Ducati. I can think of them as a tribe in a village: it does not matter who they are, the link between them is the object they love and are passionate about. We used every opportunity to engage our fans in racing. In the Ducati tribe, what is important is not winning, but fighting together. We make them feel as if they are fighting and winning with us.'

To establish a consistent new image, the company now started an identity campaign. It commissioned a new logo and used it in every possible communication medium. In 1997 it launched its first global ad campaign, 'Ducati People', featuring black and white retro photos of its employees with Ducati bikes. It aimed to allow Ducati fans to identify with young and sporty riders who were passionate about the company's Italian heritage and racing glory.

In 2002 a second 'Ducati People' global ad campaign used *Ducatisti* from all over the world to communicate the fans' passion for racing performance. Over the years of the revival, Ducati bikes have been featured in fashion and design magazines, department-store showcases, exhibitions, television series and movies: Warner Brothers bought eight Ducatis for some of the racing scenes in the blockbuster movie *Matrix Reloaded*.

Distribution, production and R&D

As back-up to the revitalization of the Ducati brand, Minoli rationalized distribution in three stages:

- **Establishing wholly owned subsidiaries** to manage overseas dealers and handle promotions and after-sales service in major European markets, the US and Japan. Some 250 professionals who had a passion for motorcycle racing and respect for customers were hired to join these subsidiaries.

- **Changing the dealer structure**, forming a new network with greater emphasis on exclusivity and quality in order to reinforce Ducati's brand image and improve sales assistance and after-sales service.
- **Creating its own flagship stores** to strengthen its brand image. The first Ducati store was opened in Manhattan in 1998. By 2004, there were over 30 stores in Italy and 20 others spread across the world.

To reinforce its cutting-edge image, the company launched a virtual store, becoming the first in the industry to sell motorbikes on the Internet. Within 31 minutes on 1 January 2000, it sold a thousand units of the limited edition MH900e online. Apparel and accessories were added to the eStore range six months later. Ducati also uses this channel to communicate with *Ducatisti* about racing news and product updates, and to form a global Ducati 'tribe' by enabling them to chat about mutual interests such as motorbike racing and maintenance. By 2003, about 8 million people had visited the website and about 140 000 racing fans were registered as users.

In the factory, as part of the second phase of the turnaround, Ducati implemented Just-in-Time and KAIZEN – a Japanese approach in which improvement is gained in small steps, with the help and collaboration of every worker involved and without any significant investment – to streamline and improve the assembly process. As a result, the time taken to build a bike was decreased by half and productivity increased by 50% in five years. The company also chose some high-quality vendors of key components as its principal suppliers and had them deal with the subsuppliers. Thus the number of dealers Ducati dealt with directly decreased from 225 in 1995 to 170 in 2003.

Phase three of the turnaround saw the introduction of new design software which reduced product development time by half and enabled the engineering team to refocus its efforts on innovation.

Results for Ducati

Ducati successfully went public on the Italian Stock Exchange in 1999. From 1996 to 2003, the company's net sales and EBITDA (earnings before interest, taxes, depreciation and amortization) increased at a compound annual growth rate of 20.4% and 21.1% respectively. Its market share grew from 3% in 1996 to 7% in 2003. It successfully expanded in the US market, where the number of motorbikes sold was up from 2000 in 1995 to 4575 in 2003. The company has grown from 500 employees in March 1996 to 1100 – including 980 factory workers – today. By 2003, Ducati had won 13 of the last 14 World Superbike Championship titles and ridden to victory in its debut MotoGP race.

Putting passion into brands: six generic key lessons

Drawing on the examples of Ducati and the other companies examined in this chapter, several valuable lessons can be drawn on how to put passion into brands and how to implement an effective 'internal brand strategy':

- **Make sure the entire senior management is behind the plan**. Creating and developing an internal brand culture only works if employees realize that it is for the long term and led by top management. Companies dedicated to building passion brands are all led by senior executives who live and communicate the brand values constantly and consistently. Their brand message is not delivered by e-mails, posters or memos but at the personal level, very often by the CEO him/herself. These senior executives display a genuine passion for their products, their customers and their brands. They create, communicate and live a compelling brand vision and mission. They don't pay them lip service.

- **Define and communicate a clear and consistent corporate brand identity** at every level of your organization. The challenge is for senior and middle management to communicate a simple and clear message based around the key components of their brand strategy (What does your brand stand for? Who is your brand targeting? What are the key benefits of your brand?) Since employees at all levels of the organization need to live, support and deliver the brand, it is essential that they have simple and credible answers to these three basic questions, consistently and over time. Executives in companies that truly live the passion for their brands also use every opportunity to communicate – in person – the values of their brands to both their staff and their partners' employees.

- **Make passion for the product and the customer** a key element of your human resources policy. As one Disney executive we met likes to stress: 'If you want to build an internal passion for the brand or a customer-oriented organization, don't hire people who love to talk to computers, hire enthusiasm!' At Ducati, 'passion for bikes' has become the number one hiring factor, almost regardless of the prospective new employee's educational or professional background. 'Passion brand companies' also spend a considerable amount of time and money educating their people. This constant effort helps to build and reinforce passion and commitment, as well as a strong sense of organizational belonging.

- **Make sure that your external and internal messages are consistent**. A recurrent problem in implementing 'internal branding' is conflicting communications. One Swiss insurance company was recently promising in its external advertising to do everything to keep its customers satisfied while at the same time urging all its employees to save costs on customer transactions. Inconsistent external and internal messages can only lead to confusion and cynical reactions from your staff. Speaking with one voice to all your stakeholders with a credible and passionate message is an absolute prerequisite for successful internal branding. As one Nokia executive says: 'In building our brand, we learnt that the following three ingredients are absolutely critical: a consistent and relevant message to consumers, a consistent transmission of this message across all channels of communications with our stakeholders, a consistent message over time!'

- **Translate the brand values** into meaningful actions and behaviours for your staff. This is another way to reinforce the credibility of your brand. Small, symbolic actions can go a long way. Think again about Federico Minoli hiring motorcycle instructors so that all employees could learn how to ride Ducati bikes, granting Ducati-owning employees the privilege of parking their bikes in front of the main building, hiring employees for advertising. The result of all these symbolic actions is a huge reinforcement of the corporate values that influence the right employee behaviour: passion for the brand and respect for the customer.

- **Celebrate the successes**. As we have seen, developing and sharing a brand philosophy that always puts the customer first, setting the example as executives, empowering and involving employees, linking incentives to customer orientation, focusing measurements on customer orientation are all necessary elements in shaping a strong brand culture.[22] However, communicating and celebrating successes are critical in bringing all these elements together and keeping the momentum going over time. At GrandOptical, the French retail chain selling optical products and services (mentioned in Chapter 4), when employees meet or exceed corporate standards, everyone is told what a difference they have made for the customer. To celebrate these successes, more than 10 000 bottles of champagne are opened every year for the employees. In many organizations, such celebrations turn out to be the 'glue' to internal brand execution.

Summary and management guidelines

- In today's highly competitive world, differentiation remains the key to producing a marketing strategy that will build a sustainable advantage for your company.
- Branding is the ultimate differentiation factor as product innovations are increasingly difficult to protect, quality is now taken for granted and customer orientation is a must.
- A brand is more than a product. While a product is essentially functional, a brand is both functional and emotional. The bigger the emotional component of a brand, the better the opportunity to build a passion brand.
- Strong brands do not happen by accident, nor do they happen in isolation. Developing passion for your brands is intrinsically linked to customer orientation, since passion for brands cannot exist without passion for the customer.
- Brand management is not only about products and services, it's also about people.

- Putting passion into brands helps to differentiate products from the competition, provides opportunities for premium pricing and reinforces internal commitment and organizational identification.
- Building passion into brands is a long journey that starts with management but entails involving your own people and making them into your best ambassadors.
- Management guidelines for effectively implementing an internal brand-building process include:

  - Make sure that the entire senior management is behind the plan and consistently leads by example by living the brand values over and over again
  - Define and communicate a clear and consistent corporate brand identity at every level of the organization
  - Make passion for the product and the customer a key element of the corporate human resources policy
  - Make sure that the external and internal brand messages are consistent
  - Translate the brand values into meaningful actions and behaviours for the staff
  - Celebrate the successes.

References

[1] Bill Fischer, an IMD professor in operations management and a specialist in China, suggests that today, close to 70% of Chinese factories are up to Western quality standards.

[2] 'Brand Building Power', *The Economic Times*, 2 December 1998.

[3] Kotler, Philip, *Marketing Management*, Upper Saddle River: Prentice Hall/Pearson Education International, 2000.

[4] Kapferer, Jean-Noël, *Strategic Brand Management: New Approaches to Creating and Evaluating Brand Equity*, London: Kogan Page, 1992.

[5] Aaker, David A. and Joachimsthaler, Erich, *Brand Leadership*, New York: Free Press, 2000; Keller, Kevin Lane, *Strategic Brand Management*, Upper Saddle River: Prentice Hall, 1998; de Chernatony, Leslie and McDonald, Malcolm, *Creating Powerful Brands*, Oxford: Butterworth-Heinemann, 1998.

[6] Adapted from an IMD presentation by Nirmalya Kumar: 'Romancing Your Brand: Are Customers in Love with Your Brand?', 2000.

[7] As quoted in Tom Peters' *The Brand You 50: Or: Fifty Ways to Transform Yourself from an 'Employee' into a Brand That Shouts Distinction, Commitment, and Passion!*, New York: Alfred A. Knopf, 1999.

[8] Presentation in Maranello, 11 December 2002.

[9] For more details on this technique, see Jacques Horovitz, *The Seven Secrets of Service Strategy*, London and Upper Saddle River: Financial Times–Prentice Hall, 2000.

[10] Carlzon, Jan, *Moments of Truth*, New York: HarperCollins, 1989.

[11] Schultz, Howard, and Yang, Dori Jones, *Put Your Heart into it: How Starbucks Built a Company One Cup at a Time*, New York: Hyperion, 1997.

[12] Quoted in 'Engaging Employees With Your Brand: Preliminary Findings', The Conference Board, 2001.

[13] See Douglas B. Holt, John A. Quelch and Earl L. Taylor, 'How Global Brands Compete', *Harvard Business Review*, September 2004.

[14] Interview by Kamran Kashani, 'The Tetra Pak Case Series (A), (B), (C), (D)', Video IMD-5-0604-V, 2003.

[15] See Manfred F.R. Kets and Raoul de Vitry D'Avancourt, 'Richard Branson: The Iconoclastic Entrepreneur: An Interview', INSEAD Case Study 495-014-5, 1995.

[16] See Pantéa Denoyelle and Jean-Claude Larréché, 'Virgin Atlantic Airways: Ten Years After', INSEAD Case Study 595-023-1; 1995.

[17] Denoyelle, Pantéa and Larréché, Jean-Claude, 'Virgin Atlantic Airways'.

[18] Interviews conducted by Dominique Turpin in Tokyo (Japan), spring 2004.

[19] Presentation at IMD, 2000.

[20] For more details see Rebecca Chung and Dominique Turpin, 'Rebuilding a Passion Brand: Ducati (A)'; Case Study IMD-5-0666, 2004 and 'Rebuilding a Passion Brand: Ducati (B)'; Case Study IMD-5-0667, 2004.

[21] To hear the sound of the desmodromic engine, click http://www.ducati.com/bikes/my2004/superbike.jhtml, choose a model and then click 'sounds'. In the 1990s

some Ducati fans in Sweden even recorded and globally released a CD of the engine sounds of about 20 different Ducati models.

[22] Horovitz, Jacques, *Seven Secrets of Service Strategy*, London and Upper Saddle River: Financial Times–Prentice Hall, 2000.

Additional references

Danielle Blumenthal, 'Internal Branding: Does it Improve Employees' Quality of Life?', Institute for Brand Leadership, http://www.instituteforbrandleadership.org/InternalBranding.pdf.

David Dell, Nathan Ainspan, Thomas Bodenberg, Kathryn Troy and Jack Hickey, 'Engaging Employees with the Brand', The Conference Board, 2001.

Jacques Horovitz, *The Seven Secrets of Service Strategy*, Harlow: Pearson Education Ltd, 2000.

Colin Mitchell, 'Selling the Brand Inside', *Harvard Business Review*, January 2002.

Angela Mohtashemi, 'Why Companies Should Brandish Their Internal Brand', *EBF*, Issue 9, Spring 2002.

PricewaterhouseCoopers and the *Financial Times*, 'Global Survey of World's Most Respected Companies', November 2001.

Howard Schultz and Dori Jones Yang, *Put Your Heart into it: How Starbucks Built a Company One Cup at a Time*, New York: Hyperion, 1997.

6
Beyond Beating Competition: Shaping Markets for Profitable Growth

Professor Adrian B. Ryans

I n many organizations marketing's role is too narrowly defined. The Chief Marketing Officer (CMO) often spends a disproportionate amount of his or her energy and time focusing on such traditional issues as product-line management, pricing, marketing communications and channels.[1] While these are important areas, they do not have the strategic impact of some of the other roles a CMO can, and should, play. If the CMO is to play a truly strategic role, he or she should be focusing on such issues as shaping the corporation's overall value proposition for its customers, helping to set the growth direction of the business by identifying attractive and profitable growth opportunities and managing the corporate brand.

The market forces tool described in this chapter is a very useful way for the CMO and his or her team to help structure some of their thinking about these critical corporate decisions. It can help them think creatively about managing the profitability of their existing markets and ensuring that new markets the company enters will be sources of profitable growth. Over the years, economists, business strategists and marketers have developed theories and concepts that provide useful insights into how to do this. However, very few companies use the approaches in a rigorous and disciplined manner, with the result that most do not reap all the benefits they might from the understanding we have gained.

In this chapter, we will attempt to bring together strategies and tactics a variety of companies in many industries have used to shape the profitability of the markets in which they compete to ensure that the growth they achieve in these markets is highly profitable. This approach can be used both in existing markets and to help the team to understand the potential profitability of new markets they are considering entering.

Conceptual framework

The Six Market Forces model is a useful way to think conceptually about managing markets for profitability. It is based on Michael Porter's 'Five Forces Model',[2] which focused on:

- rivalry among the existing players in an industry
- the power of suppliers
- the power of customers
- the threat of new entrants
- the threat of substitute products or services.

In addition, there is a sixth force which must be managed carefully in order to ensure that a market is as profitable as possible. This sixth force is complementors:[3] companies or organizations that provide products and services that make a company's products or services more useful to its customers, or to other players who are downstream from it in the market chain. Clearly a Microsoft Xbox game console is of very little value to a potential user if there are no exciting games to play on it. So one of the major challenges facing Microsoft when it launched the Xbox was to encourage game developers to write software for this new product. While Microsoft could develop some of the games itself, it also needed to harness third-party developers to work on Xbox software.

The six market forces that can impact a company's profitability in a given market are shown in Figure 6.1. In each case, some of the major factors that will contribute to a negative market environment are shown. If these forces are negative, then it is highly unlikely that a given market will be attractive for a company and will generate good profits. In some cases, even if only one major force is negative, it can make the market relatively unattractive. The challenge that management faces is to manage each of the factors that could make a market force negative in order to create as positive an overall market environment as possible.

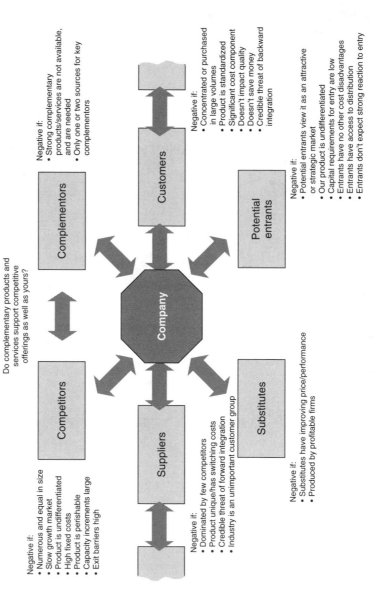

Do complementary products and
services support competitive
offerings as well as yours?

Complementors

Negative if:
• Strong complementary
products/services are not available,
and are needed
• Only one or two sources for key
complementors

Customers

Negative if:
• Concentrated or purchased
in large volumes
• Product is standardized
• Significant cost component
• Doesn't impact quality
• Doesn't save money
• Credible threat of backward
integration

Competitors

Negative if:
• Numerous and equal in size
• Slow growth market
• Product is undifferentiated
• High fixed costs
• Product is perishable
• Capacity increments large
• Exit barriers high

Company

**Potential
entrants**

Negative if:
• Potential entrants view it as an attractive
or strategic market
• Our product is undifferentiated
• Capital requirements for entry are low
• Entrants have no other cost disadvantages
• Entrants have access to distribution
• Entrants don't expect strong reaction to entry

Suppliers

Negative if:
• Dominated by few competitors
• Product unique/has switching costs
• Credible threat of forward integration
• Industry is an unimportant customer group

Substitutes

Negative if:
• Substitutes have improving price/performance
• Produced by profitable firms

Figure 6.1   Shaping the Six Market Forces

Managing customers

Powerful customers have become a major threat to profitability for companies in many markets. The massive concentration of buying power that is occurring in many sectors of retailing in many countries and even globally as large retailers such as Wal-Mart, Tesco and Carrefour expand internationally, is a major threat to profitability for many manufacturers. Similar situations can be found in many business-to-business markets, where a few major customers or consortia of customers are accounting for an increasing share of industry purchases, or where a small number of distributors control the key channels. The semiconductor manufacturing business is one example of this. As the cost of building new fabs escalates, fewer and fewer companies can afford to build state-of-the art facilities, resulting in increasing buyer power residing in a small number of big players, such as Intel, IBM, Samsung, TSMC, UMC and a few others. However, in many situations a company can take steps to actively manage its customer base and control the power of its customers.

Some of the most important ways to manage customers include:

- choosing the right customers
- actively encouraging the creation of new customers
- making sure you don't encourage customer concentration
- developing a strong brand
- helping your customers to work with other suppliers
- differentiating your solution
- developing a credible threat of forward integration.

We will discuss each of these strategies in turn.

Choose the right customers

Choice of customers is a critical decision, yet many companies do not consider its long-term consequences. For many years Federal Express (FedEx) was less interested in providing air-express service for small packages for small accounts, whereas United Parcel Service (UPS) actively sought that business. In 1990, according to a study done by an investment bank, FedEx had a gross margin of 6% on its air-express business, whereas UPS had a gross margin of 24% in the same sector.[4] FedEx's customers were more likely to be large corporations with the power to demand large-volume discounts, driving down gross margins. The analyst noted that the decision about choice of customer was the major reason that FedEx had a return on equity of 11% and UPS had a return on equity of 20%.

In some cases the structure of sales forces and sales force compensation systems encourages sales representatives to focus on the largest accounts with the biggest revenue potential. To prevent this occurring, some companies have set up special sales forces or dedicated certain sales representatives to focus on small and emerging accounts. Over time this can result in a more diversified customer base and less dependence on a few big customers. Sometimes the same result can be achieved by using the sales force compensation system to encourage the sales representatives to have a diversified customer base.

Encourage new customers

Another way to try to control the power of customers is to actively 'create' new customers. Some companies have been very effective at helping potential new customers enter the market by removing major entry barriers. Nortel Networks provided a lot of engineering support and business advice to new players entering the telecommunications business at the height of the telecom boom at the end of the 1990s. Intel has also been particularly effective at this in the personal computer business. It has made entry easy for even small, technologically unsophisticated players by taking all the challenging engineering tasks out of building a state-of-the art personal computer. Intel provides complementary chipsets, does the difficult motherboard designs and even produces complete motherboards. It also provides reference designs that ensure that manufacturers in Taiwan and elsewhere can rapidly produce motherboards for its most advanced microprocessors. By buying complete motherboards and all the other complementary products, even a new entrant can produce advanced personal computers. The strong Intel brand name and Intel Inside logo help reassure potential end users about the quality of the entrant's product and thus help the entrant build a customer base. Even very small companies are often able to build a presence in a local market, while a large company with a strong brand, relationships with contract manufacturers and established distribution can gain significant volume and pose a credible threat to established personal computer manufacturers. Consumer electronics companies and major retailers have been able to do this successfully in a number of markets around the world.

Recently Intel has extended this strategy into the more sophisticated server market. It has gradually moved from providing more and more complete server 'packages' to companies that assembled servers, to certifying that its server packages would work with hardware and software from other companies.[5] Traditionally, the server manufacturers had done this certification themselves. This was not a big issue for large manufacturers, such as Dell, IBM and Hewlett-Packard; and because it was reassuring for their customers it gave their products a competitive advantage in the market. However, certification was an important issue for smaller server manufacturers and it reduced their ability to compete. So by doing the certification for the small and medium players, Intel levelled the playing field and helped the smaller players compete effectively with the giants in this segment of the computer market. In essence Intel was helping to commoditize its customers' products, so that new customers could more easily compete in the market. Over time this would increase the amount of price competition, and helping to drive down the price of its customers' products in a price-elastic market should increase the demand for its products. Clearly, this type of strategy has to be used very carefully, since it has the potential to upset Intel's major existing customers. If they had equally attractive alternative sources of supply, they could retaliate against Intel by switching to another supplier.

In some industries companies refurbish old equipment that no longer meets the needs of their mainstream customers and sell it to new companies that are just entering the industry (sometimes in developing economies) and don't need the latest technology or equipment. This reduces the barriers of entry for these customers and serves to diversify the customer base. It also has the added benefit of driving down the cost of ownership for their leading-edge customers, who can count on a market for the equipment at the end of its lifecycle in their business. If only one competitor in the industry does this, it can give it more pricing flexibility on its new equipment. Some of the new customers will undoubtedly move up-market over time and will require more advanced equipment, giving the vendor that refurbishes its equipment a relationship it can capitalize on.

Don't encourage customer concentration

Some manufacturers selling through retail or wholesale channels unintentionally encourage their customer base to become more concentrated on a few large players by offering very aggressive volume-discount programmes. While this often stimulates revenue and market-share growth in the short run, it discourages smaller customers who cannot achieve the volumes that will result in the higher discounts. Many of these smaller customers will move to other suppliers, who provide them with some protection either through less aggressive volume discounts or special models that are not available to the large volume customers. One North American manufacturer of kitchen appliances experienced this dynamic a few years ago when, eager to grow its market share rapidly, it decided to offer a much more aggressive discount schedule than its competitors. While it was successful in growing revenues rapidly, within a couple of years it found itself highly dependent on a few mega-retailers, who demanded ever larger price concessions, seriously damaging the manufacturer's profitability.

Some companies actively work with their customer base to try to ensure that no customer or customers dominate a particular market. One large manufacturer of fast-moving consumer goods in an important national market grew increasingly concerned that its business was becoming concentrated with Wal-Mart and a large local retailer that had over a 40% share of the retail grocery business. To try to reduce, or at least slow down, the increasing concentration of the market, it seconded one of its best 'fast track' executives to work with the second strongest grocery retailer. The role of this executive was two-fold: to really understand the issues the retailer was facing so that the manufacturer could develop programmes to help it compete more effectively with Wal-Mart and the dominant grocery retailer; and to share with the retailer the best practices that the manufacturer had seen other grocery retailers using in other geographical markets.

In a similar situation in the US, many manufacturers of FMCGs are clearly concerned about the increasing dominance of Wal-Mart in their customer bases. One fast-growing, albeit relatively small, group of retailers in the United States is the so-called dollar store such as Dollar General and Family Dollar. These bare-bones retailers operate out of low-cost strip malls and sell staple and novelty items. In order to strengthen this retailing channel and improve its presence in it, Procter & Gamble has begun producing special, smaller sizes of some of its most popular products, so that Dollar General and the others can hit the price points they sell at.[6] This is helping these retailers to grow more rapidly than Wal-Mart and providing a relatively attractive channel for Procter & Gamble and its competitors.

Develop your brand

A strong brand, such as Intel's, is also a powerful tool for counterbalancing the power of a retailer or other channel member. If the ultimate purchaser is strongly influenced by the brand, the bargaining power of all the players between the ultimate purchaser and the owner of the brand is reduced. This puts the owner of the brand in a very strong position.

In some cases, of course, the value of the brand might be diminished, if discounters feature the brand to build traffic, particularly if they have little interest in actually selling the product once the customer enters the store because of the low margins. Some manufacturers have chosen to withdraw low-end products from discounters in order to strengthen the brand's image. Samsung, for example, withdrew its appliances from Wal-Mart and Target because it felt that its corporate image was being damaged.[7] This was a very tough decision given the volumes involved and the growing strength of these retailers, but one that Yun Jong Yong, the CEO of Samsung, felt was necessary to protect the future of the business.

Help your customers work with other suppliers

Some companies with a powerful position in their industry go as far as helping their customers to drive down the costs of buying complementary products and services from other suppliers. One way to do this is to ensure that there are at least a couple of sources of supply for all the other key products and services a customer might buy to complement the manufacturer's own product. For example, Intel works with suppliers of semiconductor components for the PCs that complement its microprocessors and tries to ensure that there are at least two companies able to market these parts. This has two major benefits for the manufacturer. First, by ensuring that there is competition in these other markets, it helps drive down the costs of these products and services for its customers, which in a price-elastic market encourages the customers to drop their prices, helping to increase the demand for the manufacturer's own products. Second, by ensuring that the other markets are very competitive, it may take some of the pressure off it to reduce its prices to its customers.

Differentiate your solution

A very obvious way to reduce the power of a customer is to provide a truly differentiated product that provides great value to the customer or the customer's customer and is difficult for competitors to match. While in some cases this might be a product with unique intellectual property, today it is often a complex bundle of products and associated services that provides a complete and, often, lower cost solution to a customer need. This frequently results in close integration between supplier and customer, with high switching costs, making it possible for the supplier to earn reasonable returns on the business. Dell has been very successful in doing this with many of its large accounts and is increasingly viewed as their information systems technology partner. Some of its key competitors in the computer systems market are still struggling to move beyond being providers of commodity hardware.

When a company has a truly differentiated product that is either itself in high demand or is a key enabler of a product that is in high demand, it can reduce the power of powerful customers by limiting supply. A number of companies appear to have used this tactic in recent years to strengthen their hand in negotiating with powerful retailers such as Wal-Mart. This tactic is particularly effective where there is a limited window of opportunity for the retailer, such as toys during the Christmas selling season, and where the product could be an effective traffic builder. Of course, if the tactic is used in a flagrant and obvious way, long-term relationships with the customer might be damaged.

Develop a credible threat of forward integration

Even a niche entry can keep customers honest and give you good insights into the needs of a company's customers' customers' needs. A couple of companies that have done this are Apple and Sony. Many industry observers think that Apple's retail strategy has been quite successful and that its retail stores now account for well over 10% of its total sales. Sony has adopted a similar strategy, but seems to be less focused on using its own retail channel to generate revenues directly. Rather, the stores seem to be used as a show-case for Sony's products, to build its brand image and to demonstrate to and educate consumers about the kind of integrated solutions that Sony can offer with its various products. The Sony stores also represent a credible threat of forward integration, which probably helps keep the power of major retailers like Best Buy and Circuit City in check.

Managing competitors

A great deal has been written on competitive analysis and the management of competitors. In this section we will focus on only a couple of the major and most effective ways of doing this. The most obvious one is to leverage your resources and capabilities and market a differentiated offering, so that the competition is not direct and customers find it difficult to make head-to-head comparisons. Another powerful way is to try to consolidate the market, so that there are fewer effective competitors.

Differentiate your solution and play to your strengths

If a market comprises a number of different segments with distinctive needs, relatively small players are often better positioned to develop unique solutions for one or more of the segments. The bigger players sometimes offer more generic solutions that have higher volume potential. In the industrial projector business in the 1990s, the Belgian company Barco and the Canadian company Electrohome were successful in retaining a significant share of the market by tailoring their offerings to the needs of relatively small market segments, while larger Japanese players, such as Sony and NEC, offered more generic products at lower prices.

An extreme example of a highly fragmented market was a segment of the animal-care business. This craft-oriented market had existed for hundreds of years and had developed in different ways in different countries and even different regions within those countries. This had led to literally hundreds of variations of the basic products being used around the world. In the late twentieth century there was gradual consolidation in the industry, with one company becoming the dominant player with over 80% of the market in some product segments. The Chinese market for the product was one of the largest in the world and low-cost Chinese competition was an increasing threat to the dominant player. The first reaction of top management in the dominant player was that it needed to rationalize the company's product range and encourage customers to move to globally standardized products.

This would allow the company to dramatically lower production, inventory and distribution costs and thus better prepare it to face the Chinese threat. However, after thinking more deeply about the issue, management realized that a more effective strategy might be to reinforce the fragmentation of the market. A highly fragmented global market would be less attractive to a less sophisticated, volume-oriented competitor, as it would require an understanding of all the nuances of the individual geographic markets and heavy investment in marketing and sales to try to wean the industry away from its traditional products and practices. With this insight the dominant Western manufacturer began to sponsor local and national competitions for the craftsmen in order to increase interest in the traditional practices, and to invest in a variety of other ways of reinforcing the differences between markets around the world.

Acquire or merge with competitors

In some cases an effective way to improve the attractiveness of a market from a competitive perspective is to reduce the number of players, perhaps by reducing exit barriers, so that players who are unable to make adequate returns in the market can leave it. Ryanair and easyJet consolidated their positions in the Irish and British markets for air transportation by acquiring Buzz and Go respectively. The acquisition of Buzz by Ryanair provided a face-saving way for KLM to exit the unprofitable (for it) low-cost airline segment. In some cases the exit barriers might be the result of environmental laws that require expensive clean-up of sites before exit. Lobbying to reduce the financial burden on the exiting companies might be effective here. In other cases an exit barrier might be national pride, which caused many countries to feel that they had to have a national flag carrier airline at almost any cost to the treasury. The increasing cost of supporting the flag carriers forced some countries to let them declare bankruptcy. In other cases pressure from supranational bodies, like the European Union, often abetted by the lobbying of more competitive and successful airlines through their governments, made it increasingly difficult for countries to keep subsidizing their money-losing airlines. By 2004 the Italian government was facing increasing pressure from European Union regulators to stop supporting Alitalia, which had posted an annual profit only four times in the previous 16 years.[8]

This strategy will only be effective if there are barriers to entry that prevent new players coming into the market as quickly as the old players exit. This has been an issue in certain geographical markets in the cement industry. In some cases operators have set up cement terminals on the coast or on major waterways where they can take advantage of relatively low-cost water transportation to bring in cement from low-cost sources in other countries and compete with the established players using low prices. The established cement manufacturers have sometimes responded by buying the terminals, only to see new terminals sprout up in their place.

Managing complementors

For many products and services complementors are critical. Sony introduced the Mavica digital camera in the early 1980s, but the market did not develop into a high-volume one until the mid-1990s. While part of the problem was that the initial product was expensive and did not produce acceptable results for many potential applications, a major barrier to market growth was the lack of products and services that would make the digital camera truly attractive to potential customers. By the early 1990s, however, many users had access to powerful personal computers and software for manipulating images, storage was becoming less and less expensive, inkjet printers were available to make physical copies of digital images and the Internet allowed digital image files to be circulated easily and conveniently. At this point growth began to accelerate.

In some cases complementary products and services work only with a single company's product, in other cases they support competitors' products and services as well. If you have a strong proprietary solution that you think you can drive to profitable market leadership, you may want to work with complementors who will have an exclusive relationship with you. This is the situation in the game-console business, where each of the major players has complementary games that work only on its hardware. If there are several competitors, each with its own proprietary solution, this may cause the market to 'freeze' as customers wait for a dominant standard to emerge. They don't want to get caught with a competitor who fails to attract complementors, leaving the customer with an incomplete solution. In this case all the players might be better off agreeing on one standard and sharing in the much larger, but possibly much more competitive, market that will probably emerge.

Encourage new complementors

Rather than waiting for the complementary products and services to become available spontaneously, some companies actively try to ensure that a complete solution is available for potential customers. This involves having a clear vision of what a complete solution will look like and aggressively communicating this vision to potential partners. In some cases companies will themselves produce complementors to stimulate demand for the core product. If the company does not have the interest in, or the resources and capabilities to compete in, the complementor market long term it may exit the market, when other suppliers of the complementary products or services are well established. In many cases, standards will need to be established, so that all the pieces of the solution fit neatly together. Also establishing standards enables many different players to provide each part of the solution so that no one complementor gains a great deal of power.

Hughes Space and Communication was a leading producer of satellites prior to its acquisition by Boeing. It recognized that one barrier to selling more commercial satellites was the total cost of the satellite plus the launch. Being naturally reluctant to reduce the price of its satellites, managers in Hughes decided to focus on driving down the cost of launch services. Since there were a limited number of suitable equatorial sites for launching satellites into geosynchronous orbits, Hughes encouraged Boeing to get into the sea-launch business, hoping that an additional, geographically well-positioned player would lead to increased price competition between the various launch-site operators, thus driving down the total cost for customers. Boeing did enter the satellite-launch business and the first commercial launch by Boeing's Sea Launch took place in 1999.

Nintendo did a very good job of managing its key complementors, the developers who wrote the games that ran on the Nintendo video-game player.[9] It developed some of the games itself and was successful in creating a very popular character, Mario. It also initiated a licensing programme for developers, but it only allowed each developer to develop a limited number of games, ensuring that no one developer would be too powerful. Since it was the only 'game' in town at the time, it required that each game be exclusive to Nintendo. Through these and other moves it was able to build a very profitable video-games business.

Support complementors

One company that has done a superlative job of managing its complementors in recent years is Intel, particularly with respect to its core microprocessor business. As Intel introduced more and more powerful processors with increasing capabilities over the years, it was very successful in communicating its vision of the future for the personal computer, including what it thought were going to be the next exciting applications for PCs and the hardware and software that were going to be needed to convert the vision to reality. The broad vision was often shared at major industry conferences such as Comdex. In parallel, it held Intel Developer Forums with the companies that would need to provide parts of the solution for both Intel's customers and PC end users. In these forums the discussion would be more specific and technical. Intel would also share its product road maps on a confidential basis with selected partners. Intel is more likely to work closely with partners who are willing to make their proprietary technology available to others, so that it can ensure that its customers have access to the complementary product or service from more than one source.

In many cases, Intel Capital, the company's venture-capital arm, would help fund innovative new technologies and services that supported its vision for the PC and, if successful, would fuel the demand for Intel microprocessors. Over the years Intel invested billions of dollars in promising start-ups. Even if a particular start-up was not successful, it sometimes helped create a market that would require more PCs and more processing power. In some cases Intel also invested heavily in marketing and advertising to support what it saw as critical new applications. In the case of Wi-Fi wireless networks Intel spent some $300 million on a global marketing campaign, which included advertising, conferences and support for developers wanting to make their applications work smoothly for mobile and remote workers.

One company that is counting on complementors to help it win its next battle in a key market is Microsoft. Microsoft's Xbox had a worldwide market share through 2003 in the current generation of game consoles of about 15% versus Sony PlayStation 2's 69%.[10] With those market shares game developers would much rather write games for the Sony console than the Microsoft equivalent. In order to close the gap or seize the lead in the next generation of consoles, which are expected to be launched in late 2005, Microsoft is creating a single platform of compatible programming tools that will allow developers to build games both for the Xbox and for Windows-based personal computers.[11] This new set of tools will automate many of the tasks involved in writing games software for both the Xbox and PCs, making the process quicker and cheaper for the developers. The fact that the software will run on both the games console and the PC makes Sony's current lead in consoles less important. In the early 1990s Microsoft used the same strategy of working closely with developers to help Windows win the battle with IBM and Apple for leadership in the personal computer operating-systems market.

Managing substitutes

Substitutes are competing products or services that for at least some customers and some applications meet the customers' needs to a greater or lesser extent. For an airline, substitutes include other modes of transportation such as automobiles, trains, buses and ships. Less direct substitutes, but certainly increasingly important ones from the perspective of business travel, are electronic forms of communication, such as videoconferencing and electronic networks that, say, allow engineers in different locations to work on engineering challenges together in real time.

There are a number of ways to reduce the threat to market attractiveness posed by substitutes. Among the major ways are:

- improving the price/performance of the product relative to the substitutes
- building switching costs for customers
- positioning the substitute product as a niche solution
- entering the substitute market directly to gain some control over the market.

Improve price/performance of products/services vs substitutes

In the mid-1990s Intel faced a growing challenge in the personal computer business from thin clients or network computers. Thin clients were simpler computers that were designed to work with a server, so that the client was less complex and required less local storage, processing power and maintenance. Intel partially dealt with this substitute threat by introducing the Celeron processor, which was a simpler, lower cost processor than its premium Pentium processor, but which provided the functionality that most cost-conscious customers would require. This allowed PC manufacturers to introduce sub-$500 PCs that were quite price competitive with thin clients or network PCs. With this move Intel ensured that the major threat posed by thin clients never had as big an impact as had been expected by many industry observers. This type of move often allows a company to tap into new, more price-sensitive segments of a market. These segments are often larger than anticipated and the volume they generate can help drive the product down its experience curve more rapidly, making it even more competitive with the substitute product.

Increase switching costs

An obvious but effective way to reduce the impact of substitute products is to increase the switching costs for the customer. Depending on the product, switching costs can arise from habit or investments in training, infrastructure, etc., or simply the hassle that is required to move from one supplier to another. For example, Dell has been very successful at building switching barriers for its best customers by linking their purchasing and installed base management programs with the Dell website. Dell's customers have a customized portal that allows them to order, track and manage their IT assets very effectively. This creates switching barriers that are effective against both direct competitors and any substitutes that might come along.

'Pigeon-hole' the substitute

In some situations a tactic that works is to try to position the substitute as the solution to a niche application in the market, rather than to a mainstream need. Glaxo appeared to do this when Zantac, its market-leading antiulcer drug, was threatened by a new product, Losec, which was manufactured by Astra AB. While both the drugs were antiulcerants, they used different mechanisms to control gastric acid production, which meant that they were differentially effective in treating different kinds of ulcer conditions. At one stage Glaxo seemed to be trying to 'pigeon-hole' Losec as the solution for dealing with refractory ulcers only – a relatively small, though important, segment of the overall ulcer-treatment market. This had to be done carefully, since pharmaceutical salespeople are quite con-strained in what they can say to physicians, but the Glaxo salespeople might employ the tactic of conceding that Losec was a better drug for refractory ulcers, while maintaining that Zantac had a long, strong and safe record for treating other kinds of ulcers and was therefore a better choice overall.

Consider entering the substitute market

A final approach for trying to control the effect of substitutes on the attract-iveness and profitability of a market is for a company to enter the substitute market itself, in order to influence it from the inside. Take the case of Sealed Air, a company that was the leader in the high-end protective packaging market with such products as Insta-Pak foam-packaging solutions and Air-Cap air-cellular packaging. In the early 1980s the AirCap business was increasingly threatened by lower cost, uncoated, air-cellular packaging that did not offer the same level of protection that AirCap offered, but did fully meet the needs of customers with less demanding applications. In response, Sealed Air finally decided to enter the less demanding segments of the business with its own uncoated product, leveraging its sales force and distribution system. This allowed Sealed Air to offer its customers and distributors a fuller and more complete set of packaging solutions. Through its pricing strategy for the uncoated product, Sealed Air also influenced the profitability of the other uncoated bubble manufacturers and hence their interest in, and willingness to invest further in, the uncoated bubble business. For many customers Sealed Air was the 'one-stop' solution. Over time, through acquisitions and internal development, the company increased the range of packaging solutions it offered, reinforcing its already strong position in the market.

Managing suppliers

Powerful suppliers are a huge threat to the attractiveness and profitability of many markets. Managing suppliers is therefore often a very important element in ensuring that a market is attractive.

Ensure multiple sources and manage competition between them

One of the most obvious and powerful ways of controlling the power of suppliers is to ensure that there are at least two sources for all major inputs and as far as possible that the switching costs of moving between suppliers are kept low. In some cases a very large and attractive customer may be able to demand from a supplier, even one with a proprietary solution, that there be two sources of supply. This may involve one supplier agreeing to license intellectual property to another, or some form of cross-licensing agreement between suppliers. In some cases companies will actively encourage, or invest in, new suppliers in an attempt to control the power of a dominant player. For example, Coca-Cola encouraged the Holland Sweetener Company to build a plant in Europe to produce aspartame, a low-calorie sweetener, as it was coming off patent in Europe.[12] This meant that Monsanto, the holder of the patents on aspartame (with the Monsanto brand name NutraSweet), no longer had a monopoly. With a second source in the market, Coca-Cola and Pepsi were able to negotiate much better prices with Monsanto. If a company is going to try to develop one or more strong second sources, it is usually wise to do this as early as possible before a dominant player has emerged (obviously this was not possible with NutraSweet, where Monsanto had very strong patent protection). Once a supplier has become truly dominant it may have a greater willingness and ability to retaliate against a customer that is trying to loosen its grip on a market.

Where there are two or more competing suppliers a company can take steps to reinforce the competition between them, so as not to allow one to become the unchallenged leader. In some industries, such as telecommunications, major customers often split large infrastructure orders between two or three suppliers. In high technology markets that might involve trying to slow down the rate at which new technology is introduced by suppliers, in order to make sure that when it comes to market there will be more than one supplier.

Develop a credible threat of backward integration

Another powerful approach to controlling suppliers is to maintain a credible threat of backward integration. In the telecommunications industry, Qualcomm dominates the CDMA chipset market, one of the major technologies involved in mobile phones. Qualcomm's position was well protected by patents. However, Samsung, a leading supplier of CDMA handsets, which had licensed the CDMA technology from Qualcomm, tried to control Qualcomm's power by designing its own CDMA chipsets. Even if it was not totally successful in matching Qualcomm's leading-edge products, it would help to control the power of Qualcomm.

Don't squeeze suppliers too hard

While it is sensible for any company to try to maintain the upper hand with suppliers, exerting too much power over them can backfire both on you and on your direct competitors. It may encourage the suppliers to consolidate and/or exit the business, leaving you facing a much more concentrated and powerful group of suppliers. Also, if suppliers are squeezed too hard, they may lose interest in the market and/or decide to spend less money on R&D and capital investment in that particular part of their business. In many industries companies count on their supply chain to develop innovative products and services that allow them to stay ahead of competitors and substitutors. So such a move would be detrimental to the companies' long-run interests.

Managing potential entrants

While many companies pay a lot of attention to competitive analysis and managing competitors, there is often not a similar focus on managing potential entrants to a market, who could be a major future threat to profitability. There are some powerful ways of discouraging new entrants from moving into a market, including shaping their assumptions about the market, building and reinforcing barriers to entry and attempting to compromise a potential entrant's ability to enter a market.

Shape assumptions about the market

While the most obvious way to discourage potential entrants is to build and reinforce barriers to entry, a more effective way in some situations might be to lower potential entrants' interest in a market, so that they don't even seriously consider entry, or delay entry, sometimes for years. One way some companies have done this is to manage potential entrants' expectations about the profitability and/or strategic importance of a market.

Merrill Lynch seemed to do this in the late 1970s and early 1980s when it launched its Cash Management Account (CMA) into the US market. The CMA was a bundled product which provided a Merrill Lynch customer with a Visa debit card, automatic access to 'margin' on securities held in the customer's account, unlimited free chequing and a service that resulted in any free balances in the account being swept into a money market fund, daily if the balance exceeded $1000 and weekly otherwise. The annual fee for this package of services was $26. The customer was required to have a minimum of $20 000 in cash and/or securities in his or her Merrill Lynch account to open a CMA.

Merrill Lynch began marketing the account in 1977. Given that there was some question whether or not the 'banking' elements of this product were legal for a brokerage firm, the initial marketing was very low key. However, the product got some very positive reviews in the business press and, with the high inflation at the end of the 1970s, it became very attractive, bringing in about one thousand new customers a day. About 50% of these customers had no existing relationship with Merrill Lynch.

During this period Merrill Lynch executives suggested that CMA was not a profitable product for them. On the surface this was a reasonable statement, given the very low price and the high fixed cost of developing the systems to support the product, which some analysts estimated was well over $100 million. This undoubtedly helped keep potential entrants on the sidelines, since they would face similar fixed costs and could probably not hope to amortize those costs over as many customers as Merrill Lynch, which had the largest customer base of any US stockbroker. However, given the number of accounts that Merrill Lynch was attracting from competitors and the profit that would be generated from other investment activities in these accounts, it is likely that on an incremental basis the CMA was a highly profitable and strategic addition to the Merrill Lynch portfolio. In about

1980 several of Merrill Lynch's competitors seemed to realize that this was a business that was so strategic that they could not afford not to be in it. They began to develop the systems to allow them to offer competing products. But by this time Merrill Lynch had a huge head start and had built up significant switching barriers, so that many of its new customers were likely to stick with it even as competitors began to offer similar products.

A more recent example of a company trying to manage potential entrants' assumptions and discourage their entry into an emerging market was Apple's iTunes business, which allowed customers to buy music downloads legally. Apple was partially capitalizing on the popularity of its complementary iPod product, which allowed customers to store music files digitally on a small, user-friendly, portable device. By 2004 iPod was the leader in digital music players and worked with both PCs and Macintosh computers. iPods would only accept music uploaded into iTunes from a CD or downloaded from the web or a computer file using iTunes software. In iTunes' first year on the market there were 50 million downloads from the iTunes Music Store. However, in November 2003, Steve Jobs, Apple CEO, told analysts that iTunes was not a money-maker. If Apple was unable to make money with that volume of downloads, this was not an attractive market for other entrants into the digital music download business, which could not expect to capture the same volume as Apple. Apple could, of course, make money in this market because an aggressively priced iTunes product would enhance iPod sales. And analysts believed that the iPod business was very profitable for Apple.[13]

Even if shaping the assumptions of potential entrants about the potential profitability of a market only delays the entry of the potential entrant, this may give the incumbent an opportunity to build higher barriers to entry in the interim.

Build and reinforce barriers to entry

There are a variety of ways in which companies have successfully slowed down or blocked the entry of new players into a market. In some situations protecting intellectual property can be an effective tool, but it does not usually provide an insurmountable barrier. Depending on the nature of the business, effectively locking up the key channels for reaching customers, or controlling the supply of a key component, or making the market financially unattractive for a new entrant, may be more effective.

Access to channels is sometimes a key factor influencing the success of a new entrant in a market. In some cases existing players in the market allow entrants access to their channel, when it may have been possible either to block entry or to make it much more difficult and expensive. Haier, the Chinese manufacturer of appliances, gained entry into the retail-appliance channels in the US with a niche product, low-cost wine coolers. Wine coolers had been in the US market for a number of years, but had typically been speciality products marketed through speciality channels and had not attracted much attention from the mainstream refrigerator manufacturers. Haier was successful in getting Wal-Mart and some other large retailers to carry its wine coolers, which proved to be well made and Haier proved itself to be a reliable supplier. This paved the way for Haier to begin selling small and mid-sized regular refrigerators through these same channels. As it began to build up manufacturing capacity in the US for the larger refrigerators, it became an increasing threat to the mainstream manufacturers of refrigerators in the US. One tactic these manufacturers might have used was to aggressively introduce their own competing branded wine coolers into the mass channels to slow or prevent Haier's entry.

Another potentially powerful way to build barriers and discourage or slow entry and even to make life more difficult for smaller existing competitors is to identify pressing customer needs that are best met by investing in a process that involves similar fixed costs for all players regardless of size. For example, a couple of decades ago, when reservation systems were proprietary and expensive to build and operate, large airlines and car-rental companies had significant advantages in serving certain segments of customers. A local operator found it very difficult to expand nationally or internationally without huge fixed-cost investment that most could not afford. Similarly, in many industries, the expense of setting up a nationwide service network proved to be a significant barrier to foreign competitors trying to enter a national market. Again, many of the costs were fixed and many prospective new entrants simply did not have the volume to support the fixed-cost infrastructure. However, one of the dangers in this approach is that new entrants may find ways to make the fixed-cost infrastructure irrelevant. If a company is able to make its product highly reliable, customers will no longer care whether the company has a dense service infrastructure, since service will have become an unimportant element in the choice process. Japanese entrants into the North American market in several industries were able to do this in the 1970s and 1980s. If they couldn't make their products service free, they made the technology and servicing simple enough that a non-specialist service organization (hence a more variable cost expense) could do the task, obviating the need to invest in their own fixed-cost service infrastructure.

Compromise potential entrants' ability to enter

Sometimes attacking a potential entrant's cash sources can effectively prevent or inhibit its entry into a market. An example of this occurred in one large European country. The market concerned involved a consumer product that had a large branded segment and a smaller private-label segment, where a few large retailers were the major customers. The production process for the product in question was very capital intensive and the key to profitability was running the production facilities at close to capacity. A large, highly diversified, multinational company was the dominant player in the branded segment of the market, but it dabbled in the private label from time to time to ensure that its plant was operating at close to capacity. It was believed to have a very profitable business in this market. The second and only other major player in the market was a privately held company that was focused totally on the private label segment. Because of the strategy of its large competitor, the second player's capacity utilization was fairly volatile and this, combined with its reliance on a few large private label customers, made its profitability unsatisfactory.

At one point the large multinational heard from its advertising agency that the second player was looking for an advertising agency, and naturally assumed that this meant the second player was planning to enter the branded segment of the market. After discussions among the management team, the multinational decided to undermine the entry by attacking the private-label player's cash source – its sales to existing customers – in a somewhat devious way. It used its competitive intelligence to identify the retailer with which its competitor had the closest relationship. It believed the retailer in question was the largest for this product class. The multinational approached the retailer and offered it a very attractive price for a large contract, knowing that the retailer would immediately turn to its existing supplier and give it an opportunity to take the contract at that price. This it did and the private-label supplier was basically forced to take the business at an unprofitable price. To compound its problems, word of this low-price contract was leaked and it reached the private supplier's other customers, who also demanded price concessions. Suddenly, the private-label supplier was in survival mode with all thoughts of entering the branded business put on the back burner, probably permanently.

Another tactic that has been used to compromise potential entrants' ability to enter a market is to control a key input needed to compete successfully. Minnetonka pioneered the idea of Softsoap, a liquid soap that was conveniently dispensed by a small pump. With the initial success of the product, the challenge became to delay or prevent new entrants, which would likely include such powerful companies as Procter & Gamble and Unilever. Since there were no intellectual-property barriers, the management of Minnetonka realized that the best way to slow down the entry of the giants was to buy up the global supply of the little pumps – some 100 million of them. This action helped to ensure that the big players were delayed by more than a year and gave Minnetonka a chance to build its brand equity, making it a little more difficult and expensive for the giants to enter and perhaps preventing the entry of some smaller players.[14]

Summary and management guidelines

- Many companies pay very little attention to shaping their market environment and often fail to realize the profitability they might have from their markets. In many industries, use of any one of these strategies or tactics might have only a marginal impact on the business. However, if the management team thinks about all the market forces over an extended period and implements intelligent strategies and tactics to shape these market forces, the collective impact on profitability is likely to be significant. One company that we have referred to many times in this chapter is Intel, which seems to have active programmes to manage all the market forces impacting on its extended microprocessor business. The financial results it has achieved in this market in recent years have been outstanding. In 2000, the year just prior to the beginning of the semiconductor industry slump, Intel's Architecture Group (which includes the extended microprocessor business) had revenues of $27.3 billion and operating income of $12.5 billion. Even in 2001, Intel's worst year in the recession, the Architecture Group had revenues of $21.5 billion and operating income of $6.3 billion. While we have no way of knowing what would have happened to this business without the active management of the market forces, it is highly unlikely that it would have been either as large, or as profitable.

- It is particularly important that companies begin thinking about the management of market forces very early in their decision-making with respect to a market opportunity. This analysis and thinking should begin even before market entry, in order to help the management team to decide if the market looks like an attractive one in which to play. It is critical that this be not a static view, but rather a dynamic one that looks out over a reasonable planning horizon and tries to anticipate how the market might evolve as a result of possible actions by the market players and the environmental forces that will help shape it.

- Some companies do this type of analysis prior to entry, but once they are in the market they focus too much on achieving short-run success, rather than trying to shape the market to build an attractive business long-term. Perhaps they align themselves too quickly with one or two powerful customers in order to gain market share and soon find that these customers 'own' them.

• The framework proposed in this chapter can lead to some very powerful discussions among members of the marketing and management teams, both before entering a market and on an ongoing basis as strategies and tactics are refined over time. It can help to ensure that the company focuses its scarce resources on entering attractive markets and then extracts as much profit as possible from the markets it competes in. The following are the key points to consider for each of the six market forces discussed in this chapter:

Customers

- Choose the right customers
- Actively encourage new customers, perhaps by commoditizing your current customers' offerings (but do it carefully!)
- Don't encourage customer concentration
- Develop your brand
- Help your customers work with other suppliers
- Differentiate your solution and build switching costs
- Develop a credible threat of forward integration

Competitors

- Differentiate your solution
- Play to your strengths
- Acquire or merge with competitors

Complementors

- Encourage complementors
- Support complementors

Substitutes

- Improve price/performance of products relative to substitutes
- Increase switching costs
- 'Pigeon-hole' the substitutes
- Consider entering the substitute market

Suppliers

- Ensure multiple sources and manage suppliers to maintain competition between them
- Develop a credible threat of backward integration
- Don't squeeze suppliers too hard – it may hurt you!

Potential entrants

- Shape assumptions about the market
- Build and reinforce barriers to entry
- Compromise potential entrants' ability to enter

References

[1] A review of a number of announcements of CMOs in the summer of 2004 showed, in the role descriptions, a heavy emphasis on such areas as advertising and corporate publications, sales, product development, product marketing, channel marketing, sales training and providing marketing services to support lines of business.

[2] Porter, Michael, 'How Competitive Forces Shape Strategy', *Harvard Business Review*, March–April 1979, pp. 137–145.

[3] Brandenburger, Adam M. and Nalebuff, Barry J., 'The Right Game: Use Game Theory to Shape Strategy', *Harvard Business Review*, July–August 1995, pp. 57–71.

[4] Tatge, Mark, 'Start the Ground War', *Forbes*, 26 November 2001, pp. 146–148.

[5] Shankland, Stephen, 'Intel Program to Certify Server Components', *Globe and Mail*, 15 June 2004.

[6] 'Out-Discounting the Discounter', *Business Week*, 10 May 2004.

[7] 'Yun Jong Yong: Samsung', *Business Week*, 12 January 2004, p. 65.

[8] 'Alitalia's Rescue Tests EU's Resolve', *Wall Street Journal Europe*, 12 July 2004, p. 2.

[9] Brandenburger, Adam M. and Nalebuff, Barry J., 'The Right Game'.

[10] 'Microsoft Plays Video Leapfrog', *Business Week*, 10 May 2004.

[11] Guth, Robert A., 'Microsoft Offers Programming Tools to Spur Xbox', *Wall Street Journal*, 24 March 2004.

[12] Brandenburger, Adam M. and Nalebuff, Barry J., 'The Right Game', pp. 57–71.

[13] 'iTunes Sounds the Alarm', *Financial Times*, 5 April 2004.

[14] Brandenburger, Adam M. and Nalebuff, Barry J., 'The Right Game', pp. 57–71.

7
New Frontiers in Pricing for Profit

Professor John Walsh

U ntil recently, many marketing managers grappled with setting the one 'right' price – set too high or too low and profits suffered. Opportunities to price-discriminate were few and far between. Today the combination of databases and technology presents marketers with a multitude of ways in which to offer different prices to different customers. While the opportunity here is clear – charging more to those willing to pay more – the pricing decision has become much more complex. It has moved from simply setting just one number to setting many, and to determining a plethora of payment structures. This chapter will deal with the economic and psychological factors at play in this new world that permits almost infinite flexibility in pricing. What should managers consider in setting their price structures? And how should we handle consumer perceptions of pricing?

Back to the future

You are about to make a bid for a product you've wanted for a long time. You've bought from the vendor many times before. He knows all about you. You were asked your demographic details the first time you visited this site. You said where you live, what work you do, your marital status, the number of children you have. Moreover, all your previous purchases are in the vendor's database. You can be compared to previous purchasers of this item. How much it is worth to you is easy to estimate. Bid too low and someone else may get the product. If you bid much higher than anyone else, you'll get the item, but will you be able to enjoy it feeling a bit of a sucker? As the window of time you have to make your final offer comes to a close, you pick a price and hope for the best. eBay? Priceline.com? Perhaps. But it could also be a bazaar in the Middle East or, if we were to travel through time, a marketplace in ancient Rome or Greece.

There's really nothing new about flexible or differentiated pricing. Nor is setting price with the help of accurate and exhaustive customer information truly innovative. In fact, the concept of fixed, posted prices is relatively recent. Auctions date back to the Greece of 500 BC, when Herodotus first documented a strange new way of selling he had observed.[1] Until the Industrial Revolution in mid-1700s England, prices were determined through one-on-one haggling or auctions. In the agrarian societies that preceded the steam engine and mass production, economic activity was primarily characterized by farmers bringing their products to market and taking care of sales themselves. This changed with mechanized transportation. Agricultural and mass-produced products were distributed far from their point of origin. Middlemen were needed to facilitate distribution and the producer lost contact with the purchaser. With limited ability to distribute information on the cost of production and transportation, prices had to be determined centrally rather than at the point of sale. Fixed pricing replaced dynamic pricing for most consumer products, with unique items like art and real estate remaining among the few exceptions.

Technological advances have brought us full circle. The Internet, data-mining and CRM (customer relationship management) software and sheer computing power have given new life to the old proverb 'the worth of a thing is the price it will bring'. Now, the worth of a thing doesn't have to be determined by the seller. It can evolve dynamically over time and differently across customer groups. But the price setters of today have not inherited the business acumen of their ancestors, and this return to old ways, albeit in a turbo-charged format, has proved challenging to many. The opportunity to freely change prices from one moment to another and to price differently to different customers raises many questions: Will the impact on our profitability necessarily be positive? And how will customers adjust to the phenomenon?

Coca-Cola moved to embrace dynamic pricing in 1999. Doug Ivester, Coca-Cola's chairman at the time, announced that the company was developing new vending machines with a thermometer inside. The machine would automatically increase the price of soft drinks when it sensed hot weather. Ivester said: 'Coca-Cola is a product whose utility varies from moment to moment. In a final summer sports championship when people meet in a stadium to enjoy themselves, the utility of Coke is very high. So, it is fair to make it more expensive. The machine will simply make the process automatic.'[2]

Needless to say, the announcement generated quite a bit of press. While the *San Francisco Chronicle* called it 'a cynical ploy to exploit the thirst of faithful customers',[3] the *New York Times* pointed out that 'it essentially extends to another industry what has become the practice for airlines'.[4] With memories of the failed introduction of New Coke in 1985 not yet erased, the investment community was concerned that Coca-Cola would alienate consumers. While people might tolerate paying different prices for the same seats on aeroplanes, shareholders were concerned that the marketplace might not accept this from a consumer packaged-goods company. Pepsi, sensing an opportunity, was quick to point out: 'We believe machines that raise prices in hot weather exploit consumers who live in warm climates. At Pepsi, we are focused on innovations that make it easier for consumers to buy a soft drink, not harder.'[5]

With pressure mounting and the press mostly negative, it was left to a Coca-Cola spokesman to limit the damage: 'You might be able to lower the price. It might be discounted at a vending machine in a building during the evening or when there's less traffic', he said. But it was too late. Finally the venture was killed off with an announcement that Coca-Cola would not be pursuing the variable-price vending machine.

What does this tell us? The jury is out on whether it was a bad idea or not. Clearly, people who buy Coke accept variable pricing from multiple other product and service providers, so why not Coke too? Could it be that variable pricing only applies to certain industries? Doubtful. Price discrimination is alive and well even in soft drinks, as location, package size and sales channel, to name but a few, are all utilized to vary price. Could it be that consumers simply would never accept a company varying the price of the same pack sold in the same channel over time? Doubtful also – supermarkets are forever varying prices with promotions, coupons and discounts. Besides, consumers could be educated to accept variable pricing at vending machines and surely no company would be better placed to make this work than Coca-Cola. After all, Coke's marketing group has built the world's most-valuable brand[6] with a product that's really nothing more than brown, fizzy sugar-water. Surely variable pricing would be an easy sale. Perhaps it all comes back to the way the concept was introduced to the public. Justifying a price hike through delivering increased value may work for an accountant like Mr Ivester, but not for the average consumer. If Mr Ivester had studied the work of 2002 Nobel Prize winner Daniel Kahneman, he'd have approached the announcement differently and talked of lowering prices when the weather is cold. Framing the issue as a gain for consumers, rather than a loss, would certainly have made variable pricing seem more attractive, and potentially a success for his company.

The next section deals with the economic issues involved in price discrimination. The impact of consumer psychology on pricing follows subsequently.

The economics of price discrimination

'There are two fools in every market. One charges too much. The other charges too little.' The challenge of not being one of the fools in this old proverb is illustrated in the following example. Let's say a little more than 2000 people attend a music festival where a hot-dog vendor is selling his wares. He buys his hot dogs for 20 cents each and wishes to make as much profit as possible. The demand curve he faces is given in Figure 7.1.

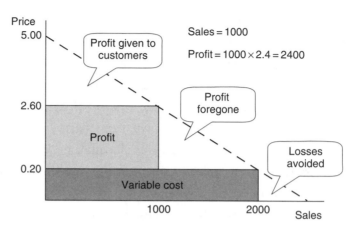

Figure 7.1 Pricing with a *single* price

What price should he put on his hot dogs? If he charges a price close to €5, the maximum price anyone will pay, he'll have a high margin, but very low volumes. A price close to his variable cost will increase volume greatly, but at the loss of margin. His profit is maximized at €2.6 but, having sold a thousand hot dogs, should he go home happy? Not if he thinks of the thousand people who didn't buy because the price was too high, but to whom it would have been profitable to sell. And certainly not if he thinks of the thousand people who bought, but who would have been happy to pay more. If he could find a way to identify those who would pay more and charge them more, and charge those who would pay less a lower price, he could go home much happier. As Figure 7.2 illustrates, he would increase his profit by 33% if he could simply charge two different prices to two 'segments' and, of course, prohibit them from trading with each other. Indeed, he needn't stop there. If he could charge each person the maximum they were willing to pay (so, one person would pay €5, one person would pay 20 cents and everyone

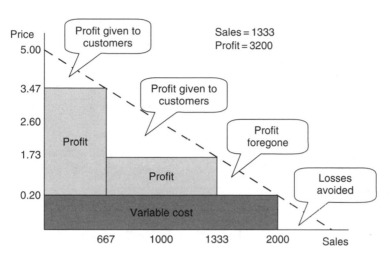

Figure 7.2   Pricing with *two* prices

else a price in between), he would double his profits over the single-price scenario.

To implement differential pricing schemes that capture most of the value created, vendors need to have information on customers' willingness to pay and they need to create barriers between customers to prevent them from paying a lower price intended for another. This also involves preventing resale between customers, as those obtaining a lower price may try to profit from the situation.

Economists have generally considered there to be three approaches to differential pricing:

- **Individualizing** prices so that each customer pays the maximum he or she is willing to pay

- **Developing a menu** of different products or services, so there are different types of offerings available at different prices, and letting buyers self-select the product/price they'd like
- **Categorizing** customers by observable characteristics and charging different prices to each based on what is known or assumed about their willingness to pay.

Individualizing

Long considered a theoretical ideal applicable to only a few situations (auctions and one-to-one negotiation, for example), personalizing price to the maximum a customer is willing to pay is clearly difficult to execute on a large scale. However, technology has recently widened the possibilities here. Take auctions, for example. Until the advent of the Internet, the cost of running an auction was very high and so it was suited to only a few expensive products. Auction websites like eBay changed that, by bringing remote buyers and sellers together in a cost-efficient manner. Clearly eBay has been a success in person-to-person sales, but auctions and the Internet have wider applications.

Auctions

Sun Microsystems started auctioning its products to small and medium-sized businesses in late 1999 and has expanded sales via auctions to this day. Scott McNealy, Sun CEO, says: 'I'm a total believer in the spot market and the auction of everything that isn't bolted down.'[7] He argues that if a product or service doesn't provide the value it is priced at, people will not buy anyway. So it is best to let the marketplace determine the price. Sun has also learned that about a third of the people who buy at auction have not bought Sun previously. Also, McNealy points out that 'on-line auctions should give us better insight into the workings of cause and effect in the marketplace. We'll be able to see, clearly and without delay, what happens when a competitor announces a new product and how that affects the demand for our products.'[8]

An interesting application of an auction was the 2004 IPO of Google. Eschewing the traditional IPO route of an offer price being predetermined by an investment bank, Google decided to run a bidding process akin to a Dutch auction. Potential investors bid a price for the number of shares they wanted to buy. Google's underwriters then used this information to determine the price that all buyers would pay – this would be the lowest price at which Google could sell all the shares it was putting on the market and all bidders would pay the same price. Thus, successful bidders bought the shares either at or below the price they bid. Those who bid a price below the market-clearing price were not allocated shares.

Having determined a market-clearing price of $85 at auction, the shares started trading on 19 August 2004 and immediately shot up to slightly over $100, where they finished at the end of the trading day. The trading volume was 22 million shares, remarkably high given that the free float of the IPO was 19.6 million shares. While commentators viewed this sharp price rise as a failure of the auction process, perhaps it was predictable, if not a certainty. Given that people bought at a price at or below the value they had already put on the shares, it is not surprising that the price should increase once the shares could be traded.

This perhaps illustrates best the dangers of auctions. Whether the design is a Dutch auction of the type used by Google or a more traditional English auction, when volumes are small, you can identify the one or two sellers willing to pay the most, or at least they reveal themselves through the auction process. When you are selling large volumes, there will be dispersion in the willingness-to-pay of potential buyers, and the one market-clearing price will be the minimum. You can sequence auctions to try to extract more from those willing to pay more, but if they expect many subsequent auctions, these efforts will have limited success. Interestingly, eBay has introduced a 'buy now' option, where sellers can set a price at which buyers can buy a product immediately without going through the auction process. This is proving popular with sellers of products available in large volumes. And, revealingly, it is being employed by Sun Microsystems.

An additional complication of auctions is that it is possible, and common, for individuals to hide their identity. Anonymity takes away the power of sellers to adjust price (in the case of auctions, the reserve price) to the buyer's willingness to pay. So, the surplus in the trade (that is, the difference between the lowest price the seller will accept and the highest price the buyer is willing to pay) ends up going mostly to the buyer. Sellers can exploit customer information to increase their share of this surplus. Some companies have been using information on purchasers to great effect in individualizing prices and even the product/service itself.

Exploiting databases

Harrah's, the US casino operator, presents its customers with a gold card, to be used every time a gamble is made. The incentive for the gambler to use the card is an accumulation of points that leads to discounts. When the collected data is analysed, the casino can estimate the potential house take from each customer. The gamblers with the most profitable behaviour receive tailored discounts and promotions. By experimenting with different offers, Harrah's can determine which incentives work best for specific gamblers. So, for example, some gamblers may be more likely to gamble more when offered complimentary dinners or tickets to shows. Others may place more value on a free room in which a spouse can remain while wagers are being made. By analysing gambling data, Harrah's can calculate the net present value of the investment in these incentives.

Even airlines, in the most competitive of industries, have benefited from using their frequent-flyer programmes in this way. For example, Clive Jones of Economics Research Associates tells us: 'Back in 1980, before the programmes started in earnest, the average business traveller had a half-hour tolerance for delay before changing airlines. Booked on American from O'Hare to LaGuardia, you would walk next door to United if your plane was more than 30 minutes late. By the late 1990s, this tolerance had increased to 3.5 hours.'[9] With this kind of loyalty has come a willingness to pay, if not from one's own pocket, then from one's company's coffers. Unfortunately, though, while frequent-flier programmes may have helped to moderate competition among established carriers, they haven't been enough to stem the tide of low-fare and low-cost airlines.

Perhaps the most interesting and in-your-face application of database utilization in pricing occurs in supermarkets. Catalina Marketing Corporation logs 250 million transactions per week at 21 000 supermarkets. They track the purchases of 100 million households who are members of store loyalty programmes and deliver 4.5 billion customized promotions per year. Shoppers receive targeted coupons based on very precise modelling of their behaviour as they check out. So, at the checkout they receive coupons for perhaps competitive or complementary products to the one they have just bought. Alternatively, if they typically buy a brand of orange juice but have bought a different, perhaps less profitable, brand on their last few trips, they may receive a coupon incentive to repurchase their old brand. Catalina claims redemption rates of between 8 and 11%, which is approximately ten times higher than traditional, untargeted coupons. Distributing coupons in this way offers unique prices to each individual based on his or her behaviour. In addition, since the discounts are not posted, it's hard for one individual to become aware of a better deal offered to another. And, as the coupons are personalized, they can be made non-transferable.

It's worthwhile considering potential consumer backlash to individualizing prices. Consumers tend not to think about the price discounts they may be offered, but rather fear that companies may require them to pay more. Amazon.com is an interesting case. Amazon.com is probably the company with the most information on its customers. It has so much information that it can recommend items customers hadn't even considered but end up buying when the suggestion is made. It was only a matter of time before Amazon used this information to its advantage in pricing. In mid-2000, the company offered different prices to different people. One customer found that after buying a DVD for $24.49, the next week he was quoted $26.24 for the same item. When he removed the 'cookies' that identified his computer, he found the same DVD priced at $22.72.[10] Amazon was set upon in the media. There was public outcry that prices could be manipulated in this way – that information about one's past shopping behaviour could be used to set prices. Amazon.com's response, in which it distanced itself from pricing based on demographics, is very interesting: 'In retrospect, this random testing was a mistake and we regret it because it created uncertainty and complexity for our customers. We've never tested and we never will test prices based on customer demographics. What we did was a random price test....'[11] We'll come back to this example later in the chapter when we talk about pricing to categories of customers.

Menus

Henry Ford was not an advocate of offering menus to customers. His mandate that you could have his Model T motorcar in any colour so long as it was black is well known to students of business history. Competition from Alfred Sloan of General Motors, with multiple brands like Cadillac, Chevrolet and Buick, in multiple colours and styles, led to the Model T's demise in 1927. Ford today is a very different company, owning many different brands (Volvo, Jaguar, Mercury to name but a few), each catering to different consumer preferences. Within each brand, different models make up a wide product line, from which all, from the young teenager to the retired old-age pensioner, can choose. Even each model can be further refined with a wide range of options.

While Henry Ford favoured a one-size-fits-all approach, his descendants prefer to put a range of product versions on the marketplace and have consumers self-select the one they prefer. The closer a product gets to a consumer's ideal, the more he or she should be willing to pay for it. The challenge for marketers is pricing these different versions to maximize profit and manage the product line for cannibalization. In addition, with multiple product versions comes additional cost. Managing the product line to maximize profit is not an easy task.

Leveraging the product line

While this isn't a new problem for marketers, we are seeing the opportunity for some new and creative solutions. Products and services now exist such that the marginal cost of making an additional change is very low. The cost of customization has diminished and the ability to price-discriminate has increased accordingly.

Information goods, with high fixed costs of creation but extremely low marginal costs of reproduction, provide almost endless possibilities for differential pricing. For example, Intuit offers multiple versions of its tax-preparation software, TurboTax. Paying $59.95 instead of $39.95 gets you TurboTax Premier instead of TurboTax Deluxe. However, TurboTax Basic, selling at $29.95, is a relative bargain. The more expensive products provide information from which only people with more complex financial situations, and therefore a greater ability to pay, would benefit. The marginal cost of creating the more advanced versions is not that great. In fact, it is probably more appropriate to think of the marginal cost of taking features away from the higher-end version than of adding them to the lower-end one.

Gettyimages, an Internet-based supplier of digital images, provides the same image at increasing levels of resolution at increasing price levels. The variance in price can be great. For example, a 1 MB image for sale at £45.99 is available in 16 MB format for £155.99. In this way, Gettyimages is imitating

IBM, which famously inserted a chip into its Laser Printer Series E. The Series E was no different from its regular laser printer, which could print at ten pages per minute – except that, as a result of the chip insertion, the Series E could print at only five pages per minute.[12] Like IBM, Gettyimages is incurring additional cost to damage or crimp products, so that it can price-discriminate and increase its profits.

In high fixed, low variable cost businesses, it is not unusual to see behaviour similar to Gettyimages. Take *Encyclopedia Britannica*, for example. The change in its cost structure brought about initially by CD-ROMs and subsequently by the Internet has brought with it myriad offerings. A visit to Britannica Online reveals many more electronic products than the traditional 32-volume print set, all available at much lower prices.

Airlines and hotels have been dealing with these issues throughout their history. Both high fixed, low variable cost businesses, it is not unusual for them to 'damage' their products. For example, demanding a Saturday night stay-over, advance purchase of 21 days, minimal flexibility to change destination, etc., reduces the value in the eye of the purchaser. It does seem unusual for a producer to willingly 'damage' his service. After all, the cost of flying a plane or providing a room-night doesn't decrease if the booking is made 21 days in advance. The firm is, however, introducing these restrictions to provide barriers to those who value the unrestricted offering. This is not a new practice in the transportation industry. In fact the following quote, dealing with ticket prices on the French railway system, comes from the economist Dupuit in 1849: 'It is not because of the few thousand francs which would have to be spent to put a roof over the third-class carriages or to upholster the third-class seats that some company or other has open carriages with wooden benches ... What the company is trying to do is prevent the passengers who can pay the second-class fare from travelling third class; it hits the poor, not because it wants to hurt them, but to frighten the rich.'[13]

A challenge for price setters of today is to set prices with the same mindset as these French transportation companies, even if they are sitting in industries not accustomed to this kind of thinking.

Bundling

Another way for firms to price discriminate is to bundle products and/or services. Variance in purchasers' willingness to pay can be exploited to maximize a firm's profit. Restaurants are old masters at bundling, by offering fixed-price menus. Let us look at an example to see how this works.

The willingness to pay for appetizer, main course and dessert for three customers is given in Table 7.1. The restaurant must leverage this information

Table 7.1   An example of three restaurant customers' willingness to pay

Customer	Appetizer	Main course	Dessert	All courses
A	$12	$18	$1	$31
B	$9	$17	$7	$33
C	$2	$18	$9	$29

to maximize profit. Assuming marginal cost is zero (which may not be too big a leap for many restaurants), the restaurant should price the appetizer at $9, yielding purchases from customers A and B, but not C, and therefore $18 in profit. The restaurant is best off pricing the main course at $17, resulting in purchases from all customers and profit of $51. As with the appetizer, the restaurant should charge $7 for dessert, yielding a purchase from both B and C and profit of $14. So, the total take for the restaurant is $83, with sales of two appetizers, two desserts and three main courses.

Is there a way for the restaurant to be better off? Yes, there is. If it prices a three-course meal at $29, all customers will buy and the restaurant will take $87, yielding a $4 profit improvement. Most restaurants offer fixed-price multiple-course meals for this reason – to extract purchases from those with a low willingness to pay for certain items. However, restaurants typically only offer this as an option, in addition to individually priced courses. Returning to the example we can see why. If the restaurant offers customers the option to buy either a three-course meal or individual courses, it should radically change its prices. It should offer the three-course meal at $33, resulting in a purchase from B. Now, since only A and C are in the market for an appetizer, it should increase the appetizer price to $12. Similarly, with customer B happily working his way through his three courses, he is irrelevant to the pricing of the main course, so that price should increase a dollar to $18. Finally, the dessert should be priced at $9, since customer A puts such a low value on it and customer C is willing to pay $9. The impact on profit of offering these two pricing schemes side by side is positive. The restaurant takes in $33 from customer B, $30 from customer A and $27 from customer C, yielding a total of $90. And, interestingly, the optimal prices for the individual courses increase over the prices that would be set if menu pricing wasn't offered.

Looking at the final price schedule for the restaurant, the menu seems like a great offer. The menu is $33, whereas the composite parts are priced such that they total $39. While diners in the restaurant will think that they are receiving a discount for buying more courses than they otherwise might, the smart proprietor knows that offering a menu allows him to inflate the prices of individual courses and drive up his total profit.

While this example may seem a little theoretical, it plays out in every town, every day. Offering a fixed-price menu allows restaurant owners to charge more for individual courses than they could if they didn't have the menu option. And this concept is being leveraged by higher-tech firms. Software, telecom, Internet service providers all offer bundles as a way to capture more of an individual's willingness-to-pay surplus. On-line subscriptions to magazines and newspapers follow this approach. The subscription charge to have access to both *Barron's* and the *Wall Street Journal* on-line is $39 annually for subscribers to the print version of either publication; it's $79 to non-subscribers.

Indeed, an interesting feature of the modern economy is the size of the bundles on offer. Bundles are growing and becoming more complicated! Products and services are being combined. The number of options is increasing and pricing is becoming more difficult for managers and purchasers alike.

Take Sky TV, the UK-based satellite TV operator, for example. Sky provides access to in excess of a hundred TV stations. Some, like say the Disney

Channel or proprietary sports channels, offer very desirable content. Other channels are simply those available for free, such as BBC1. The pricing challenge for Sky is many-fold. The marketplace variance in willingness to pay for these channels is huge. One channel – think again of Disney – could have huge value in some households, whereas in others, where visiting children are an unwelcome occasional occurrence, it may even provide negative value. One possibility for Sky would be to price each channel separately. An alternative would be to create a limited number of bundles from which households could choose. Sky, and pretty much all other satellite and cable television operators, follow the latter approach. Why? Some light has been shed on this recently.[14] Researchers at Stanford University have found that the law of large numbers averages out the high and low values individuals may attribute to specific channels. So, in general terms, the value two people put on a bundle could be approximately the same, even though they may value each of the components very differently. Hence, it is easier to predict the value that the market will put on a bundle of channels, and the resulting marketplace demand is more tolerant of price increases for the bundle. This impact is particularly noticeable, but not restricted to, situations where demand for goods in the bundle has limited or even negative correlation. So, if we go back to the example of the print and on-line versions of the *Wall Street Journal*, it is unlikely that demand for both has a positive correlation – while some readers may want both, most will want one or the other. Hence, these are ideal candidates for bundling.

This is in part why micro-payments have failed to take off. In the early days of the Internet, visionaries thought consumers would access on-line content and pay very small amounts per transaction. So, for example, instead of paying a subscription to the *Wall Street Journal*, readers would pay per article viewed. Instead, we have seen the subscription model dominate. This is essentially a version of bundling. As with the Coke vending-machine example, it may simply be an issue of giving individuals a payment structure with which they are comfortable. In any event, until now, consumers have preferred paying a bundled price, essentially a flat fee. Witness the success of Netflix, the DVD rental outfit. Initially charging a per-movie fee, they switched to a model of $20 per month for unlimited DVD rentals (e.g. a subscriber can have three movies out at a time, as the movies are returned to Netflix, the subscriber's next choice is mailed out). Subscriptions have soared and competitors like Blockbuster have imitated the pricing structure.

However, it must be said, we have seen alternatives take off too. Apple's iTunes, which we discussed in the previous chapter, offers individual songs for download (so, unbundled from an album) for 99 cents per song. Over 70 million downloads in its first year would indicate some success for this approach. Perhaps it is too early to declare the death, or more accurately stillbirth, of micro-payments. But we would need to see them more commonly used before declaring that they had arrived.

Related to bundling, software companies have discovered that a new version of a software program provides only marginal incremental value to current owners. So current owners need some enticement to buy the next version. To these, the software companies offer 'upgrades'. In a world where marginal costs are zero, the upgrade, priced below the stand-alone version, is a way for companies to capture additional sales and profit, without putting profit from the stand-alone version at risk. For example, visit the Symantec website and be offered 40% off recent releases if you are already a customer. This is hardly an act of kindness or even a reward for customer loyalty. It is offered simply because the improved version has only incremental benefit for current customers. Those who have not yet bought any version will value it much more.

The Internet has proved an effective delivery vehicle for information goods, and with it pricing has morphed the concepts we have been discussing – updates and subscriptions. While in the past there was marginal cost involved in the sales and distribution of information goods, nowadays, with Internet delivery, marginal cost of sales is truly zero. So we see more licensing of software products, where annual subscriptions are paid and updates come continuously. Take anti-virus software, for example. McAfee, one of the leaders in the field, offers an annual subscription for $34.99. Without the Internet as a vehicle to deliver updates, this business model might well be unprofitable.

Categorizing

Sellers often use characteristics of the buyer to set price. Age, location, occupation, etc., all reveal a little about the buyer's willingness to pay, and the seller adjusts price accordingly. Student and old-age pensioner 'discounts' are simply ways of extracting more from those who can pay more and increasing sales to those who can't, albeit at lower margin. Supermarkets and petrol stations charge different prices by location. They may say these differences are driven by differential labour and property costs, but some have claimed they are because of differences in willingness to pay and the availability, or dearth, of alternative stores.

However, even with pricing based on purchaser characteristics, technology has helped the seller extract a little more profit. Victoria's Secret, the US-based retailer of women's lingerie, sends catalogues with different prices based on postal code. Customers in neighbourhoods categorized as being free-spending by Victoria's Secret's database receive higher prices. More cheekily, Staples, the office supplies company, penalizes those customers who limit their information search (or rewards those who don't...) as they send multiple catalogues with different prices to the *same* customers. Those who buy randomly from the catalogues risk paying the higher price.[15] Those who give the purchase careful consideration are rewarded.

Not unlike the example of the IBM printer and Gettyimages in the previous section, sellers have used technology to reduce the functionality of the products they sell to some geographies. Take DVD players, for instance. Manufacturers have created 'regions' to fence off geographic areas from each other: a DVD movie bought in the USA, for example, is formatted not to work on a European DVD player. In doing so, they have restricted resale and flow of DVD players and disks, and have been able to extract higher prices in some areas. The effectiveness of the pricing ploy is evident in the high demand for (relatively hard-to-find) region-free players outside the US.

The Internet has not always been a friend of differential pricing. In fact, it has made traditional pricing structures obsolete and brought in new forms. Take the hotel business, for example. The establishment of travel intermediaries such as Expedia has caused a problem for hotel operators. Channels like Expedia are great outlets for disposing of 'distressed' stock, where otherwise vacant rooms can be sold at a low price. Remember, in this business, marginal cost is extremely low, so any revenue is essentially additional profit. However, it is in Expedia's interest to post and advertise the lowest prices, to encourage visitors to come to its site. With very visible low prices, hotel operators found it difficult to keep prices high with high-margin customers. As a result, hotel operators are distancing themselves from intermediaries such as Expedia.[16] However, in a twist on the discussion we had on auctions, hotel operators still happily sell through Priceline.com. Ironically, Priceline.com guarantees the seller anonymity until after the sale is made, hence limiting the information the buyer has about the seller, and the buyer's ability to price-compare.

The fact that Amazon wished to make it clear it did not experiment with price based on demographics reveals one major issue with this sort of price discrimination – people think it's unfair. This is because they can't change their demographics. They can decide whether to buy the good, better or best product in a product line, or whether to buy a bundle or individual items. It is not as easy to change their location, age or gender.

And so, price discrimination has caught the eye of lawmakers and regulators. In June 2004 the European Commission ended a six-month investigation into airline pricing. They found great disparity in the prices charged across Europe, even for the same routing. For example, a return flight from Frankfurt to Berlin, which cost €88 when purchased in Germany, cost €268 in Belgium. While it was widely believed that a legal case would be difficult to prosecute, 'a little bit of naming and shaming has achieved results', said Giles Gantelet of the EU Transport Commissioner's office.[17]

On the other side of the Atlantic, the common practice of 'ladies' night', or free admission for women, in nightclubs has been outlawed in ten US states.[18] It is worthwhile keeping in mind that laws are set by elected representatives and it is best not to upset their electorate. And the elect-orate generally doesn't like prices determined on demographics. This can have far-reaching consequences. For example, Catalina Marketing has been asked by its clients, mostly retailers, to keep a low profile and not to say too much about its couponing activities: 'This is something we'd love to talk about, but we can't...It bothers them...we just need to lay low.'[19]

Psychology in pricing

If the reaction of the masses is to drive what is acceptable (and what is not) in pricing, perhaps psychology can be just as informative as econom-ics. It is useful to review recent work in a relatively new discipline, Behavioural Decision Theory (BDT). Departing from the view held by economists – that man is a rational decision-maker – BDT has shown that consumer psychology greatly impacts the way in which consumers react to prices and price changes, and that consumers have particular, systematic biases. These should impact the ways in which companies set their prices.

The last few decades have seen much experimental work carried out in an effort to understand exactly how individuals make choices. These research-ers did not accept the premise that consumers are rational beings who choose the lowest price alternative when all else is held equal. They studied the way choices can be presented to consumers to see if preferences could be systematically altered and if prices and price changes could be presented in ways viewed preferentially by consumers.

There is a large body of literature resulting from this work. We have selected some of the most striking and most relevant results for managers in a price-setting role.

Attraction Effect

You are considering buying a new camera. You like the Nikon brand and there are two choices available to you – a low-priced alternative that is rated low by industry sources Consumer Reports and a high-priced alternative that is rated high. Let us say that, while you are mulling over the purchase in your mind, Nikon introduces a third product. This one is between the two incumbent products on quality, but it is priced even higher than the more expensive camera. This camera is clearly a dog! It is the most expensive on the market and it has only average quality. There is no way you would ever choose it, right? Right! And there is no way it would ever influence your choice, right? Wrong! Just because you wouldn't choose it, doesn't mean it won't influence you. If you are like most people, the presence of this unappealing offering will influence which of the other two you choose. It will increase the likelihood that you choose the more expensive alternative. Why? Because the new product is worse than the high-price, high-quality alternative on all dimensions (it has an even higher price and it has lower quality). And, in many studies that have investigated this, the percentage of people who choose the high-priced alternative increases when the third, even more expensive alternative is introduced.[20] Interestingly, this has been proven to be a robust effect, influencing not just novice consumers but also professionals: studies of doctors prescribing medicines have shown them to be susceptible to it.[21] We make the dominating alternative appear more attractive by introducing a dominated alternative, hence the phenomenon is called the Attraction Effect.

For many companies, exploiting the Attraction Effect is not worth it. The cost of carrying an additional product in the product line just to change people's choices a little, albeit to higher margin products, may outweigh any gains. And retailers may be unlikely to give valuable shelf space to a slow-moving product in order to increase purchases of another product. The opportunity cost of the shelf space may be too great to ignore. However, in the electronic world, with low marginal cost of changing and editing product variants, the Attraction Effect could be utilized effectively.

It may be interesting at this point to reflect on the introduction of New Coke in 1985. Changing the cherished formula of Coke provoked outrage among loyal consumers. Three months after the company had taken the old formula off the market it was forced to reintroduce it under the guise of 'Coke Classic'. Sold side by side with New Coke into the mid-1990s, Classic Coke sales steadily increased. New Coke was a disaster. Market share quickly fell to less than 1% and the product limped along for years until it was finally taken off the market in 1995.

Widely considered one of the worst marketing mistakes of the twentieth century, an interesting fact is that measures of Coca-Cola's image, stock price and market share all rose with both products on the market.[22] Commenting on the outcome of the New Coke launch, Don Keough, president of Coca-Cola at the time, said: 'Some critics will say that Coca-Cola made a marketing mistake. Some cynics will say that we planned the whole thing. The truth is that we are not that dumb, and we are not that smart.'[23] Perhaps without planning, Coca-Cola unwittingly discovered the Attraction Effect.

Compromise Effect

Closely related to the Attraction Effect is a phenomenon known as the Compromise Effect. People like to choose those items that are a compromise between the many alternatives on offer. So, for example, when presented with a choice between small, medium and large portions at a restaurant, people tend to choose the middle alternative – the medium-sized, medium-priced portion. It is no surprise that McDonald's offers 'Super Size' portions of French fries and soft drinks – even if people don't choose the largest available, they may trade up from the smaller option they might otherwise have chosen. Interestingly, this effect has been shown to be more pronounced when individuals have to explain or justify their choices to someone else.[24] So, where multiple people are involved in a decision, say for more expensive purchases such as homes, cars and large home appliances, creating a lengthy product line with one or more very expensive alternatives should cause people to trade up.

Endowment Effect

Buy a computer from Dell and you'll receive anti-virus software from Norton for a 90-day trial period. What Dell and Norton are capitalizing on is the Endowment Effect – that is, people tend to value things they already own more than they would if they did not have those items in their possession. So the computer purchaser is more likely to buy the software at the end of the free trial period than if the trial period was not offered.

The most famous demonstration of this effect was in an experiment at Cornell University in New York.[25] Students were randomly given gifts of a mug or a chocolate bar of equal value and told that they could trade with another student if they preferred the gift they did not receive to the one they did. While one might expect 50% of people to switch, given the random allocation, in fact only 10% did.

Recent work has shown that the Endowment Effect is less observable among experts in a marketplace.[26] So, Dell's ploy is more likely to work with a first-time buyer than an experienced purchaser. However, price setters seem to know this intuitively and the 'free trial' offers tend to be aimed at novices or the uninitiated, or to launch new products onto the market. Indeed, the term 'nagware' seems to have been spawned by this practice. Nagware describes software, available for free download and use, that automatically reminds users to register and pay after the free trial period is over. Offered free, trial and adoption are higher than they would be if a price were charged. And constant nagging to register and pay when the product is on one's computer will yield more purchases than if one had to pay before trial and use.

Anchoring Effect

When the 'fair' or typical price of a product is unknown, people can be manipulated in the price they would expect to pay. In addition, when the typical price is known, this serves as a reference from which they are unwilling to deviate. Let us give an example of the former condition, which is an experiment we run in our classrooms at IMD, adapted from original work by Tversky and Kahnemann:[27]

> Q1: Is the price of a tie at the IMD gift shop greater than CHF 30?
>
> Q2: What is your best estimate of the price of a tie at the IMD gift shop?

The answer to the second question usually averages CHF 50. However, when we change the value in the first question to CHF 100, the answer to the second question changes greatly and usually averages around CHF 75. If this reflects people's willingness to pay, then they are easily manipulated.

The evidence that people are indeed easily manipulated in this way is overwhelming. A study in Germany, involving the price of a used car, found that mechanics estimated the value of a car to be DM 1000 higher when the owner said he thought it was worth DM 5000 than when he put a value on it of DM 2800.[28] More disturbingly, anchoring has been shown to influence juries in personal-injury lawsuits – the more you ask for, the more you get.[29]

Anchoring is a robust and pervasive effect. For example, the starting price of an on-line auction has been shown to influence the final bidding price.[30] Consider the eBay 'buy now' option discussed earlier. Certainly it anchors the buyer such that he or she thinks he or she is getting a deal if the final auction price is relatively low.

Even when there is absolutely no relationship between the anchor and the price, anchoring is at play. In one experiment in the US, subjects were asked to write down the last two digits of their social security number. Then they were asked to assign prices to a range of products. Amazingly, those who had written down high social security numbers allocated higher prices to the products, in some cases over 100% higher than their peers.[31]

Anchoring can play a role not just when prices are unknown, but when they are known. When consumers are familiar with a product category and with the typical price for a product, it has been shown that they use the usual price as a reference (or anchor) against which to judge a change. Hence, repeated promotions can devalue the reference price and make future increases problematic.

Some recent work sheds light on the issue, as consumers hold references differently for different product attributes. Standard pack size, for example, is much less salient to consumers than price. So, when faced with the dilemma of increasing price or reducing product size, producers face much less negative consumer reaction when it is the pack size that changes.[32]

Framing

The way in which prices, or price changes, are framed can greatly impact consumers' willingness to pay. Intuitively, we know people tend to prefer thinking in terms of gains than losses. It is best if we 'frame' a purchase, price or price change as a gain for the consumer, rather than a loss. This is why it is better to offer 50% of your customers a discount than to offer 50% a surcharge! However, despite how obvious this seems, it is still common to be charged a surcharge if using a credit card in some stores. Had Doug Ivester at Coca-Cola remembered this when introducing variable-price vending machines, the introduction might have been a success instead of a flop.

It is important to keep framing in mind when pricing bundles, and here the old quote of Niccolo Machiavelli is as true now as it was in his day: 'Severities should be dealt out all at once, so that their suddenness may give less offence; benefits ought to be handed out drop by drop, so that they may be relished the more.' Highlighting the multiple discounts involved in a bundle of products conforms to Machiavelli's advice and is common practice today, as viewers of late-night infomercials will attest. On the other hand, when multiple components of a bundle increase simultaneously, it is the increase of the bundle that should be communicated, rather than the multiple individual increases.

People tend to think in relative rather than absolute terms. Consider the following problem:[33]

> You are buying a watch for €1000 and the sales assistant tells you the same model is available for €980 at a different outlet located five minutes' walk away. Would you walk to the other store?

While you are contemplating that decision, let us ask you another question:

> You are buying a watch strap for €30 and the sales assistant tells you the same model is available for €10 at a different outlet located five minutes' walk away. Would you walk to the other store?

If you are like most of our IMD participants, you will answer no to the first question and yes to the second. In both cases you are essentially walking five minutes to be 'paid' €20, not a bad hourly rate. But consumers lack the ability to reframe the problem this way. If they had that ability, there would be no difference in the responses to the two questions. So, when setting a price, it might be best to reframe it for them. For example, if offering a discount on a large-ticket item where the discount is a small percentage of the price, but still a reasonable amount of money, perhaps you could remind consumers what they could do with the money saved.

Interestingly, framing can impact individuals' appetite for risk. When outcomes of risky opportunities are framed as positives, people tend to choose the more certain option. When they are framed as negatives, they tend to choose the risky options.

Consider the following two questions:

> Q1. Would you rather receive €50 with certainty or a lottery ticket with a 50/50 chance of winning €100?
>
> Q2. Would you rather lose €50 with certainty or a lottery ticket with a 50/50 chance of losing €100?

Most of our participants choose the certain option in question 1 and the risky option in question 2. The unfortunate consequences for manufacturers of loss-avoiding products such as burglar alarms, for example, is that people are more likely to risk a loss than to pay the expected value of the loss. So, if the loss incurred by being burgled is likely to be €5000 and the chance of a burglary is 1%, economists would predict that consumers should be willing to pay up to €50 for a burglar alarm or insurance. Unfortunately, the finding of behavioural research is that they are typically unwilling to do so, and would rather incur the risk.

Summary and management guidelines

- Technology is bringing with it more opportunities to price-discriminate.
- Price setters have more opportunity to

  - individualize prices
  - leverage customer information to ascertain willingness to pay
  - manipulate a product line to increase both margins and sales.

- Opportunities to price-discriminate based on observable customer characteristics may be declining as customer access to information increases and political and legal challenges are raised.
- Psychological phenomena impact customers' reaction to prices and can manipulate their willingness to pay.
- The biases covered in this chapter are:

  - **Attraction Effect** Consumers' willingness to pay more for a product after the introduction of another product that is worse on all dimensions
  - **Compromise Effect** Consumers' tendency to pick mid-priced products, regardless of the price range
  - **Endowment Effect** Consumers' tendency to place a higher value on products they possess or have experienced

- **Anchoring Effect** Consumers' willingness to pay being manipulated by initial or reference prices
- **Framing Effect** Consumers' willingness to pay being influenced by the way the transaction is described: in terms of a loss or a gain; or risky or certain options.

- Guidelines to management are the following:

  - Try to calculate the spread in the willingness to pay among your consumers. Experiment with price to capture this information, but be aware that consumers may react negatively. So be prepared to offer the lowest price to everyone, or discounts, after the experiment is over.
  - Leverage pricing to capture as much of the consumer surplus as possible through individualization of the price or the product/service, or through offering a menu of alternatives from which more and less price-sensitive consumers can choose.
  - Be cautious when employing differential pricing based on demographics – consumers generally view this as being unfair.
  - Keep in mind the psychology of pricing so:

    - Be prepared to introduce low-volume, 'phantom' products to make your higher-margin product seems more attractive to consumers.
    - Try to have your highest margin products in the mid-range of your product line.
    - Increase the perceived value of your products by offering trial and free versions with reduced features.
    - Anchor consumers at high price points, by comparing your products to higher priced competitors, higher priced versions or more expensive seasons or times.

➤ Try to induce a price increase by manipulating less salient product attributes, like pack size or weight.

➤ Introduce price increases all at once and price reductions separately.

References

[1] Cassidy, Ralph Jr., *Auctions and Auctioneering*, University of California Press, 1967.

[2] 'Coke's Chilling Concept', *The Irish Times*, 29 October 1999.

[3] www.argmax.com, John Irons, 3 November 1999.

[4] Hays, Constance L., 'Coke Tests Vending Unit That Can Hike Prices in Hot Weather', *New York Times*, 28 October 1999.

[5] Hays, Constance L., 'Coke Tests Vending Unit That Can Hike Prices in Hot Weather'.

[6] 'The World's 10 Most Valuable Brands', *Business Week*, 2 August 2004.

[7] Senia, Al, 'Sun's McNealy Envisions an Auction Economy', www.varbusiness.com, 2 June 2000.

[8] McNealy, Scott, 'Welcome to the Bazaar', *Harvard Business Review*, March 2001, pp. 2–3.

[9] Jones, Clive B., 'Applications of Database Marketing in the Tourism Industry', Economics Research Associates Issue Paper, September 1998.

[10] Haggblom, Ted, 'Pricing Psychology', *Honolulu Star-Bulletin*, 18 April 2004.

[11] 'Amazon Price Test', www.pricingsociety.com

[12] Denerke, R. and McAfee, P., 'Damaged Goods', *Journal of Economics and Management Strategy*, Vol. 5, No. 2, 1996, pp. 149–174.

[13] Ekelund, R.B., 'Price Discrimination and Product Differentiation in Economic Set Theory: An Early Analysis', *Quarterly Journal of Economics*, Vol. 84, 1970, pp. 268–278.

[14] Bakos, Yannis and Brynjolfsson, Erik, 'Bundling Information Goods: Pricing, Profits and Efficiency', Stanford University Graduate School of Business, Research Paper 1427, December 1996.

[15] 'I Got it Cheaper Than You', Forbes.com, November 1998.

[16] Garrahan, Matthew, 'Hotel Giant Set to Sever Links with Expedia', *Financial Times*, 16 August 2004.

[17] Castle, Stephen, 'Airlines Told to End Price Discrimination', *Independent*, 8 June 2004.

[18] Williams, Walter, 'What's Wrong with Price Discrimination?', *Augusta Chronicle*, 18 June 2004.

[19] O'Harrow, Robert Jr., 'Behind the Instant Coupons, a Data-crunching Powerhouse', *Washington Post*, 31 December 1998.

[20] Huber, Joel, Payne, John W. and Puto, Christopher, 'Adding Asymmetrically Dominated Alternatives: Violations of Regularity and the Similarity Hypothesis', *Journal of Consumer Research*, Vol. 9, June 1982, pp. 90–98.

[21] Schwartz, J.A. and Chapman, G.B., 'Are More Options Always Better? The Attraction Effect in Physicians' Decisions about Medications', *Medical Decision Making*, Vol. 19, pp. 315–323.

[22] Fournier, Susan, 'Introducing New Coke', Harvard Business School Case Study 9-5000-067, 31 October 2001.

[23] Pendergast, Mark, *For God, Country and Coca-Cola*, New York: Collier Books, 1993, p. 365.

[24] Simonson, Itamar, 'Choice Based on Reasons: The Case of Attraction and Compromise Effects', *Journal of Consumer Research*, vol. 16, September 1989, pp. 158–174.

[25] 'To Have and to Hold', *The Economist*, 30 August 2003.

[26] 'Does Market Experience Eliminate Market Anomalies?', *Quarterly Journal of Economics*, February 2003.

[27] 'Judgment under Uncertainty: Heuristics and Biases', *Science*, Vol. 185, 1974, pp. 1124–1131.

[28] Galinsky, Adam D., 'Should You Make the First Offer?', *Negotiation*, July 2004, pp. 3–5.

[29] Chapman, Gretchen B. and Bornstein, Brian H., 'The More You Ask for, the More You Get: Anchoring in Personal Injury Verdicts', *Applied Cognitive Psychology*, Vol. 10, 1996.

[30] Ariely, Dan and Simonson, Itamar, 'Buying, Bidding, Playing or Competing? Value Assessment and Decision Dynamics in Online Auctions', *Journal of Consumer Psychology*, 13 (1&2), 2003, pp. 113–123.

[31] Ariely, Dan, Loewenstein, George and Prelec, Drazen, 'Coherent Arbitrariness: Stable Demand Curves without Stable Preferences', *Quarterly Journal of Economics*, February 2003, pp. 73–105.

[32] Gourville, John, 'The Consumer Psychology of Rates', *Advances in Consumer Research*, Vol. 30, 2003, pp. 106–108.

[33] Adapted from J. Edward Russo and Paul J.H. Schoemaker, *Decision Traps: The Ten Barriers to Brilliant Decision Making & How to Overcome Them*, New York: Doubleday, 1989.

8

Beyond the Matrix: An Organization-wide Solution for Creating and Sustaining Customer Value

Professor Seán Meehan

F or decades companies have struggled with what exactly is the role of the marketing function and indeed what is its role, if any, in driving or realizing their vision of being a 'customer-centric' organization. The startling evidence from several studies is that Drucker's concept of focusing the entire firm on customer-value creation simply hasn't caught on in practice. At best, customer satisfaction and retention rates are mediocre, companies struggle with implementing a customer-value orientation and CEOs often subjugate it to the interests of other stakeholders. This chapter examines how a company's structure and culture work hand in hand to focus the entire organization on customer-value creation. It will argue that, counter to prevailing notions about empowerment and network organizations, customer-value orientation thrives in environments where clarity and simplicity are highly valued and hierarchy is appreciated.

This organizational vision demands that we revisit traditional notions of structure. The central recommendation is that executives reconsider the traditional matrix organization, don't replace it with a more sophisticated alternative, but rather ensure that it works to enhance customer responsiveness. Executives are urged to radically respecify the role of marketing in their organizations.

Companies are failing customers

Great companies do fall short of the mark. One such company is Allstate Insurance. With 2003 revenues in excess of $32 billion, it is the largest publicly held personal-lines insurer in the US, selling cover to over 16 million households. It had provided returns well ahead of the market indices since going public 11 years earlier. In 2003/4 *Fortune* magazine recognized it in its Most Admired Companies list. Nevertheless, in June 1999, disaffected customer Gary Weingardt, having exhausted all obvious avenues, created a website, Allstateinsurancesucks.com, to share his disappointment and anger with a wider audience – the general public. At that time he had little idea what he was tapping in to. Just over four years later the site had attracted nearly 900 000 visitors (a rate of around 18 000 per month). It offers merchandise such as mugs, t-shirts, bumper stickers and so on. Using donations from sympathetic visitors it has even been able to afford to sponsor sports teams. *Forbes* selected it as its number one corporate-complaint site.

Allstate is not alone; complaint sites are popular because a lot of people are so disappointed with their experiences as customers. Think back over the last few months. How many articles have you read in the business press about customers who are horrified at the treatment received from banks, airlines and hotels? And service companies do not have a monopoly with regard to failing to meet fundamental and reasonable customer expectations. Customer dissatisfaction is widespread. While anecdotally this is not hard to believe, the hard data is staggering. In 1994 Claes Fornell and colleagues at the University of Michigan Business School started to report what is probably the world's most comprehensive indicator of customer satisfaction. Some 65 000 customers are interviewed annually, enabling the researchers to create what they call the American Customer Satisfaction Index (ACSI). When this was first published in early 1994, the overall national score was 74.8, well short of the theoretical maximum of 100. For around five years it fell consistently from quarter to quarter, then started a somewhat unsteady recovery. At the time of writing it still had not recovered its initial level.

Although the index quantifies overall satisfaction, a reasonable interpretation of it (in a world in which we are frequently reminded that the only 'reliable' customers are those with whom we have somehow bonded or whom we consider behaviourally loyal) is that the incidence of less than committed customers could be as many as one-quarter of all customers.

Think about that in terms of your own business – even if you assume the effect is half as severe! Think about the economic impact of one-quarter (or one-eighth) of all your customers leaving you. This could well happen if customers had reasonable alternatives and were not tied in by what they might perceive to be heavy and therefore unreasonable costs of switching from one brand or supplier to another. Many companies can thank mediocrity of competition rather than so-called 'loyalty' for the relative stability in their customer base.

In short, customers feel their expectations have not been met. Some executives may feel justified in hiding behind the claim that customer expectations are out of control – that is, no matter what you do, the customer always wants more for less. This is very short-sighted. Instead, those executives should look inside and think through the extent to which their own organizations are getting in the way of customer-value creation. After all, it is 50 years since Peter Drucker first espoused the notion of the customer-centric organization. Back then, he proffered that marketing was not a function at all; rather it was the whole enterprise seen from the customer's viewpoint. This is clearly right. Customers do not interface with any department, never mind the marketing department. They buy a product or service in expectation of the receipt of fairly specific tangible or intangible benefits. And it is in the name of delivering on that promise, the value proposition, that companies engage so much organizational energy and consume so many organizational resources.

Customers thankfully have better things to do than sweat about how a supplier is organized or why it is organized the way it is. So, if your objective as a company is to enhance customer-value creation – whether through more effective interpretation of customer needs or wants, more effective business-system delivery or more effective interface with the market in your communications and presence – the solution isn't about relocating or redetermining the nature and scope of the marketing function in any traditional way. Enhancing customer orientation is an organization-wide mandate in which marketing has a special role. Given the grim realities of so many customers' experiences, we can safely infer that implementation is difficult and that many firms continue to struggle in their efforts to become more customer oriented.

Perhaps we can begin to understand why implementation of such a simple idea has proved so problematic by reflecting on the analysis of Marvin Bower, legendary leader of consulting firm McKinsey & Co., in 1985.[1] Based on his observations of companies he believes are exemplary in their embracing of the marketing concept, Bower identifies seven characteristics that distinguish these companies from others. One of these seven stands out as being particularly challenging: Bower points out that exemplars implement a structure or process for co-ordinating all company functions toward the achievement of marketing ends.

Before deciding that this is inherently straightforward, think about your own organization and all the people, forces and conditions that get in the way of co-ordination and co-operation. Co-ordination and co-operation across multiple entities within any social structure, not just a business, are political, lead to conflict and are just hard work – often for little personal short-term benefit. Indeed, Professor Frederick Webster Jr. characterizes the marketing challenge as a top management task of resolving the conflicts inherent in managers' responsibilities to their own, different constituencies.[2] This, he explains, is further complicated by so many executives within any firm believing they know best what is in the customers' interest. During the 1990s scholars working under the auspices of a research initiative from the renowned Marketing Science Institute began to report a number of studies of the nature and effectiveness of market orientation. Researchers converged on an understanding of market orientation as having two behavioural elements:

- **a set of market-sensing capabilities** relating to understanding customers (customer sensing) and understanding competitors (competitor sensing)
- **strong interfunctional co-ordination** which ensures that what is learned through the customer- and competitor-sensing mechanisms is widely shared and thus an appropriate, orchestrated response is forthcoming.

The studies provided the first solid, empirical evidence supporting the positive impact of being market oriented.

Knowing more about the market should help – but it doesn't

The present author's own studies suggest that the stimulus of these insights has contributed to the rush of companies claiming to be serious about taking whatever steps are necessary to become truly market oriented. They suggest that, rightly or wrongly, companies have chosen to go for the low-hanging fruits. As reported by global market research authority ESOMAR, investment in understanding customers and competitors has experienced huge growth throughout the 1990s and into the new millennium. A longitudinal study this author carried out in UK companies supported the view that those companies that had adopted a market orientation were likely to be superior performers; it also highlighted organizational issues, such as interfunctional co-ordination, rather than the development of customer- and competitor-sensing mechanisms as characteristics distinguishing high- from low-performing companies.[3] (Customer-sensing mechanisms included making customer satisfaction a key performance indicator, measuring it frequently and giving close attention to after-sales service, while competitor sensing included sharing information across functions and departments concerning competitors' strategies, regular top management discussion thereof, and strategic fit of target selection and pursuit.)

Of particular interest in this context was how the profile of high performers, with respect to adopting market-oriented behaviours, changed over the five years covered by the study. By 2001 the *persistent discriminators* between high and low performers were the presence among high performers of (1) *values that supported change, dynamism, innovation, entrepreneurship, and risk taking* and (2) *behaviours that effectively achieved co-ordination between all parts of a business critical in developing and delivering the value proposition.* To summarize, the characteristics that distinguished high performers from the low performers at both points in time were that the respondents from high performers agreed that:

- their business was very dynamic and entrepreneurial
- effective leaders in their company were generally considered to be innovators or risk takers
- their business was held together by a commitment to innovation and development
- their businesses emphasized growth and the acquisition of new resources

- their top managers from every function regularly visited current and prospective customers
- they freely communicated information about successful and unsuccessful customer experiences across all functions
- all functions were integrated in serving the needs of target markets
- all managers understood how everyone could contribute to creating customer value.

The 'take-away' is that there cannot be a chequebook approach to becoming customer oriented. Investing in building market-sensing capabilities, often the initial kneejerk reaction of an overanxious but underinformed or fundamentally uninterested CEO, simply does not make sense without the underlying desire to focus the entire organization on customer-value creation. Interfunctional co-ordination, and the structure and critically the shared values that permit it, are core to a successful reorientation of an organization onto customer-value creation. In the next section, we will distinguish between the structure *per se* and the enabling values required to achieve a customer orientation. In doing so, it becomes clear why so many companies find such a reorientation so difficult.

Companies seek to enhance customer responsiveness with structural solutions

Many companies we at IMD work with tell us that while in theory they buy into the notion of being customer focused, in the 'real world' they find it hard to achieve. The classic co-ordinating mechanism of the matrix clearly frustrates them in their quest for speed and responsiveness to customer requests and requirements. As if supporting the story emerging from this author's longitudinal study, it is clear that lack of effective co-ordination is one of their biggest challenges in achieving the kind of customer centricity they aspire to. These symptoms are further exacerbated by industry consolidations and globalization. Consider the challenges and experiences of US-based consumer-goods manufacturer Bausch & Lomb (B&L), the industrial GE Plastics (GEP) and computer giant Hewlett-Packard (HP), who all reorganized in the pursuit of enhanced customer focus.

Successful forays internationally provided B&L with a serious challenge: how to manage its brands globally.[4] In the early 1980s each of the company's international subsidiaries was headed by a country manager, with a product manager and sales organization for each product line. The product managers reported directly to a worldwide product division manager, based in the US, in addition to their locally based country manager. This solution, simple on paper, relatively easy to put in place and therefore commonplace, is inefficient and cumbersome. Having a product manager in each subsidiary for the same product line resulted in duplication of selling efforts and administrative inefficiencies. Critically, however, decision-making was complex and slow.

In an attempt to overcome this, B&L created a new international division (ID), within which country managers had unprecedented decision-making authority. Market share increased in most countries and responses to local market needs were much faster. However, as B&L kept growing during the 1980s and early 1990s, the design weaknesses of this elegant solution became evident. The US domestic divisions and ID made separate marketing decisions that sometimes impacted the global image of famous brands such as Ray Ban. A further reorganization, in 1992, therefore attempted to increase the autonomy of international subsidiaries. Three regional headquarters replaced ID. Marketing, product planning and operational support functions were transferred to the regions in order to be closer to customers. Each region notably had its own product development team. Global business networks were established to ensure co-ordination among regions and with the US divisions.

This approach seems to have been successful, as at the time of writing B&L is still organized along these lines. From the customer perspective, the company added value through local adaptation of products, higher service levels and new products for specific market needs. For B&L, however, higher customer focus has also meant higher structural complexity (co-ordination among units in terms of product development, pricing, brand positioning and cultural clash between decentralization values and co-ordination needs), and consequently less agility and responsiveness.

Co-ordinating mechanisms such as B&L global business networks are a ubiquitous theme in the pursuit of customer orientation. In implementation, however, finding the right form of such mechanisms is difficult, as GEP could attest. It went through a commonplace reorganization designed to bring it closer to customers. The consequences of the reorganization were, however, unexpected.

At GEP, as with so many companies, product focus had provided a positive sense of ownership and accountability in each product line, but had also fostered internal and external conflict. Competition among products was fierce and confused consumers, who often asked to talk to the 'real GEP'. In addition, as each product division possessed its own marketing, finance and purchasing department, there were clear cost inefficiencies. To overcome this, a new organization featuring three geographic regions was put in place. This was a matrix based on geography and function, as each area had its own manufacturing, technology, sales and marketing divisions. The product division-based competition was ended and market development reps working directly with customers could choose from the whole range of products to best meet the customers' needs.

This new matrix structure had achieved a major goal: it stopped competition among products and created a unique marketing interface with customers. But it also caused problems. With little or no authority, product managers had to rely on influence and networks to get things done and resolve conflicts. Another problem was the impact on the company's culture. Previously, employees had been able to identify with a product division. Now there was a global sense of identity loss, and bureaucracy was spreading. Nor was the new structure a perfect solution for many important customers. Larger accounts wanted global solutions, leading to the need for global account managers who could provide consistency.[5] In a nutshell, GEP had won synergy but lost speed and creativity, two key ingredients of success in an industry where product lifecycle was short. As one manager put it: 'We might make better decisions, but we definitely make slower ones.'

Creeping bureaucracy and lack of speed are frequently recurring themes in discussions on what it takes to achieve real customer focus. When Carla Fiorina became president and CEO of HP in July 1999, she announced her intention to reinvent HP with a view to attaining customer intimacy.[6] She had identified two major obstacles to this objective: HP's organizational

structure and its long-cherished 'HP way of management', which emphasized teamwork and respect for co-workers, but had over the years been
distorted into a culture of weak consensus that bogged down the decision-
making process. A former executive at HP recalled that he left because he did
not want to spend 80% of his time managing internal bureaucracy. At one
point, he had to go through 37 different committees to clear an operational
change. The bureaucracy was also affecting innovation. Fearing to miss their
quarterly targets, most managers preferred not to invest in radical ideas. As a
result, HP had not had a breakthrough product since the inkjet printer.

Fiorina launched her effort to change the company's culture by creating the
'rules of the garage'. The rules were simple: no bureaucracy, no politics, and
if a new idea does not serve our customers, it should not leave the garage.
The new culture was performance oriented, valued discipline and accountability, and encouraged employees to be open and to resolve conflicts in order
to move things forward quickly.

Structurally, Fiorina reorganized HP's 83 independent product divisions into
six centralized divisions. Following the merger with Compaq, this became
17 units under four divisions, but the main idea remained as at GEP: a single
point of contact with the customer for efficiency. The centralization would
provide clarity and, perhaps surprisingly, more hierarchy for faster decision-
making. The initial indications were indeed positive. At the time of writing
HP continues with the challenge of implementing the PC industry's biggest
merger integration ever.

In stark contrast, Siebel Systems achieved the apparently desirable simplicity
and speed with its culture of customer satisfaction, rapid execution and

quick action. Mistakes were tolerated as long as decisions were based on facts and people were flexible enough to change their course of action immediately. During a meeting, employees could challenge each other freely, but at the end a decision had to be made. Senior managers were the final arbiters when a consensus did not arise; decisiveness was paramount in order to satisfy customer request as fast as possible.

From the preceding examples it is clear that achieving an appropriate level of customer responsiveness is challenging for many large and otherwise accomplished companies. As they grow revenues, most companies struggle more and more to remain customer focused – unless, like Siebel, they were built on the core value of customer satisfaction that drove all future developments. The many different solutions highlighted in the different circumstances and industries all seek to facilitate speed and quality of response through more effective co-ordination. A lot of energy is spent searching for an elegant structural solution to provide a co-ordinating mechanism. However, our contention is that the solution is not structural at all, but rather that it lies in the norms and values that guide decision-making and behaviour within any given structural solution.

How values enable structure to enhance customer responsiveness

It is not easy to establish any helpful measure or description of a given organization's values, but one successful approach is known as the 'competing values' framework.[7] This provides a lens through which to understand that any organization is governed by the way it resolves inherent conflicts such as choosing between often attractive alternatives (see Figure 8.1). Although it apparently describes four archetypes – the clan, the hierarchy, the adhocracy and the market – it is more helpful to think of any business as being to some extent compliant to each of the types. Researchers using this framework ask managers, or employees and managers, to assess the extent to which the competing descriptions, each consistent with a clan, hierarchy, market or adhocracy, helpfully describe their organization's attributes, leadership style, bonding or strategic emphasis.

However, because we can see that the conflict is heightened across the diagonals, businesses have to resolve this by tending to either end. For example, a business unit will tend towards either the adhocratic type (external/flexible) or the hierarchy (internal/rigid). Clearly no business can be at its most effective when it is in equal measure internally and externally oriented, rigid and flexible.

Using the competing values framework, this author's studies suggest that companies which value openness and flexibility and are more concerned with external rather than internal matters, i.e. the so-called adhocracies, are more likely to be customer-responsive and enjoy superior performance. Elsewhere, General Electric and Citibank are cited as good examples of adhocracies that value 'flexibility and adaptability while maintaining a focus on the external environment'.[8] Their dominant values are entrepreneurship, creativity, adaptability, autonomy and willingness to experiment. They value growth/acquisition of new resources, innovativeness and competitiveness, combined with a healthy dose of respect for people. They are diametrically opposite to the bureaucratic archetype, the hierarchy.

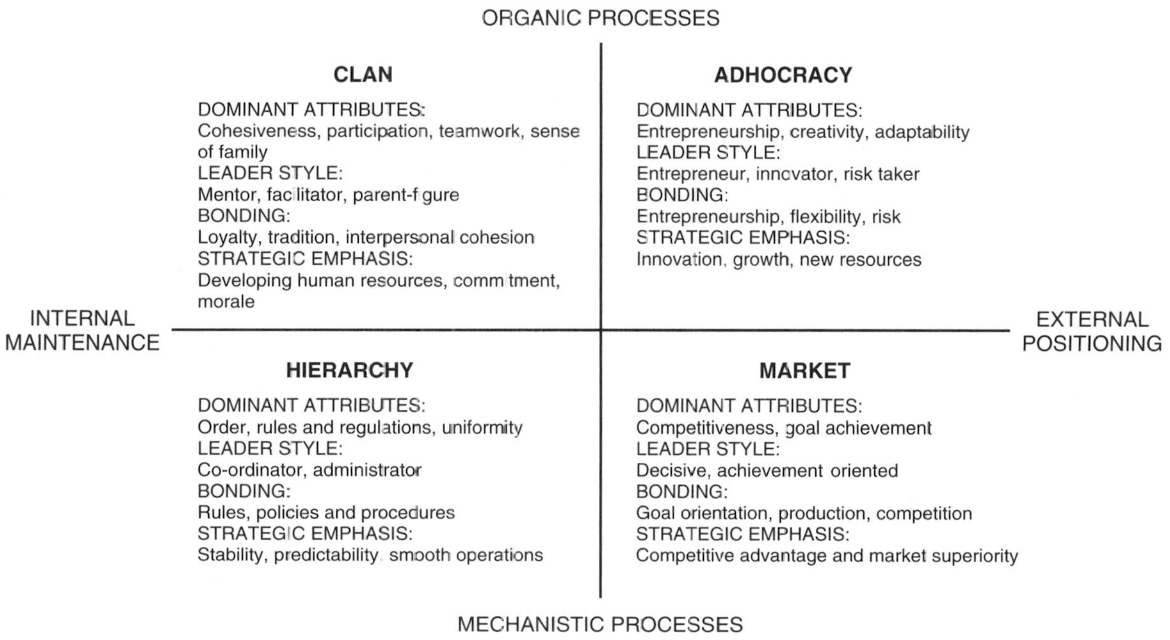

ORGANIC PROCESSES

CLAN

DOMINANT ATTRIBUTES:
Cohesiveness, participation, teamwork, sense of family
LEADER STYLE:
Mentor, facilitator, parent-figure
BONDING:
Loyalty, tradition, interpersonal cohesion
STRATEGIC EMPHASIS:
Developing human resources, commitment, morale

ADHOCRACY

DOMINANT ATTRIBUTES:
Entrepreneurship, creativity, adaptability
LEADER STYLE:
Entrepreneur, innovator, risk taker
BONDING:
Entrepreneurship, flexibility, risk
STRATEGIC EMPHASIS:
Innovation, growth, new resources

HIERARCHY

DOMINANT ATTRIBUTES:
Order, rules and regulations, uniformity
LEADER STYLE:
Co-ordinator, administrator
BONDING:
Rules, policies and procedures
STRATEGIC EMPHASIS:
Stability, predictability smooth operations

MARKET

DOMINANT ATTRIBUTES:
Competitiveness, goal achievement
LEADER STYLE:
Decisive, achievement oriented
BONDING:
Goal orientation, production, competition
STRATEGIC EMPHASIS:
Competitive advantage and market superiority

INTERNAL MAINTENANCE

EXTERNAL POSITIONING

MECHANISTIC PROCESSES

Figure 8.1 Competing values model (Source: Adapted by Deshpande, Farley and Webster (1993) from Cameron and Freeman (1991) and Quinn (1998))

Hierarchies, on the other hand, tend to be inward-looking and rigid, prioritizing order and routine. However, we must be careful to distinguish the *characteristics* of a hierarchy from the *fundamental notion* of a hierarchy. A hierarchy is simply a chain of command, usually accompanied by a standard process and procedure governing information flow and decision-making. It offers reasonable certainty and clarity. While de facto not necessarily producing qualitatively better decisions, it does produce decisions. Hierarchy is frequently confused with bureaucracy simply because hierarchies can become multi-layered, and therefore slow and cumbersome. Let us make it clear: in business bureaucracy is bad – always. As if we need the reassurance of empirical support, various studies this author has examined show clearly that irrespective of the industry (high tech/low tech, products/services, B2B/B2C) the more bureaucratic an organization is, the less likely it is to be commercially successful. However, it is worth remembering that a firm with no hierarchy or bureaucracy would suffer from insufficient direction and control. A properly functioning hierarchy can, for a customer, be a thing of beauty.

Effective hierarchies

A clear sense of hierarchy can deliver efficiency and effectiveness, and actually *reduce* unhelpful bureaucracy, according to Jacques Dubois, chairman and CEO of reinsurer Swiss Re America.[9] Dubois demands that his executives focus on precisely what delivers customer value. He observes that managers often see their job as delegating, which he believes is dysfunctional, since it puts decisions in the hands of potentially inadequately qualified people. Dubois goes further: 'By raising decision-making to the highest level possible, we get to see our people in action. It motivates them. They deal with the top.' There are no standing committees, but meetings happen as needed. Decisions get made.

With a total sense of hierarchy, Carlos Zambrano, CEO of giant cement producer Cemex, has at the same time shown how it is possible and even attractive to use information systems to cultivate an entrepreneurial and energetic organization.[10] Cemex's systems place Zambrano in direct contact with all elements of the massive organization. He can monitor plant productivity globally and in real time. If he detects that a plant's operating levels are below the benchmark for the other 49 plants, he can call a worker directly to find out why. If he wants to check out how sales worldwide were in the last 24 hours, he can. That capability has changed how Cemex people manage their time and work. They no longer have to stop what they are doing to look for information. The data is readily available.

Critically, as with Swiss Re and Cemex, both of whom find virtue in sensible hierarchy to enhance customer responsiveness, the high-performing companies this author has observed tended to be flexible and claimed to have the ability to respond and adapt to changing market conditions. Their employees also felt that they were treated well and were part of the 'deal'. Respondents suggested that in terms of those values that provided a shared sense of purpose in their companies, these high-performing companies valued loyalty and tradition as well as innovation and development over mindless micro-management characterized by an overemphasis on goals, tasks, rules and policies. Creating a flexible organization that is responsive, focused and efficient thus involves managing a duality.

It is reasonable to attribute companies' ability to manage the duality – flexibility plus order and efficiency – to their transparency and inclusiveness.[11] Concurring with this is one CEO who has tracked his employees' morale in great detail for over a decade and dug deep to better understand variances across his organization. He believes that the two most critical drivers of employee morale are:

- **understanding the firm's strategy**, i.e. being able to make sense of what it is doing day to day
- **having faith in the ability of your immediate boss** to contribute effectively to making the strategy a success.

This combination has a decisive impact on how information is treated and the rate at which the organization learns about and responds to events in the market. It helps that in high-performing companies trust is high and market insights are relatively depoliticized.

Implementing a customer-value orientation

With these lessons in mind and building on the observations prompted by the foregoing, we at IMD propose an agenda, in the form of three questions for managers struggling with how to approach implementing a customer-value orientation. They are:

- **Responsiveness** How well does the organizational structure facilitate fast decision-making and action in customer-service encounters?
- **Measurement** How well is the organization measuring performance that is aligned with customer needs?

- **Simplicity** How effective is the organization at keeping unnecessary complexity out of systems?

Let us look at each of these three in turn.

Responsiveness

How long does a typical customer wait to get the product/service they expect compared with their needs and expectations? Two root attributes of responsiveness are speed of decision-making within an organization and relevance of decisions being made to customer experience. These are key drivers of customer satisfaction and perceived advantage.

To better understand the other elements of such responsiveness, this author, together with Charlie Dawson, interviewed ten high-profile UK CEOs with marketing backgrounds.[12] They told us they defined customer responsiveness as 'accurately and insightfully giving customers what they need, want or don't yet know they want. And . . . consistently doing so more quickly than anyone else and rapidly enough to retain the value of the decision or idea for the customer.'

To paraphrase, customer responsiveness means being fast and right in the eyes of customers.[13] The value of being right about customer needs is obvious. However, the value to both the customer and the business also depends on the speed of the response. Satisfying customers is usually not that hard – it simply takes time and money to get things right. Enough testing and piloting and most companies will get there in the end. Being fast is not that hard either. It is being both fast and right that presents a challenge.

'Fast and right' is not a risk-taking, 'failure is good' culture. Interviewees conveyed both intolerance of doing the wrong thing and impatience about responding too slowly. Practically speaking, to enhance customer responsiveness, companies should embrace three key sets of behaviours that lead to decisions being both faster and better. We call these:

- **direct learning** (comprising immersion, intuition and fact-based market research)
- **hard-work decision-making**
- **accountable experimentation**.

These behaviours are supported by what we call a 'pure air' culture (see Figure 8.2).

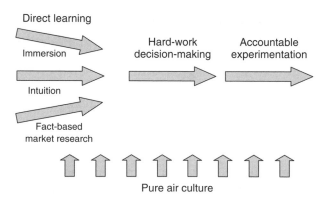

Figure 8.2   The elements of customer responsiveness

Direct learning

This behaviour enhances a team's ability to make the right decisions using its judgement, avoiding the need for continual research. Although it has three elements, the first, *immersion*, is of particular interest here. It is the primary source of customer knowledge. It was common practice among the executives we interviewed to spend considerable time in direct contact with customers. At its most extreme, this meant spending one day a week out of the office and on the 'shop floor', speaking to customers about complaints or just about how they were getting on. Immersion is powerful because it provides:

- **an unarguable version of the truth** for the individuals concerned. This has real power in subsequent discussions and debates.
- **a filter through which to view indirect data** such as more conventional market research. It helps the management team to process data and to direct challenges at interpretations of the information that do not fit its own observations in the field.
- **an excellent source of storytelling and anecdote**, crucially important in managing large organizations where the ability to persuade people to follow can hinge on engaging them emotionally with specific, human expressions of what is required of them.
- **a learning catalyst**. If your boss sees customers for a day a week, then unless you do too, he or she is going to know more than you. That could mean you won't win arguments and you won't get on.

Further, the absence of this direct contact with customers and channel partners is liable to lead to complacency and insulation from reality.

Remarkably, it is true even in the case of understanding the real impact of major market shocks. Consider the strange case of Sun Microsystems (whose on-line auctioning we discussed in the previous chapter), an organization dominated at the top by engineers and considered to be highly entrepreneurial. The impact of the bursting of the 'dot com' bubble and the resulting cutbacks at many of Sun's core customers was compounded as Sun increased its work force to 44 000 employees from 37 000. It wasn't until mid-2001, when sales had dipped, its market share fell 3.8% and it began to report net losses, that it was ready for the kind of change it needed. With the recovery plan in full force senior executives were storming North America trying to keep everything on track. In September 2002 one executive visited Sun's largest distributor, GE Access, and discovered to her surprise that she was the first senior Sun executive ever to meet this distributor's sales reps. Mr Hendrix of GE Access opined that Sun had lost its customer focus and suggested that it wasn't until he complained directly to a top Sun executive that he began to see improvements.

Executives at the top of and throughout a hierarchy are there to make important decisions and allocate scarce resources, and their decision-making ability is enhanced by their knowledge of the day-to-day realities of their customers' experience in dealing with their organizations. In one of the studies mentioned earlier, this author asked managing directors of the business units being examined to reflect on how they allocated their time. Although there is no magic number, given the strength of customer-first rhetoric today, he was somewhat surprised to find that on average they spent only 15% of their time directly with their customers or consumers. How they spent this time, though, was very revealing. High performers wanted to go to the point of value realization. They took this contact as a fantastic opportunity to reflect on and learn about their own performance, particularly how they could do better. Their lower performing counterparts had a clear preference for social settings. Their focus was on 'developing' the contact for the purpose of selling more product. The moral of the story is clear. Get out of your office, immerse yourself in your customer's reality and seek to do better.

In situations where 'rightness' is valued above speed, the skill of *intuition* can get lost in the need for certainty. Given enough 'facts', people will override their instincts – not always a bad thing but *in extremis* the loss of a valuable capability.

Fact-based market research is the final aspect of direct learning. The gap in the first two aspects, immersion and intuition, is breadth. Gathering information across large numbers of people, without which decision-making would take on an aspect of educated guesswork, requires some reliable sources of data. This, in the context of enhancing understanding together with immersion and intuition, has a completely different value to the organization than fact-based research on its own.

The hard-work decision-making process

While ultimately a successful organization would have many empowered individuals all capable of making the right decisions swiftly and effectively, it is valuable to proactively limit dissipation of effort by replacing frantic activity with debate among a better-informed team, holding all accountable to high standards. This is far from being an egalitarian approach. Rather it is characterized by a very directive, top-down guidance of thought and action. It works because it is based on objectivity and on what is right for the customer, not on some power-crazed individual who believes he or she has all the answers.

Accountable experimentation

The combination of widespread, good-quality learning and setting high hurdles for decision-making ensures that, when trials do happen, they are already building on considerable reflection and thought. Two very important benefits flow from this approach.

First, having a set of well-informed, bright people totally in touch with the reality of the marketplace thinking through a business case is a lot faster than running multiple trials; it is also likely to produce some excellent results. Too often, frenzied activity replaces more thoughtful decision-making, and once a company is off down the road of some ill-considered trial it can take a huge effort, financially and emotionally, to rein it in again.

Second, conducting fewer experiments means that each one is carefully planned and has more energy and less cloudy judgement applied to it, compared to an incubator-style environment with higher numbers and less consideration. As a result, each stands a better chance of success.

A 'pure air' culture

This approach prevents executives becoming removed from or out of touch with the realities of the marketplace. It prizes rigorous debate and remains objective in pursuit of swiftly getting things right. Challenge and debate are seen as forces for good. Because the process of discussing conflicting ideas and views is based on facts and objective observation, it helps to share learning and build judgement. Further, no one expects an easy 'yes'. By requiring a lot from people if they are to be given the go-ahead, an organization toughens up and fully values opportunities when they do arise. The consequence of all this is the purging of poor argument and lack of rigor. While a balance must always be struck between fast and right, a feeling of compromise is avoided. There are not fewer ideas being discussed and progressed, just fewer bad ones. Like purer air, this is a richer environment within which strong people and strong thinking can thrive.

Measurement

One of the most frustrating things confronting a researcher interested in understanding what works and why in relation to achieving a customer orientation is a glib proclamation by senior executives such as 'the year of the customer', or a proud announcement in an annual report that their business has successfully developed deeper relationships with clients.[14] While such proclamations are generally ignored by dispassionate observers and the general public, analysts, customers and employees are more critical. Analysts with fairly detailed knowledge of the specific companies and their executives will question the judgement of a management willing to make empty and meaningless statements such as these. Customers living with the brunt of incomplete or late orders, substandard performance or disappointing after-sales support and service are incensed. Employees, who know the dirty truth better than anyone, are at best discouraged and at worst deeply sceptical.

Recently this author received a corporate calendar from an angry employee. It was intended to support an initiative to become more customer focused. Each month carried a personal message from an executive explaining what the initiative meant to him or her. The employee reported that the calendar had been greeted with derision within the company, that what employees wanted was to see concrete steps and above all maybe hear from customers in the company's internal communications.

The bottom line is that executives can get ahead of themselves and in doing so expose themselves to uncertain actions and reactions of customers and employees. When embarking on a series of initiatives designed to enhance customer orientation, it is critical therefore that management, having determined their value proposition, map all key processes underlying their value delivery. They must set up concrete systems and measures to monitor performance and whenever possible improve it. This, to all, represents reality – what are you measuring, what are you rewarding? Measuring early and often is also the best way to identify problems while they are small. Down the line, managers will naturally focus on improving performance in those key areas that are measured. Measurement of your own company's performance against that of competitors on key customer-value drives focuses everybody on what matters most – value.

Professional service firms (PSFs) appear to have done more than most to achieve alignment in this regard. Client contact drives PSFs' measurement and reward systems. Most veterans of PSFs can recall clearly their first exposure to the time sheet during their induction programme. The time sheet is the key platform of the 'time and billing' system, allowing the firm to track the extent to which anyone is 'utilized', i.e. working on fee-paying assignments. In at least one firm the practice of publishing the utilization rates of the top and bottom 10% at each level has had a defining effect on the company's culture. A related measure is the 'recovery rate', the extent to which the hours spent on an engagement can be turned into fees actually paid by the client. Its effect is to focus the engagement on delivering services that the client values. In turn, this encourages spending time with clients in order to really understand their business and how the firm can add value. The lesson is to measure what really matters.

It is insightful to examine Ryanair's management system in this regard. Ryanair, a so-called 'budget' airline, has become one of Europe's leading airlines of any kind and needs to be respected for its growth in passenger numbers, revenues, profitability and market capitalization. It has become so thanks to a relentless focus on delivering on its value proposition. Its CEO, Michael O'Leary, captures it well: 'Our customer service proposition is about the most well defined in the world. We guarantee to give you the lowest airfare. You get a safe flight. You get a normally on-time flight. That's the package. We don't and won't give you anything more on top of that ... We care for our customers in the most fundamental way possible: we don't screw them every time they fly.'[15]

O'Leary is utterly focused on delivering his value proposition. Thus when he receives complaints he doesn't panic, because generally he does not get complaints about failing to deliver on Ryanair's *actual value proposition*.

Some travellers are upset by the airline's failure to deliver on what they *imagine* the value proposition should be. O'Leary, on the other hand, focuses on what it *is*. So obsessed is Ryanair with performing according to its promise that it publishes its performance against its competitors on news-wires every month. For example, in May 2004, it published data showing that 93% of all its flights were on time (up from 91% a year earlier), complaints per thousand passengers were 0.48 (nearly half the level of a year earlier). Similarly, data on the level of baggage complaints is published, as are rankings showing Ryanair in number one position relative to other major European carriers (including the other successful budget airlines) on percentage of flights arriving within 15 minutes of the scheduled time, bags lost per hundred passengers and percentage of flights completed. Finally, the airline clearly takes great pride in measuring its punctuality relative to what many perceive to be its closest rival, easyJet (see Table 8.1).

There is a further moral in this Ryanair story. It is the remarkable clarity of the value proposition and belief in its validity, reinforced by the positive marketplace reception that provides Michael O'Leary with his most valuable asset – his confidence. This makes the hierarchy at Ryanair work exceptionally smoothly. Everyone knows what is expected and the signals from the top are completely consistent over time. Although O'Leary is often criticized in his native Ireland, where he is a bit of a celebrity, for being arrogant and unreceptive to customers' concerns, he is in fact simply standing firm in the face of customers' demands to give a little more.

We should always remember that there is no shortage of customers with the mother of all requirements – more for less. We operate in a world where customers are militant and articulate, and this is great. But executives need

Table 8.1 Ryanair and easyJet punctuality records 2004

	Week ending	Ryanair	easyJet
1	05-Jan	90%	73%
2	12-Jan	91%	80%
3	19-Jan	95%	84%
4	26-Jan	95%	89%
5	01-Feb	85%	64%
6	08-Feb	93%	81%
7	15-Feb	95%	84%
8	22-Feb	91%	84%
9	29-Feb	89%	69%
10	07-Mar	93%	80%
11	14-Mar	93%	80%
12	21-Mar	92%	82%
13	28-Mar	95%	88%
14	04-Apr	94%	87%
15	11-Apr	93%	88%
16	18-Apr	95%	85%
17	25-Apr	96%	92%
18	2-May	94%	85%
19	9-May	93%	81%
20	16-May	95%	84%
21	23-May	94%	87%

to decide early on whether they are in business simply to score high on customer-satisfaction indices (like the ACSI described earlier) or to create customer value. Although there is plenty of evidence that there is an important relationship between the two and other key metrics like market capitalization, it is nevertheless critical that, like Michael O'Leary, you are very clear on your business-system delivery as well as your value proposition and that you focus all your organizational energy on delivering on your promises to customers. In a world where this appears to be surprisingly exceptional, you will be rewarded for doing so.

We can imagine that Ryanair benefits from this competitive approach internally – it keeps the organization focused. But behind these customer metrics must also be, as with Southwest Airlines, a sophisticated system and process map with all key levers being measured carefully. Southwest Airlines utilizes measurement with the Balanced Score Card (BSC) to focus all employees on its strategic goal of being number one in 'operating efficiency'. The four perspectives embodied in the BSC were linked together by a series of relatively simple questions and answers:

- **Financial** What will drive operating efficiency? Answer: More customers on fewer planes.
- **Customer** How will we get more customers on fewer planes? Answer: Attract targeted segments of customers who value price and on-time arrivals.
- **Internal** What must our internal focus be? Answer: Fast aircraft turn-around time.
- **Learning** How will our people accomplish fast turnaround? Answer: Educate and compensate the ground crew regarding how they contribute to the firm's success. Also, use your employee stockholder programme if you have one.

The goal of Southwest's BSC is to encourage improvement by identifying key performance measures in each domain for the operating personnel. Some of the non-financial metrics that have emerged on a departmental level include:

- **load factor** (percentage of seats occupied)
- **utilization factors** on aircraft and personnel

- **on-time performance**
- **available seat miles**
- **denied-boarding rate**
- **lost-bag reports** per 10 000 passengers
- **flight cancellation rate**
- **employee head count**
- **customer complaints** per 10 000 passengers filed with the Department of Transportation.

The BSC by design shows how all critical operations and initiatives interact with one another and highlights interdependencies. In a sense it is exactly this that overcomes the barriers sometimes presented by any organization structure – matrices included. Kaplan and Norton, the creators of the BSC, have long argued that its power comes from the discussion executives have in designing their own system, discovering the interdependencies, collectively agreeing what matters for value creation, value delivery and value capture.

However you design your business system, it is critical that all employees understand their role in its execution. Measurement is a key lever that helps create and maintain such clarity. Clarity allows for decisiveness and engagement. It goes together with one overriding consideration in achieving responsiveness – simplicity.

Simplicity

Perhaps the biggest gift any company can give to a customer is delivering exactly what it has agreed to when it said it would. Providers are paid to spend a lot of time agonizing about every aspect of their company and even those who like to think that they are genuinely customer oriented often fall into the biggest trap of all – overestimating the overall importance of their product or service in the life of their customers. Maybe it is natural. But customers have very different expectations. They want to acquire the value you promised them and then move on. Anything you do to slow up or complicate the acquisition process or underdeliver on your promise will frustrate, annoy and complicate your customer's life. In stark contrast to widespread executive delusion that customers are available for some kind of relationship with them or their brand, customers actually crave simplicity and predictability. Call that a relationship if you want, but understand what it really is.

Almost everyone reading this will have bought a book on Amazon.com. One of the reasons we go back so much is not to satisfy a need for a relationship. Rather it is because Amazon has successfully invested in understanding what we want from a (mainly) book-shopping experience. Speed, simplicity and security really matter. Just as they do for many more mundane shopping experiences such as our visits to the food store. Our time is limited, shopping around is usually a chore, and as favourite brands are generally satisfactory, routinized buying behaviour works well.

Think about the last time you shopped for yoghurt. Not only did you most likely buy it at the same store you normally buy it at, you probably just went to that same spot in the cold section and picked up the same brand and same flavour as the week before. Thus customers rationalize their brand choices, rarely bothering to compare all the competing brands or to use all the available information, even about those brands they do consider. This means that their behaviour falls short of economic 'rationality', which would ordinarily assume that they would use all the information on every brand before making their choice. The buyers' shortcuts are the reward for not disappointing them and they are of great benefit to customers because they simplify their lives.

In the words of mathematical philosopher Alfred North Whitehead: 'It is a profoundly erroneous truism . . . that we should cultivate the habit of thinking of what we are doing. The precise opposite is the case. Civilization advances by extending the number of important operations which we can perform without thinking about them.'[16]

This reflection is surely true of us as individuals also: we advance partly by increasing the number of things we can do without having to think hard about them, from walking and talking to driving – and shopping. With most of these, we sometimes do stop and think a little, but our lives are greatly enriched by the fact that, most of the time, it is only a little.

Maximum value is created when organizations are designed in a way that simplifies operations while also simplifying customer transactions with the company. Customer value is increased when the complexity of transactions is reduced for them. Speed to creating customer value is increased when the company's operations are streamlined and simplified. Creating simplicity, however, is itself deceptively simple! Although we all want our companies' operations to be as simple and efficient as possible, it is challenging to achieve this in such a heavily regulated world. Again we revert to utter clarity in what is and is not within your value proposition as the key to designing a business system that nails the customer's sweet spot and that's all. Consider the approach of In-N-Out, a hugely successful US fast-food chain.

In-N-Out is a privately held, 182-outlet burger chain located in the western United States. Each outlet has annual revenue of around $2 million of which 20% is profit. Industry analysts claim that although In-N-Out pays its employees more than either McDonald's or Burger King, it beats them in terms of per-store volume and net earnings. It also consistently outperforms competitors in customer-satisfaction surveys. According to restaurant consultant Edward Engoron the key to In-N-Out's success is simplicity. It offers 'only' fresh hamburgers, French fries and soft drinks in a fast and friendly manner. There are none of the 'innovative' products like fish, chicken and salads that you will find at McDonald's or Burger King. The only complexity allowed into the system is driven around getting customers the food and drinks they want. There are several 'secret menu' preparations that loyal customers know about. These include 'protein-style' bunless lettuce-wrapped burgers compatible with the Atkins diet that has taken the US by storm in recent years. These variations are minor and do not add materially to the complexity of the kitchen operation.

Additionally, businesses would do well to ensure their front- and back-office operations – that is, those operations the customer sees, experiences and indirectly consumes as well as those operations invisible to customers – are kept in check. Any business today needs to really challenge itself on whether it needs all its brands and SKUs. Emblematic of this manifestation of the concern for simplicity is global marketing powerhouse Unilever. It pruned its brand line from 1600 to 400. In addition to yielding financial saving from operational synergies in areas such as production, design, distribution and promotion, this enabled the company to focus its energy and brand-development resources on fewer assets, thereby increasing the potential impact of each.

Similarly, during the restructuring at Sun referred to earlier, a major programme was launched with the aim of reducing the company's catalogue of more than 200 software products to six. This also simplified software pricing so that corporate customers paid a fixed price per user, instead of varying amounts based on the number of processors in a computer and other factors.

Orange, the mobile telephone service provider, when it was launched in the United Kingdom, had as its brand platform the demystification of services provided by incumbents. Its call tariffs were very simple compared with those of competitors. And it focused utterly on delivering what its competitors were failing on – getting a signal when desired, not dropping the calls when connected. It launched very successfully and was sold ten years later at an enormous premium of some £13 billion to head-to-head rival One 2 One.

If the critical starting point in realizing the benefits of simplicity is understanding that customers really just want you to do as you promised, a key milestone on your journey is to design an uncomplicated business system that does just that. Simplifying your offering is actually only the more obvious part of the appropriate organizational response. The less obvious supporting mechanism is to keep the organization itself simple. Not necessarily in terms of layers, departments and procedures, as documented earlier regarding HP, but rather in terms of the behaviour of executives.

Executives derive pleasure from applying smart solutions and seeing them succeed. Smart product developers obtain satisfaction from overdesigning products with clever gadgets and gizmos. Smart salespeople enjoy explaining a product's 'clever' utility. Similarly, market researchers, accountants and human resource personnel all crave personal satisfaction from mastering complexity. They get paid appropriately. This creates a mindset that fosters overindulgence in debate and discussion and unnecessarily complicates decision-making processes, thus slowing down time to market and impeding customer responsiveness.

So, what is the role of marketing?

Given the sorry market evidence of customer dissatisfaction, there is surely time for a rethink. Not for a 'radical breakthrough' in organizational design, rather a sensible reaction to the stark truth – we've overcomplicated our worlds. Those worlds are already fairly complicated – structures and systems rely on behaviour (that's good old human intervention) to make them work. Unpredictability is a reality. The solution lies in effective implementation of a three-point agenda: *customer responsiveness*, *measurement* and *simplicity*. The new role of marketing is to leverage the CEO in his implementation mandate. The Chief Marketing Officer (CMO) should not be concerned with the effectiveness and efficiency of the provision or contribution of traditional marketing services such as the technical-support processes. Neither should he or she be overly concerned with the 4 Ps that have distracted customer-value creation discussions forever – that is the job of business managers (à la the P&G 'school' of brand management). There is a huge change-management job to be done driving the customer agenda, understanding the implications of all decisions from the customer's perspective. And when the job is done, perhaps there is no role. The greatest compliment to any organization interested in achieving customer centricity is to make 'marketing' redundant.

Summary and management guidelines

- High levels of customer dissatisfaction suggest that companies have fallen short of the mark in implementing the marketing concept. Various studies converge on the critical importance of achieving excellence in market sensing as well as ensuring that market data flows around an organization efficiently and effectively.

- While many companies appear to make great strides in fixing market sensing, at least superficially, the real stumbling block seems to be getting all parts of the organization to focus on doing whatever it takes to deliver on its value proposition.

- Experiences of highly credible companies operating successfully on the global stage suggest that organizational structure *per se* is not the issue; rather it is values and behaviour that can effect a true customer orientation.

- Pivotal seems to be the capturing of all that is good in being externally focused and flexible and combining it with the speed and lack of decision-making ambiguity that emerges from hierarchy. Customer responsiveness can be achieved by managing this duality if measurement systems are aligned and simplicity becomes the watchword in all aspects of value creation, delivery and capture.

- At the heart of achieving customer responsiveness is the way senior executives go about experiencing the day-to-day realities of the marketplace. It is not simply a question of the information that emerges from the activity. Rather, the very process of immersion impacts how the emergent understanding is received by other executives. Further, it changes the discussion, debate and decision-making process. It blows through organizational bureaucracy and thus aids speed and responsiveness.

- Critical enablers of the model of customer responsiveness proposed are measurement systems and simplicity throughout the organization.
- Marketing management needs to understand the unusual consequences of success. The real role of marketing is to support the CEO in driving the three-point agenda: customer responsiveness, measurement and simplicity. Success is, therefore, for the marketing department in the way we think of it today to become redundant.
- There are four broad guidelines for management:

  – Be prepared to look beyond structural solutions and organizational charts in order to enhance customer responsiveness.
  – Be willing to translate your business's value proposition into simple mandates for all employees.
  – Having designed a business system that theoretically should be effective in the marketplace, be willing to design simple decision-making governance mechanisms that enhance speed.
  – Learn to discriminate between customers who are whiners always looking for something extra (beyond the initial offer) and those genuinely aggrieved because companies have failed to deliver on their promise.

References

[1] Bower, Marvin and Garda, Robert, 'The Role of Marketing in Management', *McKinsey Quarterly*, Autumn 1985, pp. 34–46.
[2] Webster, Frederick E. Jr., *Market Driven Management*, Chichester: John Wiley & Sons, 1994, pp. 26–27.
[3] The data reported was generated from two surveys of CEOs of businesses comprising the population of public limited companies in UK businesses in 1996 and 2001.

These yielded responses from 434 and 157 chief executives (or their designates), representing response rates of 31% and 16% respectively. A self-administered questionnaire allowed respondents to evaluate their organization's adoption of market-oriented values and market-oriented behaviours (customer orientation, competitor orientation and interfunctional co-ordination) and rate their business performance relative to their main competition on dimensions such as sales growth, market share, and return on assets. In both surveys the sitting chairmen of the Marketing Council, Sir Colin Marshall, then chairman of British Airways, and Sir Michael Perry, formerly chairman of Unilever, endorsed the study (see: 'The Evolution of Market Orientation in Public Companies 1996–2001', Seán Meehan, *Irish Academy of Management Conference Proceedings*, 2004, Dublin).

[4] This case is summarized from the HBS case 'BAUSCH & LOMB: regional organization', Quelch, Ja. and Laidler, N., 1 December 2003.

[5] Day, George, 'Aligning Organizational Structure to the Market,' *Business Strategy Review*, Vol. 10, No. 3 (1999), pp. 33–46.

[6] Perlow, L. and Kind, L., 'The New HP: The Clean Room and Beyond', Harvard Business School case study, 22 February 2004.

[7] For the competing values framework, see R.E. Quinn and J. Rohrbaugh, 'A Spatial Model of Effectiveness Criteria: Towards a Competing Values Approach to Organizational Analysis', *Management Science* 29 (1983), pp. 363–377; and R.E. Quinn, *Beyond Rational Management*, San Francisco: Jossey Bass, 1988. This operationalization of culture as values has been adopted in the market orientation literature (see R. Deshpande, J. Farley and F. Webster Jr., 'Corporate Culture, Customer Orientation and Innovativeness in Japanese Firms: A Quadrad Analysis', *Journal of Marketing* 57, January (1993), pp. 23–37; and C. Moorman, 'Organizational Market Information Processes: Cultural Antecedents and New Product Outcomes', *Journal of Marketing Research* XXXII (1995), pp. 318–335.

[8] Day, George, *The Market-driven Organization: Understanding, Attracting, and Keeping Valuable Customers*, New York: Free Press, 1999, pp. 54–55.

[9] Barwise, Patrick and Meehan, Seán, *Simply Better*, Boston: Harvard Business School Press, 2004.

[10] Marchand, Donald, Chung, Rebecca and Paddack, Katarina, 'Global Growth Through Superior Information Capabilities', Case GM 953, Lausanne: IMD, 2003.

[11] Day, George, *The Market-driven Organization*, pp. 54–55.

[12] These included Sir Peter Davis (CEO Sainsbury), Luc Vandevelde (chairman, Marks & Spencer), Peter Burt (CEO, Bank of Scotland) and Eric Nicoli (chairman, EMI).

[13] Meehan, Seán and Dawson, Charlie, 'Customer Responsiveness: Getting it Fast and Right Through Impatience and Intolerance', *Business Strategy Review*, Vol. 13, No. 4 (Winter 2002), p. 26.

[14] See Tom Robertson's excellent review of corporate rhetoric, 'Corporate Graffiti', *Business Strategy Review*, Vol. 6, No. 1 (Spring 1995), pp. 27–44.

[15] Chesshyre, Tom, 'It's Cheap But Why Not More Cheerful?', *The Times*, 5 January 2002.

[16] Whitehead, Alfred North, *An Introduction to Mathematics*, New York: Holt, 1911.

Index

Index compiled by Annette Musker